Routledge Revivals

Capitalism in the UK

First published in 1981, *Capitalism in the UK* clearly states the Marxist position arguing that capitalism dominates the world economy, and that the world's trade and multinational enterprises favour the capitalist system. It shows how orthodox economics is not value-free and how orthodox economics implicitly assumes that capitalism is the only possible form of economic organisation for society. Designed for students on Political Economy and Marxists Economics courses, this comprehensive and concise volume provides an important counterweight to traditional first- and second-year introductory textbooks.

Capitalism in the UK

A Perspective from Marxist Political Economy

Mike Campbell

Routledge
Taylor & Francis Group

First published in 1981
By Croom Helm

This edition first published in 2022 by Routledge
4 Park Square, Milton Park, Abingdon, Oxon, OX14 4RN
and by Routledge
605 Third Avenue, New York, NY 10017

Routledge is an imprint of the Taylor & Francis Group, an informa business

Publisher's Note
The publisher has gone to great lengths to ensure the quality of this reprint but points out that some imperfections in the original copies may be apparent.

Disclaimer
The publisher has made every effort to trace copyright holders and welcomes correspondence from those they have been unable to contact.

A Library of Congress record exists under ISBN: 0709900899

ISBN: 978-1-032-42212-1 (hbk)
ISBN: 978-1-003-36174-9 (ebk)
ISBN: 978-1-032-42215-2 (pbk)

Book DOI 10.4324/9781003361749

Capitalism in the UK

A Perspective from Marxist Political Economy

Mike Campbell

CROOM HELM LONDON

© 1981 Mike Campbell
Croom Helm Ltd, 2-10 St John's Road, London SW11

British Library Cataloguing in Publication Data

Campbell, Mike
    Capitalism in the UK.
    1. Capitalism
    I. Title
    330.12'2'0941

    ISBN 0-7099-0089-9
    ISBN 0-7099-0090-2 (Pbk)

Printed in Great Britain by Photobooks (Bristol) Ltd,
and bound by Redwood Burn, Esher

CONTENTS

Preface and Acknowledgements

1. A Critique of Orthodox Economics   9
   1. Introduction   9
   2. Apologetics and Ideology   12
   3. Appearance and Reality   15
   4. Methodology   17
   5. Behaviour and Motivation   19
   6. Individualism   20
   7. Social Harmony   23
   8. The State   25
   9. Conclusion – Can We Assume Reality Away?   29
      Further Reading   30

2. Marxist Political Economy: An Introduction   32
   1. Introduction   32
   2. Historical Materialism – Economic Change and Class Structure   33
   3. The Nature of Capitalism – Capital and Labour Opposed   36
   4. How Capitalism Works (1) – Surplus Value and Profit   39
   5. How Capitalism Works (2) – The Capital Accumulation
      Process   45
   6: The Breakdown of Capitalism – Theories of Economic
      Development and Crisis   49
   7. Conclusions   55
      Further Reading   56

3. Big Business   59
   1. Introduction   59
   2. The Growth of Market Concentration in the UK   60
   3. The Growth of Aggregate Concentrationin the UK   66
   4. Mergers and Concentration   69
   5. The Concentration and Centralisation of Capital   72
   6. Ownership and Control of Capital   75
      Further Reading   78

4. Inequality – The Distribution of Wealth, Income and Power   81
   1. Introduction   81
   2. Class and Inequality – Elements of a Theory   81

3. The Distribution of Wealth   84
4. The Distribution of Income   90
5. The Impact of the State on Inequality   97
6. The Distribution of Power   100
7. Further Aspects of Inequality   102
   Further Reading   104

5. Economic Crises, Unemployment and Inflation   108
   1. Introduction   108
   2. Unemployment: The UK Experience   109
   3. The Nature of Capitalist Crises — Accumulation,   113
      Restructuring and the Demand for Labour Power
   4. Inflation in the UK   132
      Further Reading   137

6. International Perspectives — Trade, Multinational Corporations
      and the EEC   141
   1. Introduction   141
   2. International Trade and the UK Balance of Payments   143
   3. The Multinational Corporation   147
   4. The European Economic Community   155
      Further Reading   161

7. The State   164
   1. Introduction   164
   2. The Market System and State Intervention   165
   3. The State in Capitalist Society: A Marxist Perspective   170
   4. The Growth of the State: Capital Accumulation and the   173
      Class Struggle
   5. The State and Capital: Contradictions and Responses   179
   6. Capital and the Welfare State   183
      Further Reading   189
Bibliography   193
Index   201

PREFACE AND ACKNOWLEDGEMENTS

This book is intended to provide a relatively self-contained and intelligible analysis and critique of capitalism in the United Kingdom from a marxist perspective. It begins with a critique of orthodox economics and an introduction to marxist political economy. These are followed by five chapters that relate and apply marxist political economy to contemporary 'economic' problems and issues in the UK, thus linking theory to the concrete analysis of problems and offering an 'alternative' to orthodox treatment of these problems.

This book has been designed with two groups of people in mind. Students and lecturers in polytechnics, universities and colleges should find it useful in their studies, particularly on degree courses in economics and the social sciences, wherever 'alternative' views and perspectives are considered. It should also be relevant for individual courses in areas such as applied economics, economic systems, marxist political economy, and for the increasing number of multi/interdisciplinary 'issue' or 'problem' based courses. I also hope it will be valuable to activists and groups in the labour movement and communities, in providing a context for their struggles and an analysis of the economic system which generates them. As such, trade union, political, WEA and Adult Education groups will, I hope, find it useful.

I am grateful to a number of people who have typed various drafts and chapters of the book, usually under severe time constraints — Barbara Stirk, Anne Lock, V.P. Rex and especially to Phyllis Campbell who typed most of the final draft. My thanks are also due to several friends, colleagues and students on the Economics and Public Policy degree at Leeds Polytechnic who make teaching and writing seem, after all, worth while. For helpful comments on this book I would like in particular to thank Richard Stead, John Sutherland, Reg Chapman and Tom Burden. Thanks are also due to the Leeds WEA 'Political Economy and Everyday Life' group and to Nick Foster of Sheffield City Polytechnic.

The singlemindedness required to write this book has meant that it has been an essentially selfish endeavour. Thanks then to all my friends who have had to put up with me during the writing of it, and apologies for my neglect of them; thanks especially to Liz for her help and support and thanks, finally, to T.R.B.

Mike Campbell

1 A CRITIQUE OF ORTHODOX ECONOMICS

'All science would be superfluous if the outward appearance and the essence of things directly coincided' (Marx)

1. Introduction

Orthodox economics is in deep crisis. There is widespread dissatisfaction with economics even from its adherents: 'Faced with the policy issues of the modern world economics in its present state is either inadequate or irrelevant and economists are the practitioners of that art.'[1] The growth of interest in alternative approaches to economics also bears witness to this fact, with an increasing number of academics, students and activists turning to marxist political economy for analyses of the operation of contemporary capitalism, and correspondingly a growth in articles, pamphlets, journals, books and courses that adopt a marxist framework in attempting to understand contemporary economic and social problems.

It is essential to construct a fundamental critique of orthodox economics, one that strikes at its very roots, because it provides the 'scientific' basis that underpins the capitalist economic system. The subtitle of Marx's *Capital* was *A critique of political economy*, for the construction of an alternative perspective on society implies a critique of orthodox perspectives. It is up to today's marxist economists to challenge contemporary orthodox economics, just as Marx challenged nineteenth century orthodox political economy. The aim in this chapter is therefore to present a critique of orthodox economics which demonstrates that objective, neutral, value-free economics is, in reality, a value-laden, mystifying apologetic for capitalism. In particular it aims to present a critique of orthodox economics' methods and assumptions, which direct it into a specific ideological position. It is a critique of orthodox economics as conventionally presented to students. Naturally economics is not a totally homogeneous body of knowledge and there are both disagreements between economists as well as internal criticism of the discipline itself. However, this chapter represents a critique of the 'received wisdom' in economics, a critique not so much of individual theories, nor one that rests on technical disagreements between economists nor on 'value judgements' as to the desirability of state intervention in the system, but rather a fundamental, radical critique of its assumptions, often implicit, that serve an ideological function.

In the remainder of this introduction first we outline some of the *common* characteristics of orthodox economics, many of which are taken up in later sections of the chapter, before going on to briefly argue that Keynesian economics is not so radically different from neoclassical economics as to shield it from the critique that follows. Finally, we mention the resurgent neo-Ricardian economics which we do not include as part of orthodox economics.

Orthodox economics, whether neoclassical or Keynesian, shares a common lack of concern with the social relations that *underlie* market and exchange relations. It is preoccupied with the level of appearances, with the visible form of such relations. For example, as we shall see in the next chapter, it concentrates on the formation of prices and ignores the class relationships that underlie wages and profits. The production process is seen as a technical relationship between 'inputs' and 'outputs' and the relationships between classes involved in it are ignored. The social relationships that arise out of the distinction between ownership/ non ownership of the means of production, and the phenomena to which this gives rise, is hence by-passed. There is no distinction between what is specific to capitalism, that is the existence of wage labour and privately owned capital, and what is general in all societies that indulge in exchange transactions. Hence there is no analysis of the class relations of specifically capitalist production, and the view is therefore at at best partial.

Related to this, because society is not divided into classes, there is no real analysis of power in society and it is then a short step to assume social harmony rather than social conflict as an underlying feature of the system. A broad consensus is assumed to exist where the main issue is 'how to get the most out of what we've got'. All individuals seem to be on an equal footing, whether in production or consumption, in their contractual relations. All individuals are equally free to indulge in market exchange. Given this concentration on exchange, it is inevitable that orthodox economics is primarily concerned with the efficient allocation and utilisation of scarce resources and how markets can be used, at a micro- and macro-level, to achieve this. Two other characteristics of orthodox economics that set it apart from marxist political economy are first the view that economic theory can be 'neutral', that it can somehow stand outside, and can be isolated from, society and secondly that the economic system is somehow separate from the rest of society. Marxist political economy, by contrast, stresses the relations between the institutions of society and the form of economic organisation.

As for specifically Keynesian economics, it is true that its analysis of economic fluctuations is different from that of neoclassical economics, though of course as it is an analysis of the macro-economy it has not displaced neoclassical economics in the analysis of resource allocation, micro-economics. However, the Keynesian analysis largely locates the cause of economic fluctuations in capitalists' expectations of falls in the rate of return on capital, which in turn are put down to pessimism or other psychological explanations which adversely impact on the 'animal spirits' motivation of capitalists. It thus does not locate such fluctuations as an inherent part of the mechanics of capitalist development. It differs from other orthodox analyses of economic fluctuations only with regard to whether the system tends to equilibrium and is self-stabilising, or whether state intervention is required to correct disequilibrium tendencies caused by expectations and uncertainty. Like the rest of orthodox economics it is rooted in the analysis of exchange and thus concentrates on 'aggregate demand' and its control, the realisation process as marxist political economy calls it, and *not* on production and its method of organisation, the accumulation process, where deeper problems and threats to profitability and output reside.

Neo-Ricardian economics is not part of the received wisdom of orthodox economics, and in fact challenges much of the basis of orthodox economics. However, it still shares certain common assumptions with orthodox economics in that it too views production as an asocial and ahistorical process. It does not deal with the organisation of production and the generation of surplus value. It sees production as a purely technical relationship between inputs and outputs abstracting from what is specific to capitalism. It only analyses social relations – class relations – in the sphere of distribution: the struggle between capital and labour over the distribution of the surplus.

The critique which follows is a critique of orthodox economics as a whole, defined as neoclassical and Keynesian economics. Where the criticisms are applicable only to individual schools of thought within orthodox economics, this will be identified. However the internal differences within orthodox economics are much less than between marxist political economy and orthodox economics as a whole, as we shall see in this chapter and the next. (For an evaluation of neo-Ricardian economics, which is not considered in the rest of this chapter, see the references to Rowthorn and Fine at the end of the chapter.)

The chapter proceeds as follows. First, we outline the case against

viewing orthodox economics as ideologically neutral, as a value-free
objective social science. Secondly, we make the charge that it obscures
the nature of reality by concentrating attention on observable and,
literally, superficial phenomena rather than on the underlying structures and features of capitalism. Thirdly, we attack the empiricist and
positivist methodology of orthodox economics before, in the next
section, analysing the assumptions made with regard to the motivation
and behaviour of economic agents, and the implicit acceptance of
capitalism as the only relevant form of economic organisation for
society. In the next two sections (5 and 6) we take two implicit assumptions — the nature of behaviour in capitalism (individualism) and
the organisation of capitalist society as a whole (social harmony) — and
seek to demonstrate the ideological basis of these assumptions. In the
final section, prior to our concluding comments, we outline the role of
the state in capitalist society as seen by orthodox economics, and
briefly contrast this with the role of the state as envisaged by marxist
political economy.

2. Apologetics and Ideology

It is not surprising that orthodox economics gives support and credence
to capitalism, nor is it surprising that it is the dominant and widely
accepted system of economic thought for 'the ideas of the ruling class
are in every epoch the ruling ideas . . . the ruling ideas are nothing
more than the ideal expression of the dominant material relationships'.[2]
Thus ideas, whether economic, political or social, reflect the prevailing
system and sets of economic relationships. It could hardly be otherwise,
except in a potentially revolutionary situation, for if it were there
would be a basic conflict between the prevailing economic and social
system and the ideas/views of its members; a distinctly unstable situation. It is in this sense that the economics is ideological, for it serves
the class interests of the owners of capital.[3] Views other than the conventional consensus ones are strongly discouraged. It is in this sense too
that the battle for ideas, the ideological battle between the objective
interests of capital and labour, is of such importance in the struggle for
economic and social change.
    A substantial ideological achievement of orthodox economics is
the 'proof' from neoclassical micro-economics that a free market system, with private ownership of the means of production, will achieve
an optimum allocation of resources. That is, within the constraints

imposed by a scarcity of resources it can maximise society's material well being. Where the supply of a commodity exceeds the demand for it price falls, which acts as a signal to the producer of the commodity to reduce output and a signal to consumers to increase their demand for it, thus bringing supply and demand back into balance. The same argument applies to 'factors of production'. Markets, therefore, through relative price and profit changes allocate resources to their most efficient uses, resulting in maximum possible total output and maximum total consumer satisfaction, as well as minimising costs of production, prices and profits in the process. Moreover, in terms of the distribution of income from production each 'factor of production' gets a reward in proportion to their contribution to production.[4] This represents a powerful intellectual defence for capitalism. For if the market system in association with the private ownership of the means of production can 'solve' the economic problem of scarcity efficiently (in other words if it gives us the best of all possible worlds) how can it be challenged as an economic system, by others that would abolish both these key features of capitalism? There are two basic ideological and apologetic implications of this free market model. We deal with each in turn.

First, because it can be shown that the capitalist system is capable of allocating resources optimally, the basic features of capitalism are taken as given and the analysis proceeds on this basis. The analysis is therefore ahistoric. It takes capitalism as given, as well as abstracting from the particular features of capitalism compared to other systems. Fundamental questions about the economic organisation of society are hence by-passed, and concern centres on the operation and administration of these given data. Consequently, orthodox economics is constituted on given legal and institutional foundations, within a fixed socio-economic environment. It concentrates therefore on the problem of allocating resources within these constraints and as a result can become a technical study of the attempt to maximise or minimise the value of some objective function subject to constraints. Indeed the rationality of action becomes defined in terms of minimising the use of scarce resources which have alternative uses. That is to say, that decisions and choices are made on the basis of what is efficient (or 'economic') and the analysis of goals, of what is desired and for whom, becomes secondary. Thus orthodox micro-economics concentrates on means (efficiency in the use of scarce resources) rather than ends/goals (what gets produced and who gets it). Moreover it is supposed that considerations of distribution/equity are not value-free, whereas questions of efficiency are, and in its search for a spurious neutrality, interpersonal

comparisons are ruled out as they involve value judgements with regard
to comparing the satisfactions different people obtain from, say,
income. Consequently there is no way of saying that a redistribution of
income from the rich to the poor is more likely to increase society's
welfare than vice versa, without taking an ethical perspective. Thus
economists cannot say whether a more equitable distribution of income
makes society as a whole 'better off'. Clearly this is a powerful inbuilt
mechanism to preserve the existing unequal income distribution.[5]

Secondly, though the market system can theoretically be shown to
be capable of achieving an optimum allocation of resources, the necessary conditions for this to be achieved are highly unrealistic, restrictive
and large in number. It has been shown that there are no less than 17
assumptions necessary for the system to achieve optimality.[6] It
would seem that the model of perfectly competitive capitalism is
nothing more than a *normative* model wherein the optimum situation
is compared to reality and recommendations are made to adjust reality
towards the model i.e. recreate the assumptions (of which more later)
on which the model rests, in the real world. Now this model is set up in
orthodox economics and is used as the starting point for the analysis
of all manner of problems in the various branches of economic analysis, whenceforth policy prescriptions pour forth from comparing the
model to reality, each one taking us supposedly a little nearer to the
'optimal' (and therefore presumably desirable) situation of a perfectly
operating free market system. For example, many policy prescriptions
revolve around the need to increase competition which will erode the
'imperfections' in the market system that exist in reality, and which
prevent the market from working smoothly. With regard to international trade, for example, barriers to the free movement of goods, for
example tariffs and subsidies, should be abolished so that 'free' trade
can occur. With regard to the operation of the labour market, near
monopolies like trade unions, should be curtailed to improve competition for jobs so that wages reflect the extent of excess labour supply.
Regional growth disparities will be narrowed by breaking down barriers
to labour and capital mobility; no restrictions should be placed in the
way of either. Similar arguments are applied to monopoly, unemployment . . . *ad nauseam*. The political implications of so-called value-free
orthodox economics are here absolutely blatant. The long list of
assumptions that have to be fulfilled for the market to work in such a
way are, moreover, unrealistic and systematically at variance with
reality. These include perfect competition in the markets for goods,
services and labour and capital; perfect mobility of human and physical

resources (between uses and over space); and perfect information on all alternatives available to buyers and sellers. Moreover, there are circumstances where even if all the assumptions hold markets will fail. (The operation of the market is treated in more detail in Chapter 7.)

The orthodox economics textbooks' 'distortions' and 'imperfections' inevitably arise out of the natural development of capitalism, as we shall see in later chapters. Nevertheless orthodox economics analyses capitalism *as if* it were an inherently self-regulating system. Unemployment, inequality and so on are regarded as imperfections in the market, rather than as fundamental and endogeneously determined features of the system. They are therefore treated as if they can be eliminated by piecemeal changes at the level of markets designed to remove these imperfections in an otherwise perfect system, even though many of the necessary assumptions are the complete opposite of what exists in reality. Take, for example, the assumption of perfect information. The competitive process between firms actually creates uncertainty and barriers to the free flow of information and, more generally, such an assumption implies such knowledge about reality as to be an impossibility for any individual or organisation. It is also the case that the language used by orthodox economics, the 'imperfections' of markets, the 'deviations' from ideal conditions, the 'interference' of the state and so on, contain an innate ideological bias in favour of the unregulated operation of markets i.e. *laissez faire.*[7]

Thus it would seem that the model of the perfectly competitive free market economy plays a powerful ideological and apologetic role in its 'explanation' of the workings of the capitalist economy. It would seem it is designed less to reveal the truth about such economies and rather more to reassure those who study it about the status quo.

3. Appearance and Reality

In this section we argue that orthodox economics concentrates attention on the observable, surface phenomena of markets and their relationships rather than the underlying social relations that lie behind these observed relations, which emanate from the prevailing mode of production. In consequence it ignores and obscures social and class relations and so neglects the significance of power and conflict, thus mystifying for example the nature and origin of wages and profits. Orthodox economics concerns itself with the operation of markets and deals therefore only with the observable, immediately apparent relationships in the sphere of market exchange (circulation). This, literally, superficial perspective sees the links between individuals solely as buyers and sellers of commodities on the market. It sees the relationships between 'things' and not between people, even though the relationships between 'things' in the market (i.e. commodities) are nothing more than the outward form or expression, of the underlying *social* relationships between the owners of the commodities that are exchanged. It is these social relationships that determine the conditions underlying the exchange, and it is these social relationships, expressed in terms of value and surplus value which are not observable at the level of exchange, that underlie the observable categories of prices, wages, profits and so on with which orthodox economics deals. Hence the concentration on appearance at the level of exchange conceals the real relationships and the processes at work in a capitalist economy.

Let us exemplify this point in relation to two essential categories of economics the nature of, and payment to, labour and capital i.e. wages and profits.[8] On the labour market all the participants *seem* to be on equal footing in their contractual relations. Labour, unlike in feudal times, is free to dispose of labour power (the ability to work) as desired. There are no legal constraints, visible force or coercion involved and people can work or withdraw their labour power as they please. However this freedom is apparent rather than real, which becomes clear once we dig beneath the illusory *appearance* of freedom and into the underlying structure of the labour market. Coercion exists in reality because of the nature of property rights under capitalism. Though not physically coerced to work for others labour does not possess the means to work on its own account and thus, of necessity, must work for others. The workers have no access to the means of production, they are monopolised by another class. This class relationship is concealed at the level of exchange, where relationships seem fair and equal and wages seem to be paid for all the labour contributed by the worker. In reality, however, the exchange relationship is unequal for capitalists own the means of production and labour does not, and in consequence labour is exploited in the sense of being paid a wage for his/her labour power which is less than his/her contribution to production. This 'surplus' labour is expropriated by the capitalists and forms the source of profit. Here the reality behind the forms is exposed, and the labour market is seen as merely the outward expression of the class relations underlying the condition of exchange. Thus the market for labour is not the independent arbiter of rewards that it seems, bestowing 'flexible' value on labour according to variations in demand and supply

and ensuring that everyone receives their just deserts from their contribution to production – a fair day's work for a fair day's pay.

   With regard to capital, orthodox economics again conceals the underlying rationale for, and source of, its payment by confusing the meaning
of capital – capital *goods* are productive but *ownership* of them is not.
Capital thus has two meanings, one of which is concerned with capital
as physical objects, as means of production, whilst in the other sense it
is the property of certain individuals the ownership of which entitles
them, in a capitalist society, to a portion of the total product. Capital
in the first sense, as a physical material object cannot produce social
categories such as profit; it is capital in the second sense that produces
profit, due to monopoly ownership of the means of production. All
that is supplied in return for the payment of a profit is the ownership
of capital, a fact which gives such owners the right to part of the social
product. Profit is thus not a natural, inevitable payment stemming
from the material nature of capital, but rather it is a result of the particular social relations of production in capitalism. The ability to earn
profit is not a physical property of capital, profit is only yielded
because of the organisation of production.[9]

   The existence then of the categories of profits and wages are not
in doubt, but such categories are not inevitable, natural or eternal. This
cannot be recognised at the level of market exchange and demonstrates
the importance of analysing economy and society at levels other than
that of the market. Moreover, a market approach not only mystifies the
source and nature of wages and profits, but also implies that any 'problems' that arise in the distribution of income, between wages and
profits or within either category, can be corrected 'at the level of
exchange' without affecting, of course, the basic nature of the economic
system.[10]

4. Methodology

The methodology of orthodox economics is essentially *empiricist* and
positivist. The principles and methods of natural science are applied to
the study of economy and society. It proceeds first by making a series
of assumptions i.e. definitions of terms and hypotheses about human
behaviour; then by making logical deductions from the assumptions, a
(or several) prediction is generated. Finally, these predictions are tested
against the real world by observing and analysing empirical data. Theories
then are justified only in terms of their predictive success and

discrimination between competing theories is handled by appeal 'to the facts'.[11]

The implications of this methodology are as follows. First, knowledge is only acquired, and theories verified, through observation. Thus no theory is ever conclusively proved, for it denies that knowledge can be acquired *a priori* and thus there is no necessity about causal relationships – everything could be otherwise. Secondly, theories are merely the logical implications/deductions from a set of assumptions. The logical reasoning itself says nothing about the world, this is contained in the assumptions (explicit and implicit), some of which are analysed in this chapter and contain, in many cases, dubious, ahistorical and asocial hypotheses about human behaviour. In passing we may note, that this shakes the notion of the universality in time and space, of orthodox economics and illustrates the importance of subjecting the assumptions of orthodox economics to close scrutiny. Thirdly, it implies that no statements of any significance or meaning about the world can be made except those that can be verified by observation. Empirical evidence is the ultimate arbiter. Any other statements are invalid. However, this assumes that there exist distinct facts which observation and experiment can reveal and that these constitute all that has to be explained. Moreover, there are major difficulties involved if competing theories *both* explain the observed facts. How is one to distinguish between them? Further, verification of theories by appeal to the facts is extremely difficult, for ceteris paribus (all else being equal) clauses are necessary in this methodology to allow of under which conditions the theory holds. Thus theories become statements of what *would* happen if certain conditions held, and thus cannot be tested against actual observations. It is impossible then to distinguish between the failure of the theory, and the failure of ceteris to be paribus.[12] Fourthly, questions of value and morality are not only unanswerable in this framework, but also are meaningless, because they cannot be verified by recourse to facts. Thus orthodox economics is both empiricist (poses that knowledge can only be gained through empirical data) and positivist (proceeds by generating predictions by logical deduction from a series of assumptions).

Finally it is tempting to make the charge of orthodox economics that on its own criteria – the ability of theories to predict/explain reality successfully – it has not been, to put the point gently, entirely successful.

5. Behaviour and Motivation[13]

The central concern of orthodox economics is scarcity — the allocation
of scarce resources between competing uses. Because, under capitalism,
the basic institution used to perform this function is the market where
buyers and sellers of commodities exchange them for money, attempting to maximise their utility and profits respectively, then the dominant motivator of individual behaviour is assumed to be market conditions. The stimuli and constraints of the market are seen as the motive
force behind human behaviour, on the basis of which universally applicable theories of resource allocation are constructed. This motivation,
and the behaviour by individuals in response to it, is seen as being
rational. Behaviour based on other criteria is treated as irrational and as
an imperfection in the operation of markets. Moreover self-interested,
maximising behaviour of this kind is often treated as if it were universal
and 'natural' i.e. an innate characteristic of people and society.

   This is a very narrow view of human behaviour where people are
viewed as *things* — inert and passive — and thus where people respond
mechanically to external impulses and stimuli. It not only neglects the
social, political and psychological causes and consequences of individual
and group behaviour, but also is completely ahistorical (historically
specific) and asocial (specific to particular organisations of the
economy and society).[14] For if behaviour is conditioned by the organisation and values of society then different societies will give rise to
different behaviour patterns on the part of its members. This point will
be taken up again in a moment, but it suffices for now to note that in
pre-capitalist societies market exchange and the maximisation of
material well being (utility for consumers, profits for producers)
through self interest was *not* a dominant characteristic. It is capitalist
society that has turned people into 'economic' animals; individual,
rational market behaviour is not eternal or even 'natural'.[15] All this
arises because orthodox economics, unlike marxist political economy,
abstracts from the historically and socially specific relations of a capitalist society, and fails to recognise that the relationships between
people, between economic actors, are conditioned by the organisation
of production in society, and that it is these relations that in turn
determine the economic phenomena of society.[16] As these relationships
change, as the organisation of economy and society change, so too does
the behaviour of the individuals and groups within it. For example, the
motivation of the capitalists, to maximise their profits or the extraction
of surplus value, is not a universal phenomenon. It does not arise from

an inborn desire on their part. Rather it is determined by their social role and the 'laws' of capitalist development.[17] This applies equally to the behaviour of workers and unions under capitalism, in their struggle over the appropriation and distribution of the surplus.

A further implication of this view of human behaviour which concentrates on individuals as economic units responding rationally to, for example, economic stimuli, is that motivations are expressed through 'preferences', for example, of one commodity for another which are accepted not only as 'given' (as we've argued above) but also as 'exogenous' to the economic system. That is they are regarded as being individually formulated, or even as emanating from 'human nature', rather than as being 'learnt' from the economic system or affected by the behaviour of others. For a subject so inbred with empiricism this is a remarkable view, for it clearly contradicts observed behaviour as well as studies of preference formation – a study of which orthodox economics shifts to other disciplines and ignores. To take one example, individuals may express, through the market, a preference for private rather than public transport. This preference is determined by the availability of alternative transport modes, the spatial separation of work from the home and other characteristics and norms of society. Clearly such a preference is neither individually formulated nor independent of the structure of society. It is the organisation of society that conditions individual behaviour, for individuals live and develop in society and the relations within it. A further problem arises in orthodox economics as a result of preferences being taken as given. There is a mutual dependence between ends (preferences) and means (courses of action), for preferences are shaped in the actual course of action.[18] If this is true then orthodox economics is faced with a major problem, for the efficiency of the market system is judged to the extent that it satisfies preferences and these preferences are not independent of it i.e. are in part determined by it, then to say that the market system is efficient in terms of satisfying preferences, is not to judge it from an independent perspective. In the next section we criticise (inter alia) one other particular assumption about human behaviour, the assumption of 'individualism'.

6. Individualism

It was argued in the previous section that behaviour is in part developed and conditioned by the market, and that capitalism relies on people to behave in response to such economic stimuli. It thus encourages an *individualist* rationality of isolated individuals in competition with one another, be they capitalists, workers or consumers. Indeed the history of orthodox micro-economics is largely that of the elaboration of theories of consumer behaviour and business behaviour based on the assumption of individualism. Such a thesis of individualism implies that people behave egoistically. To use Adam Smith's own words, it is 'self interest' rather than 'benevolence' that guides the 'invisible hand' of the market system. Individuals act in their own self interest in an attempt to maximise their own individual gain in competition with each other as buyers and sellers of commodities. It is this behaviour which results in changes in the supply of, and demand for, commodities, and hence in prices and profits, which in turn guides the use of resources in a free market economy. The motivation, the driving force of the system, is thus to maximise one's own gain. Individuals are seen as isolated instruments of gain responding to the forces of the market. As Marx said: 'The only goals that political economy sets in motion are greed, and the war amongst the greedy.'

Thus in explaining human behaviour and in guiding the system the focus is not on man's social role, but rather on individuals choosing between alternatives according to maximising principles. 'Man' as a consumer is seen as an individual bundle of desires, whose behaviour is explicable in terms of the rational calculation of self interest. We don't know *what* he wants, but we do know he is a 'maximiser'. Man is thus treated as being egoistic, but he is also seen as being 'intellectual' and 'inert'. That is, he must be capable of making a rational calculation of his own self interest so he knows what is best for him, and as we've seen above, he is also treated as if he is not strongly influenced by the institutions of society — there is no analysis of the way in which society constrains the range of effective choice available to individuals.

In consequence the basis of behavioural analysis is the individual decision-maker making choices. Society is, as it were, constructed out of individual behaviour and is explained in terms of the individual, rather than the individual in terms of society. This type of explanation of behaviour, in terms of the attitudes and behaviour of individuals rather than in terms of the structure of society, is sometimes called *psychologism*, and it leads to a very particular explanation of behaviour. For example, such a perspective would view the process of capital accumulation as a result of individual capitalists' rates of 'time preference', in the pursuit of their own individual attempt to maximise their own profits rather than as being the result of the 'laws' of capitalist development which *require* them to expand their capital, and which operate irrespective of the characteristics of the individual capitalists themselves. It would view unemployment as often being a result of an individual 'over pricing' him/her self in the market, his/her lack of skills, or even laziness, rather than as being due for example to changes in technology and levels of demand which are outside the individual's control. In short this perspective sees problems, and their solutions, at an individual level rather than at the level of the economic institutions of society. Social problems, created out of society, thus easily become individuals' problems, a fault of the individual. This perspective is associated with neoclassical views. There is one extremely important corollary of this view of man's economic behaviour. It implies that individuals should be left 'free' to pursue their own interests with the minimum of interference, regulation or restriction from the state, for unrestrained individual behaviour on the market can be shown to lead, under certain conditions, to an optimum allocation of resources. Thus the individual becomes the basis for economic organisation and 'freedom of choice' the ruling ideology. Freedom of enterprise and private property become central to the system, with a presumption against regulation and in favour of freedom — after all individuals are the best judge of their own self interest. Hence the implications of the necessity for 'free' competition and 'free' trade, on the presumption that the maximising of economic 'liberty' and the minimising of state 'interference' is both efficient and desirable.

Individualism then implies an economic system based on the unfettered self interest of individuals operating in a competitive market framework with private ownership of productive resources. It also implies a particular concept of 'freedom' referring to the absence of constraints on individual action and choice; the ability to follow one's own interests without interference from others. Hence, the so-called threats to freedom that develop from state invention in the economy and society — land use controls, abolition of pay beds, restriction of private cars in cities, comprehensive education and so on, for all such actions 'interfere' with individuals' own freedom of choice. This freedom of choice is freedom only at the level of exchange. It conceals the lack of freedom at the level of production, where freedom (of enterprise) for the few means the freedom to be a wage slave for the many.

This freedom is the freedom to operate a society based on private ownership of the means of production, and hence to operate a class society, where freedom is restricted and controlled by those who benefit most from it. It is freedom for those with the power, money and influence who are able to exercise it. For marxists freedom refers to 'man's' ability to adapt and control his social conditions of existence, which he is unable to do in a class society where power, income, and wealth, and thus freedom of action, are concentrated and where the ownership and control of the productive system is in the hands of a dominant class.

In this section we have tried to show that a major implicit assumption of orthodox economics is not ideologically neutral but rather that it is a normative doctrine which implies, and attempts to justify, a particular form of economic organisation. In the next section we question the implied assumption of orthodox economics that capitalist society exhibits a harmony of interests between capital and labour.

7. Social Harmony

This assumption about the economic and social organisation of capitalist society implies that there is no divergence of interest between different social classes but that there is rather, apart from some minor difficulties, a coincidence of interests. The idea that capitalist society produces no irreconcilable clashes of interest, that the interests of capital and labour are harmonious, or even identical, is naturally very convenient for orthodox economics (and for capitalist society) as there is then no necessity to recognise the existence of competing classes. Everyone is deemed to have interests that can be reduced to a common consensus about what is desirable and what is not. One implication of this is the emergence of such slogans justifying economic policies as being 'in the national interest' and 'for the common good'. The economic goals, and the economic policies aimed at reaching these goals, thus become *national* ones aimed at increasing national affluence. Yet how can there be a national interest when society is divided into owners of the means of production, an ownership which confers the right of appropriation of the surplus product and the ability to make strategic decisions in society, and those whose only means of living is to sell their labour power for a wage to the owners of capital who appropriate the surplus produced? This is a situation of objective conflict of interest.

For example, the problem of inflation may become national enemy number one and its reduction the major aim of policy. The success of such a policy would be measured in terms of the reduction in the rate of increase in prices. Yet rarely is the question asked, what is the distribution between different social groups of the benefits and especially, the costs of such a policy? For example the period of various incomes policies and restrictions on public spending between 1975 and 1978 certainly reduced the rate of inflation, but at the 'cost' of reduced real wages and reductions in the 'social wage'. Thus the costs of such policies were largely borne by working people, and the beneficiaries were the owners of capital whose labour costs were controlled and profitability, at least partly, restored.

To take another example, economic growth is a major economic goal, probably the ultimate economic goal, in capitalist society, which is deemed to be in everyone's interest yet there is much less concern, in economics and in capitalist society, as to the distribution of gains and losses from the growth so achieved. Growth is assumed to be in everyone's interest, whereas in fact, the issue is how different group's and individuals' quality of life improves absolutely *and* relatively. Who gets what share of increased national 'prosperity'?

A second implication of the assumption of social harmony, in addition to the non-recognition of conflicting interests over the social product, is that economics regards 'change' as gradual and non-disruptive (the preface to Marshall's seminal work in economics is 'nature makes no leaps') rather than as disruptive and sudden due to inevitable clashes of economic interest. The problems of capitalist society are seen as blemishes on an otherwise acceptable visage that can therefore be overcome within the system. They are not seen as structurally related inherent contradictions of the system itself, which can only be overcome by changing the system.

The associated technique of economics is thus 'marginal' analysis which concentrates on marginal adjustments on the edge of the large aggregate of capitalism whose basic character is accepted. It concentrates on choice at the margin within a fixed economic environment, hence diverting attention from fundamental issues about the nature of the aggregate itself. It is essentially therefore a conservative analysis abstracting from fundamental or qualitative change in the structure of the economic system.

In addition, much of orthodox economics is obsessed with the associated concept of, and tendency to, *equilibrium*. This implies a notion of inbuilt regulation and stability in the economic system, where disturbances are only oscillations around equilibrium, prior to a new one being reached. Change cannot be regarded as inherently destabilising and uncorrective for this would imply the possibility of major 'catastrophes' in the system (like crises), which naturally cannot occur endogenously; they can only be countenanced as being due to sunspots, poor harvests, Arabs, subversives or wars! Social harmony, as we shall see again in the next chapter and in Chapter 4, is not a characteristic of capitalist society, for the interests of capital and labour are essentially in conflict. Once again, a central assumption of orthodox economics is shown to be essentially ideological.

8. The State[19]

Is the state in capitalist society an institution established in the interests of society as a whole with the role of reconciling antagonisms that inevitably arise in human society? Does it perform the function of neutral referee between various groups in society? Is it an impartial arbiter (for example in industrial disputes) unattached to any particular class or group? In short, is there a *pluralist democracy* where power is distributed between different groups and the state arbitrates in cases of disagreement in an attempt to reconcile these differences? The comfortable, implicit assumption of orthodox economics is that the answer to these questions is yes. Orthodox economics treats the state as an external, exogenous black box that comes into the economic system 'from outside' as it were intervening or even, as it is sometimes put, interfering, in the economy to correct markets, internalise externalities, stabilise demand and so on. It then disappears again until further 'distortions' or 'imperfections' of the capitalist system appear again to be corrected by the neutral paternalist state which is assumed to be committed to achieving full employment, low inflation, raising living standards and so on!

The analysis of the nature of the state is sidestepped and left to other disciplines to analyse, whilst economics takes a very particular view of its operation. Indeed it would be difficult for orthodox microeconomics to see the state as an inherent part of the economic system, as endogenous and essential to it, for it would strike at the heart of the ideology of the self-correcting free market basis of capitalism. This is, of course, a major difference between neoclassicists and Keynesians — the necessary extent of state intervention. The implicit assumption in this view of the state is that the basic class structure and system of property relations in society is taken as given and immutable and it merely sets out to ask what arrangements can the different classes in society make to get along in this situation. However, as we've argued above, and will again throughout the book, the class structure of contemporary capitalism is not immutable, it is not part of the natural order of things. The means of production can exist in other forms than private ownership!

Our view of the state, which is developed in Chapter 7, is that it ultimately serves the interests of the controlling class in society, rather than the interests of society as a whole, because it preserves and supports the basic capitalist institutions. It thus protects the interests of capital. Behind the façade of democracy lies its class nature and the class nature of capitalism in general. The state, in this view, has essentially three functions. First, it regulates the economy as a whole at the macro-economic level through demand management, incomes and other policies. Secondly, it guarantees private property rights, regulates the relations between capitals, and between capital and labour, as well as regulating imperfections in the operation of the law of value. Thirdly, it has an ideological and political role, in encouraging acceptance of the social order and setting the outer limits to change or reform. It thus attempts to legitimate capitalism through its activities and propaganda as well as through concessions to working people, designed to stabilise and diffuse conflict, and ultimately if necessary through coercion and repression.

The state then is viewed by marxists as part of the superstructure of society and thus reflects the pattern of economic power in society. Any other situation would bring the state into direct conflict with capital. But the state is more than an 'elected government' which could conceivably have interests opposed to those of capital. A government is only able to operate the state for a given time period. The judiciary, police, army and civil service — the permanent state — is not up for election. Moreover, governments must preside over a 'successful' economy and to do this they must not act against the long run interests of capital, for otherwise the controllers of the means of production can sabotage such policies, through their own (in)activity. It is they who ultimately have power in society, for it is they who make the decisions about prices, employment, investment, output and so on. Power rests essentially with capital and not in parliament. The state thus preserves capitalism, through preserving private ownership of the means of production and hence the exploitation of labour and the continuance of a class society.[20]

Thus, reformism is severely limited by the dominant power of capital. Major government policies not approved of by the capitalist class either fail, are greatly changed or are dropped from social democratic/ reformist government programmes altogether.[21] This is so for the additional reason that, given the basic capitalist institutions are not to be challenged fundamentally, then capital must be allowed to compete, nationally and internationally, which means that policies (if they are to be successful) cannot ultimately challenge the profitability of capital. To the extent that they do, they will almost certainly fail. For example, a government policy to severely limit or freeze prices would lead to economic collapse, as capitalists would react to cuts in their profitability by reducing employment, cutting back production, holding back investment plans, investing abroad where returns are higher and so on.

The structure of the state itself to a large extent mirrors the concentration of power, wealth and decision-making in society at large.[22] The occupational background of individuals in government, parliament, the judiciary and the Civil Service, illustrates this point. For example, in the 1970/74 parliament, Conservative MPs between them held an average of four company directorships each whilst only eight MPs had been manual workers. This is hardly a cross-section of the nation able to act in the 'national interest' and shows, even in parliament, the overwhelming representation of the ruling class. But parliament does not govern, it does not master the power of the state, which rests to a large degree in the permanent non-elected institutions of the state that are isolated from changes in the pattern of voting, e.g. the army, police, judges and top administrators of government departments. Here again members of the ruling class directly participate in the state apparatus. As important as their class origins is their class position; that is they belong to the state apparatus and their objective function becomes that of the state. Furthermore, there are strong and increasing links between the private sector and the state, in the form of key positions in public and semi-public bodies e.g. chairmen of the nationalised industries. It is, however, often argued that even if it is accepted that at *one* time the state was, as it were, the organised power of the capitalist class for the suppression of working people, that it was used as an instrument of enforcing the dominance of the capitalist class, that role of the state has *changed* in the more advanced stages of capitalism and, further, that it has changed to such an extent that capitalism itself has changed as a result. It is argued that the state has modified the failures and excesses of nineteenth century and early twentieth century *laissez faire* capitalism, and that as a result capitalism today is a rather different, and more humane, animal than of old. Such arguments point to the role of demand management policies in regulating the economy and reducing (sic) unemployment; the growth of the Welfare State; state provision of housing and transport; and so on. We here briefly refute these arguments, both in so far as they are supposed to have changed the face of capitalism, and in particular, in so far as they are supposed to reflect the role of the state in advanced capitalism. For an extended discussion of the state, the reader is again referred to Chapter 7.

These policies have *not* altered the fundamental nature of the capitalist system. Such measures are corrective only, in that they attempt to make the system work 'better' rather than changing the system itself. They have not replaced the key defining institutions of capitalism.[23] Such actions are 'interventions' in the economy to stabilise capitalism economically and socially, but still allow firms and individuals to pursue the same interests, altering only the arithmetic of market calculation. Indeed, far from interfering with the interests of private capital, state policies protect and enhance capitalists' interests:[24] for example, attempts to stabilise demand, so-called 'incomes' policies, the expansion of technical education and government training services, membership of the EEC, measures to control trade unions, subsidies to private industry and so on. The rationality remains that of the market system, where firms and individuals act as the calculation of their own private gains dictate and where relative prices and profits move in response to these decisions guiding the allocation and distribution of resources. At the most, in some circumstances, the system is 'guided' and stabilised and the arithmetic of some of the calculations may have been changed but it has not altered *who* makes the decisions and for *what* purpose. It has not altered the essential characteristics and dynamics of capitalist economic development and the 'laws of motion' to which, as we will see it is subject. Moreover, as we've seen state intervention must not go so far as to threaten individual freedom, destroy work incentives or threaten profitability. Thus capitalist values are preserved.

Nevertheless, it is true that the form and actions of the state in contemporary capitalism do reflect to some degree, the modifications to the relations of production and the changing balance of forces in the class struggle. The state is no longer the simple agent of capital. Concessions have been won by the actions of the labour movement. Concessions are made by the state, depending on the relationship of forces at any point in time, and as such an organised, united and militant trade union and labour movement can modify the parameters of the capitalist system. But it must be remembered that these are concessions; concessions won by struggle, and concessions only — which are often given to diffuse the objective opposition of capital and labour, to restrict the scope for fundamental change, to reduce class antagonisms and consciousness. Such concessions are necessary to maintain the system in the face of its increasingly obvious contradictions.

The capitalist state rules out attacks on the roots of problems, for they are the roots of the capitalist system itself. It rather attempts to alleviate the symptoms of a problem in order to camouflage the nature and extent of the problem, diffuse discontent and maintain order. For example, in order to alleviate growing unemployment in the period 1975 to 1979 'temporary' employment subsidies, job creation projects and training programmes were introduced which, at one time or another, preserved/created around 500,000 jobs. Similarly, attempts to reduce inequality do not tackle its root causes but rather introduce reforms that are perfectly compatible with capitalism. For example action on pensions, social security, unequal access to education and training facilities because of sex or race, and so on. Such action is taken partly because such situations may threaten the system, and partly under pressure, particularly when such phenomena (like unemployment and inequality) are such a necessary feature of the capitalist economy. But always the emphasis is on secondary factors, on symptoms not causes.

9. Conclusion — Can We Assume Reality Away?

In this chapter we've attempted to undertake a fundamental, radical critique of orthodox economics as it is conventionally presented to its students. It is a critique that strikes at the very heart of orthodox economics, questioning its ideological neutrality, its methodology, its assumptions about the nature of reality, individual motivation, social harmony and the nature and role of the state. We have tried to show that behind the façade of neutrality and objectivity orthodox economics is deeply ideological, and that this serves to direct its communicants into a specific view of reality with regard to the organisation, operation and efficiency of contemporary capitalist society. It conceals some elements of the system, and obscures and mystifies others. The crisis of economics and of other orthodox social sciences reflects the crisis of capitalism. In the following chapters we attempt to understand the reality that is contemporary capitalism in the United Kingdom from an alternative perspective: a critical marxist perspective.

Further Reading

A useful introduction to many of the issues raised here is the introduction in Hunt and Scwartz (1972). Indeed the whole book contains
critical essays on economic theory though most are quite difficult.
Sweezy (1972), Chapter 4 covers similar ground whilst Scwartz (1977)
contains a number of penetrating, but on the whole difficult, articles
which are critical of orthodox economics *and* neo-Ricardian economics: see especially Chapter 2 by Hunt on individualism and welfare
economics. Fine (1980) exposes orthodox economics to a powerful
critique and contains chapters on Keynesianism and neo-Ricardian
economics. For a critique of orthodox economics from the inside see
Heilbronner and Ford (1971). Hunt and Sherman (1978), Chapters 4,
7 and 8 deals with the evolution of capitalist ideology and Gordon
(1972) Chapters 2 and 5 compares and contrasts orthodox and
essentially marxist approaches and applies them to the analysis of
poverty and unemployment. The chapter by Nell in Blackburn (1972)
gives an outline critique of the orthodox perspective especially in
relation to its ignorance of class relations whilst Hollis and Nell (1975)
is one of the most powerful contemporary critiques of economics with
regard to its methodology and its view of 'rational man'. In terms of the
areas closest to the ground covered in this chapter see the introduction
and Chapters 1, 2 and 8. Rowthorn (1975) is a valuable critique of
orthodox economics and of neo-Richardian economics. For a debate on
the critique of orthodox economics, see the debate at the back of
Lindbeck (1977); part one is a defence of orthodox economics. The
article by Mohun in Green and Nore (1979) is an excellent reference on
ideology and economics. For more detail on individualism see Lukes
(1973). On the state see Miliband (1969), Mandel (1971), and Gamble
and Walton (1976) especially Chapter 2. For a fuller guide to references
on the state see the guide to further reading at the end of Chapter 7 in
this book. However the last word must go to Fromm (1963): see
especially Chapter 5.

Notes

1. Winch (1971), p. 200. This chapter is essentially a critique of the overall
perspective of orthodox economics as conventionally presented to students. It
does not imply that, conceptually, parts of orthodox economics are useful, or
that orthodox economists have not done concrete work which aids an understanding of the economic system. See Green and Nore (1979) and the remarks
later in this section.

2. Marx (1970).

3. See Chapter 2.

4. See Chapter 7 for an analysis of the market system and Chapter 4 for an analysis of inequality and the distribution of income.

5. On this issue see Nath (1973), Chapters 1 and 4.

6. See Graaf (1957), p. 142 ff., and Chapter 7 in this book.

7. See Rowthorn (1975).

8. See Chapters 2 and 4 for more detail.

9. A useful analysis of the contrast between orthodox and marxist approaches to the payment of profit using the 'circular flow of income' approach can be found in Hollis and Nell (1975), pp. 14-20 or Nell in Blackburn (1972).

10. Naturally this also applies to orthodox analysis and policy prescriptions on other issues as well, for example unemployment.

11. See, for example, the discussion of the methodology of orthodox economics in Lipsey (1971), Chapter 1.

12. For more detail on this line of argument see Hollis and Nell (1975), Chapter 1.

13. See also Sections 6 and 7 of this chapter for an analysis of two key assumptions made by orthodox economics about individual behaviour and social organisation.

14. It is, therefore, not a very sophisticated view of human behaviour under capitalism, though the system does seek to encourage such behaviour.

15. See Mauss' (1970) study of 'gift' relationships in neolithic civilisations, particularly Chapter 4 where the economic, as well as moral and political, implications of such behaviour is outlined.

16. To take one example, the categories of Keynesian economics are defined ahistorically and asocially in this way – liquidity preference, marginal efficiency of capital and so on. The method of marxist political economy, historical materialism, is outlined in Chapter 2.

17. See Chapter 3.

18. See Gintis (1972).

19. This section is a critique of the orthodox theory of the state. The marxist theory of the state, as well as an account and analysis of its growth and functions, is the subject of Chapter 7.

20. See Chapter 2.

21. Witness the examples of the National Enterprise Board and the Planning Agreements System in the 1974/79 Labour government.

22. See Urry and Wakeford (1973) and Roth (1972).

23. On which see Chapter 2. It's worth noting in passing, that they have done less in their corrective role than is often supposed by orthodox economists and social commentators. See, for example, Chapters 4 and 7.

24. See Chapter 7.

2 MARXIST POLITICAL ECONOMY: AN INTRODUCTION

1. Introduction

In this chapter we introduce and explain the key categories of marxist
political economy as well as giving an overall perspective on the marxist
approach and its explanation of the dynamics of economic systems in
general and capitalism in particular. These categories, perspectives and
explanations are applied and concretised in later chapters in the analysis of contemporary capitalism in the United Kingdom. Consequently
this chapter should be treated as the starting point for the analysis,
theoretical and empirical, of contemporary capitalism in the UK undertaken in this book, and thus echoes Engels' view that 'all concepts of
Marx are not doctrines but methods . . . they do not provide complete
doctrines but starting points'.

It will become clear in the course of this chapter that the approach
of marxist political economy is fundamentally different to that of
orthodox economics[1] in that it digs beneath the surface appearance of
the economy in an attempt to uncover the inner, hidden, 'laws of
motion' of the system. Thus it analyses many features of capitalism
that are often assumed to be eternal, or taken for granted, like private
ownership of the means of production and people's relationships to it,
the existence of production for exchange, and the existence of categories and 'rewards' to economic actors like profit and wages.

One aim therefore of this chapter is to begin to uncover the laws of
motion of capitalism — its origins, operation, development and eventual
decline. Moreover, this study of the birth, life and death of capitalism
demonstrates that capitalism is not eternal, that it has been preceded by
different economic systems, or modes of production, and will be
succeeded by others. Clearly therefore, this perspective is more than an
academic study of economy and society. A heightened understanding
of the operation and deficiencies of capitalism encourages an awareness
of the need to change it.

This chapter proceeds as follows. In the next section the basic
methodology of historical materialism is set up, and thus the process of
transition to and from capitalism explained, and the role of the class
struggle identified. In section 3 the major features of capitalism are
delineated prior to analysing, in sections 4 and 5, how capitalism works

through the study of the core of marxist political economy, the generation of surplus value and the capital accumulation process. Section 6
deals with the breakdown of capitalism associated with the tendency to
crises and is followed by some concluding remarks.

2. Historical Materialism – Economic Change and Class Structure

An appreciation of historical materialism demonstrates the fundamental
importance of the economy in explaining and understanding society,
for it emphasises the central role played by the mode of production. To
understand society one must start with people's productive activity,
how it is organised and how they relate to it. For it is through productive activity that people obtain their means of subsistence and ensure
their survival, and in the last analysis it determines the broad structure
of society as a whole. Indeed the 'laws' of marxist political economy
result from the historically specific structure of relationships between
people in the process of production. All societies must find a way of
organising production, a way of allocating human labour between
different uses and distributing the proceeds of that labour between
them, and different societies historically do this in different ways. Thus
these different *modes of production* are central to understanding the
development of society.

The mode of production, or economic base of society, consists of
two elements. The *forces of production* refer to the machines, tools
and equipment used in the production process and the technical skills
and abilities of the people involved i.e. the technical ability or capacity
to produce. The *relations of production*, on the other hand, refer to the
way production is organised, the relations between those involved in
the production process. In organising production people enter into
relations with each other, and these relations differ from society to
society. For a long time productivity, because of the development of
the productive forces, has been sufficient to produce a surplus, i.e. an
amount over and above what is necessary to replace or reproduce the
means of production as they wear out (machines etc.) and reproduce
the means of subsistence for the labour force. With the existence of
such a surplus the question arises as to who appropriates this surplus
and how. Forms of appropriation differ between modes of production,
and are associated with different relations of production, which themselves may change as productive forces develop. Whatever form it takes
however, whatever are the relations of production, they are *class*

relations i.e. relations between groups of people who have a different
relationship to the means of production — some will have access to the
surplus, whilst others will not. A class is thus a strata of society grouped
in accordance with their relationship to the production process e.g.
lord and serf, master and slave, capitalist and worker. In each case one
class is able to appropriate the surplus by virtue of their relationship
to the production process (their ownership of one element of the forces
of production) and thence to the other class. As soon as an element of
the forces of production is *not* owned by the producers a class society
emerges by virtue of appropriation of the surplus by one group necessarily implying that others will not receive all they produce.

This may be, as in slavery, where the producers themselves are
owned by the slave owners; in feudalism where the land is owned by
the landlords; or in capitalism where machinery and factories (capital)
are owned by capitalists. In all cases one element of production is
owned by, and has become the property of, one class of people who
now by virtue of this particular relationship to the means of production and thus to the other class, are able to appropriate the surplus. The
relations between those involved in the production process are thus
class relationships. In capitalism, for example, the labourer is deprived
of access to machinery and factories, is separated from the means of
production, and thus must sell his only remaining contribution to production, the ability to work, to the capitalist, who does own the means
of production. This relationship, between capitalist and labourer, is
more than a legal one (ownership or non-ownership of means of production), it is economic too for as we have seen it allows the surplus
to be appropriated by the class who possesses the means of production
as their own private property.

Clearly in any such class society there are then antagonistic relationships between the appropriators and the appropriated. Their
interests are opposed, for the former naturally benefit from the existing organisation of production at the expense of the latter. Moreover,
it is clear that these class relationships are social and economic rather
than part of the natural order of things; that they are historically
specific to the particular mode of production and therefore are capable of being changed. The means of production can after all exist in
other forms than the private property of capitalists!

The importance of historical materialism is not only that it defines
this situation, but more importantly it explains how social change
arises out of it. The motive force of change is the contradiction between the forces and relations of production. The former are

continually changing in so far as the technical ability to produce becomes greater over time due to innovation and technological change, giving the potential capacity for continuous increases in the production of goods and services. The dynamism and rapid and continuous change in the productive forces is in contradiction to the inflexible unchanging relations of production. The latter hold back, and act as a brake on, the former because they increasingly become inappropriate for the level reached by the productive forces. For example, at the present level of development of productive forces many unmet material needs of society *could* be satisfied (for example housing, health care and heating) but the existing relations of production (private ownership of the means of production, the existence of wage labour and the quest for profit) forbid it, for goods and services will only be produced if it is profitable to do so.[2] Thus, as the forces of production develop they come into conflict with the existing relations of production. Moreover, those who benefit from the existing relations will use their power to defend them, for it is on these relations that their income, privilege and dominance depend. The dominant class thus have a common objective interest in preserving the status quo. There is thus likely to be increasing strain on the relations of production, as they fail to correspond to the changing forces of production. This internal conflict, this contradiction, is inherent in the process of historical development. From a correspondence between the forces and relations of production, the latter eventually become a hindrance to the former and for economic progress to be made the latter must give way. As the relations though are inflexible and the appropriating class will not readily give up their class dominance, a struggle between classes will ensue over the transformation of the relations of production. Thus social change results from the conflict between classes which arises out of the limits and class nature of the existing mode of production.[3] It therefore arises not as a result of historical accident or the deeds of great men but out of the developing contradictions inherent in the mode of production. Needless to say this conflict may not result in changes in the relations of production and the transition to a 'higher' mode of production (e.g. capitalism replacing feudalism, or socialism replacing capitalism). That depends on the balance of class forces in any particular historical epoch and whether the hegemony of the dominant class is increased, reduced, or eliminated in the process of the struggle.

How does *social* change, however, emanate from changes in the relations of production? Historical materialism seeks to demonstrate that changes in the economic base of society, because they are primary, will change the social and political *superstructure*, for it is argued that each mode of production has a corresponding superstructure and thus changes in the former bring about, in their train, changes in the latter. However, though it is argued that forms of social organisation primarily reflect the nature of the economic base, the relationship is nevertheless a *dialectical* one, i.e. the connections and interdependencies between them are important, and so the effect of economic change is not determinant. The superstructure is not treated as a pure derivative of the economic base, though the chain of causation is predominantly from economic base to superstructure, and the dialectical relationship between them implies that they cannot exist independently of each other.

Two major elements of the superstructure operate so as to strongly resist social change however; the state and the system of ideas, or value structure, in society. According to historical materialism these are powerfully influenced by the existing mode of production and, like the relations of production are resistant to the underlying force for change. The state is treated in a later chapter[4] but it can be noted here that views of society other than the conventional ones which correspond to the relations of production are discouraged, because the dominant ideas, or ideology, serve the class interest of the dominant class. Indeed one manifestation of class conflict is an ideological struggle. These ideas are deeply embedded in society and it is arguable if economic change *alone* is a necessary and sufficient condition for their overthrow.[5]

It is in the context of this methodology that the rest of this chapter on the capitalist economy and how it works, and ultimately fails to work, should be seen.

3. The Nature of Capitalism — Capital and Labour Opposed

Given the framework of historical materialism outlined above we naturally treat capitalism as (a) emerging historically from the development of a previous mode of production, (b) being identified and characterised essentially through its economic base, and in particular its relations of production and (c) experiencing contradictions in its development.

Capitalism shares certain similarities with its precursor, simple commodity production (SCP). The latter was essentially a mode of production characterised by individual producers, artisans, who owned and worked their own means of production. That is, they themselves owned all the requirements for production; the tools, materials and naturally their own labour. There were no relations of production, as production was organised on an individual (or family) basis. There were however relationships not in the production sphere, but in the circulation, or exchange, sphere. That is to say, that the production of goods and services under SCP takes the form of production of *commodities* i.e. production is for exchange not use.[6] Producers produce commodities to sell in exchange on the market in order to buy different commodities. Thus people relate not in production, in the workplace, but in the market, in buying and selling the individually produced commodities. The existence of markets therefore is a characteristic that SCP and capitalism share, and consequently an analysis of capitalism at that level alone (i.e. in the sphere of circulation/exchange/markets) fails to get to grips with the distinguishing features of capitalism. The other characteristic that both SCP and capitalism share is that the productive forces are at a level which makes possible the production of a surplus over and above the needs of the producers for otherwise there would be nothing to offer on the market to exchange, through the medium of barter or money, for other commodities. This naturally involves a developed division of labour where individuals undertake different occupations and produce different commodities. The market will operate, through changes in supply and demand and thus price, so as to channel producers to temporarily 'profitable' areas of production where there is excess demand and vice versa.

Capitalism, however, differs from SCP in the sphere of circulation in one respect for a new commodity appears on the market, *labour power*. Workers sell their capacity for work on the labour market. How does this situation come about? In order to understand how this occurs and what its implications are we must return again to the underlying sphere of production. Whilst in SCP producers owned their own means of production and consequently there could be no exploiting or dominant class, in capitalism the producers are *separated* from the means of production, they can no longer work for themselves. This is so because the essential characteristic of capitalism, like any mode of production, is its relations of production. The relations of production under capitalism are that there is a class monopoly of the means of production. The means of production, the machines and factories, are owned not by the producers but by another class, the capitalist class.[7] Relations of production then are characterised by the separation of producers from the means of production. In such a situation where producers become propertyless they are no longer able to work for themselves and must, in order to live, sell their only remaining element of production to the capitalist i.e. they must sell their ability to work. If they owned, or had access to, the means of production there is no reason why they should sell themselves to the capitalist because they could then sell their own commodities that they had produced on the market, instead of selling their day's labour.

Their ability to work, their day's labour, is thus offered in return for its price, like any other commodity, in this case the wage. At the level of circulation this relationship between 'worker' and 'capitalist' seems free and equal. There is no coercion involved, both are selling commodities on the market, capitalists are buying workers' ability to work, and workers are willing to sell it. Yet at the level of the relations of production, it becomes clear that this system of wage labour, where capitalists buy labour power (the ability to work) in return for wage, is an unequal and inherently exploitive one. Like all commodities labour power has an exchange value, its price (the wage), yet again like all commodities, it also has use value to the purchaser. Once purchased, like any commodity, it can be used as the owner of it sees fit. Labour power is owned therefore, like a machine, and is put to work. Thus social relations are involved in production, and these relations are not free and equal, but coercive and hierarchical, for it is the capitalists who organise the production process, and determine the pattern and pace of work, as well as whether to employ the wage labour at all and at what price. Capitalists' ownership of the means of production, indeed, gives them the right to decision-making as well as an income. An income which is squeezed out of the employment of wage labour.[8]

These relations of production are the central characteristic of capitalism, and distinguish it from other modes of production. Two further aspects of these relations, as well as the separation of producers from the means of production and the consequence of labour power being a commodity, are the organisation of the capitalists and their objectives. The owners of capital are separate, competing organisations which individually decide on what to produce, at what price and so on. There is no social direction or control of capital as a whole. The question arises then, that given this 'organisation' and given that production is for exchange not use, what guides and motivates the capitalists to undertake production? It is the desire (in fact as we will see later the need) for individual gain; the desire/need to profit from the activity. It is competition between capitalists in the search for profit that is the dynamic of the system. Unlike SCP where commodities are sold in order to buy *different* commodities, in capitalism commodities are sold to buy more of the *same* commodities.[9]

All this is very different to orthodox economics where the relations between capital and labour are seen only in the 'superficial' sphere of circulation, and not in the underlying sphere of production, where the motivations of the economic actors are defined in ahistorical and asocial ways, implying that they are eternal/natural features of life rather than historically and socially specific to the capitalist mode of production; and where the economic categories themselves, for example capital and labour, are treated also in an ahistorical and asocial manner as if 'nature' produced owners of the means of production on the one hand and wage labour on the other.

The nature of capitalism as we have identified it above, whilst being 'progressive' compared to earlier modes of production in some ways (for example increased material abundance, increased development of productive forces), is nevertheless fundamentally antagonistic to the further development of people. This is due to the relations of production in capitalism, where the relationship between people is not one of person to person but servant to master, subordinate to commander, exploited to exploiter. People lose then the ability and power to control their own lives. People become *alienated*. Workers are alienated first from their own product, because they have no access to the means of production and must sell their labour power to those that do. They thus have no control over what is produced or how it is produced and sold on an 'impersonal' market. Secondly, they are alienated from the work process itself. Labour power has become a commodity, like any other to be bought and sold, and workers have thus no control over their conditions of work i.e. how the workplace is organised, the introduction of new machinery and so on. They become an appendage of a machine. Thirdly, they are alienated because, whilst work should be people's greatest pleasure and give meaning and purpose to life, it instead becomes only a means of existence, a means of subsistence. This problem increases as workplaces become larger, labour becomes de-skilled and workers have less and less control over their working lives. Compare for example the position of an independent handloom weaver with a textile worker.

4. How Capitalism Works (1) – Surplus Value and Profit

The central purpose of this section is to examine the origins of capital, surplus value and profit. This will be done through setting up the labour theory of value: but first let us examine briefly the perspective from orthodox economics and compare it with our perspective. Orthodox economics abstracts from the relations of production and concentrates its attention on the sphere of circulation. Thus capital is conceived of as a 'thing' that produces and earns profit due to 'its' productivity, even though such technical characteristics of things cannot possibly produce essentially social categories like profit, which are rather specific to particular relations of production. The focus on circulation/exchange again concentrates on literally superficial appearances, rather than digging beneath them to the production sphere. For at the former level the relationship between capital and labour seems equal it is only in the sphere of production that the nature of class domination becomes clear. In contrast therefore to orthodox economics we concentrate here on the sphere of production and the specific relations of production in capitalism.

The objective of undertaking production in any society is to produce useful things, or use values. But in capitalism, as we have seen, production is undertaken for exchange on the market. Therefore the question arises as to what determines the ratio of exchange between commodities. That is, what determines the exchange value of a commodity? At the level of circulation in a capitalist economy it is clear that commodities exchange through the medium of money, and thus they have prices attached to them. The question is however what determines these prices. Orthodox economics answers that the forces of supply and demand determine prices; increases in the former and/or reductions in the latter will reduce prices, and vice versa. Whilst it is without doubt that changes in the supply of, or demand for, a commodity may alter its price on the market, particularly in the short run, this does not help us understand what determines the long run, underlying exchange relationships between commodities; the axis around which prices move up and down. The *labour theory of value* attempts to do this and simultaneously provides us with the explanation of the origin of profit. It states that the exchange value of a commodity is determined by its labour content. The only property that all commodities have in common is that they are the products of human labour, indeed commodities can be considered to be the 'material envelope' of the human labour that went into producing it. The value of a commodity is thus the socially necessary labour time (i.e. the time under average existing conditions of productivity and average skill) required to produce it. This takes account of *all* the labour that went into it, both the direct or living labour inputs, and the indirect or dead labour inputs.

These latter indirect inputs refer to the labour time necessary for creating the means of production required to produce the commodity, whilst the former refer to the labour time necessary for producing the commodity itself.

Thus the exchange value of a commodity may be measured by the amount of labour spent in the production of other commodities which can be exchanged for it. In practical terms this is an extremely difficult and cumbersome method for arriving at rates of exchange between commodities, and advanced societies express a commodity's exchange value in terms of other commodities (a barter system of direct exchange, where for example one book is exchangeable for five litres of beer) or, yet more conveniently, in terms of prices (a money system, where for example one book is exchangeable for five units of money). Thus the difference, in principle, between values and prices is that the former is measured in labour time, the latter in labour time valued in money.[10]

However, our main interest is in the explanation of the origin of profit, and in order to understand this we must return to a major difference between SCP and capitalism. This difference, and the origin of profit, can most clearly be understood by reference to the *circuit of capital*. In SCP producers exchange one commodity (C) for another through the medium of money (M). They first of all exchange the commodity they have produced for money (C → M) and then this money is exchanged for another, different, commodity (M → C). Thus the exchange process begins and ends with commodities which have the same value but are different things (use values). In capitalism, on the other hand, capitalists begin with money (M) which is exchanged for commodities (C) which are the inputs to the production process. These inputs consist of the means of production and labour power, and are put to work to produce new commodities (C′) which are the property of the capitalist, and whose value *exceeds* the value of the commodities which were inputs. These commodities are then sold on the market and their value thus realised (M′). The circuit thus begins and ends with capital in money form, and not with commodities. Thus both 'extremes' of the circuit are the same thing, and consequently the only purpose of this activity by the capitalist is if C′ > C and thus M′ > M i.e. the sum of money at the capitalist's disposal is greater at the end of the circuit than at the beginning. The purpose therefore of capitalist production is to *expand* value, and production is thus undertaken in the expectation that the money capital started with will be enlarged in the course of production. It should be noted that this expansion of value is of no use to capitalists until the commodities are sold, their value realised, on the market.[11] Thus the faster the entire circuit of production and circulation is completed, the sooner a new one can begin to expand value further. This expanded value, this extra money capital may be consumed by capitalists (i.e. they may purchase commodities other than means of production and labour power for their own personal consumption) in which case the circuit cannot be expanded, but can only be repeated on the same scale, so-called *simple reproduction*. On the other hand the extra money capital may be accumulated (i.e. they may purchase more means of production and labour power), in which case the circuit can begin again on a larger scale, so-called *expanded reproduction.*[12]

Whatever choice capitalists make, and they may of course divide the money capital between consumption and accumulation (though as we'll see in the next section this is not a free choice for them), the question arises as to what is the source of this expanded value, this extra money capital? Where does it come from? Why does it accrue to capitalists? And how does this stimulate production?

It cannot arise in the sphere of circulation of commodities by, for example, buying cheap and selling dear, because if all capitalists tried to gain in this way, what each gained as a seller he would lose as a buyer. It must therefore arise in the production sphere as a result of one of the commodities bought by the capitalist creating more value than it cost him. This takes us back to the distinction drawn earlier between labour and labour power. Because the means of production are owned by one class, the vast majority of the population have no choice but to sell the only element of production they own to capitalists (i.e. their ability to work, their labour power) in return for its exchange value, the wage. However, in return the capitalist receives its use value, the right to put the worker to work as he wishes. He can thus expand value by making the worker work for more hours, and thus create more value, than is paid in the wage. The value of labour power is the cost of its purchase (the quantity of labour time necessary to produce the wage) yet the value it creates is the quantity of labour time exercised in return. The value contributed by the worker thus exceeds the wage. The difference between the two is *surplus value*.

The worker's day can thus be divided into *necessary labour* (the labour time necessary to produce the wage) and *surplus labour* (the unpaid labour time). If we denote the former as V and the latter as S then the ratio S/V, surplus to necessary labour time, can be called the rate of surplus value or the *rate of exploitation* (E). For example, if

a worker works for eight hours and the necessary labour time to produce the wage is five hours, then for three hours he works for nothing,
he works 'free' for the capitalist. Thus if

$$V = 5$$
$$S = 3$$
$$\text{then } S/V = E = 3/5 = 60\%$$

and the rate of exploitation is 60%. It is this surplus labour then that
produces surplus value, and means that workers only receive part of the
value they create. Capitalists, on the other hand, appropriate this surplus value as it is embedded in the commodities they sell and forms
the basis of profit as we shall see in a moment.

What determines the value of labour power, the wage? Like every commodity it is determined by the socially necessary labour time required
to produce it, in the case of people this cost of production is its means
of subsistence. This will be more than a physiological minimum required for survival for it must include the ability to bring up future
workers (costs of reproduction) and will include an 'historical' element
i.e. the ability to purchase commodities that have become an accepted
part of daily life in that particular society, and thus means that workers
must live in what is regarded as 'socially acceptable' conditions, which
themselves are a function of the class struggle over the surplus in
previous time periods. Moreover, again like any commodity, its price
may temporarily exceed its value if the demand for labour power
exceeds the supply. Thus labour shortages and the class struggle may
limit the appropriation of the surplus.[13] Though all new value is created
by labour, because the capitalist owns the means of production, it is he
who has access to the surplus. Thus capital is nothing more than part of
labour appropriated by the capitalist class. Surplus labour forms the
'property income' of the capitalist class.

The value of the commodities produced has three components. So
far we have only discussed two – necessary labour which produces the
value of labour power or *variable capital* (V) and surplus labour which
produces *surplus value* (S). In addition however the capitalist advances
constant capital (C), the value of the means of production which
consists of *dead* or indirect labour. Part of the value of a commodity
is thus the value transferred from constant capital in the production
process. It is called constant capital because, unlike variable capital,
it does not contribute more value to the product than it costs as an
input. This is because whilst workers were exploited in producing the

means of production that are advanced as constant capital, it was sold at its value, like any other commodity, including the surplus value. Only variable capital can confer new value on commodities and thus expands value.

Thus the rate of profit is not the same as the rate of surplus value or the rate of exploitation,[14] for the former refers to the rate of return on the total amount of capital advanced (constant and variable) whereas the latter refers to the return on the amount advanced to purchase labour power only, and reflects the extent to which workers produce value over and above what they are paid for. If we denote profit as (Π) and the value of a commodity as m then,

$$m = C + V + S$$
$$E = S/V$$
$$\text{and } \Pi = \frac{S}{C + V}$$

The amount of surplus value is a function both of the rate of exploitation and the amount of labour employed, so clearly capitalists have an interest in expanding their labour force and also in increasing the rate of exploitation. How can the rate of exploitation be increased? In the early days of capitalism one important method was to increase the length of the working day and hence squeezing more output from workers at a given wage (this is so called *absolute* extraction of surplus value) thus increasing the rate of exploitation, providing of course that wages are not increased *pari passu*. Clearly there are limits to this process, and thus as capitalism develops a more important method becomes the *relative* extraction of surplus value involving increased productivity through investment in the means of production, especially machinery, i.e. changes in production methods as a result of technical progress. This will have the effect of reducing the proportion of the total value produced (m) that the capitalist has to pay the worker as a wage and thus increases the 'unpaid' (S) portion of the working day.[15] This is due to increased 'productivity of labour' and clearly if V, for example, because of increased wages doesn't increase by the full amount of the increase in S, then E will increase. Speed-ups and indeed any increased throughput will have a similar effect. Hence, once again, the crucial importance of the class struggle at the point of production over how the increased surplus is shared between capital and labour.[16]

Production under capitalism is directed to the purpose of expanding value. Production is undertaken in the expectation that money capital will be expanded in the course of production. This then is the driving force of the system, this is how commodities are produced in capitalism — a continuous process of the creation of, and search for, surplus value and hence profit. The need for capitalists to accumulate capital, rather than consume it, and thus lead to continual expansion of production is considered in the next section.

The analysis of this section has once again demonstrated the importance of the relations of production under capitalism for an understanding of the economic system and how it operates. There is an objective conflict of interest between capital and labour, manifested in the class struggle over the surplus. In the last analysis the extent of exploitation depends on the class struggle, in particular the struggle over wages and working conditions. Whilst concessions are possible in periods of high or rising rates of surplus value/profit, the diffusion of conflict is impossible in other conditions. For if wages bite too deeply into the surplus, or if the surplus is already small, capital accumulation may collapse and effectively leave workers with a choice of moderating wage claims or facing unemployment. The objective conflict between the interests of labour and capital becomes clearer in such crises. The conflict is manifested through capital trying to increase workloads; appropriate the benefits of increased productivity; keep wage increases down and reduce the organisation, power and militancy of working people, whilst labour attempts to reduce the workload; reduce the working day/week with no loss of wages; increase wages as much as possible and strengthen their organisations. It is capital that stands in their path.

5. How Capitalism Works (2) — The Capital Accumulation Process

We consider here how capitalism develops over time, that is how capitalism reproduces itself. We begin by outlining a simple model of reproduction where the scale of production does not change through time (simple reproduction) and then consider more realistic reproduction where there is economic growth (expanded reproduction). Then we consider some of the implications of this capital accumulation process for capitalist development.

In simple reproduction the scale of production does not increase over time. However, as in all economic systems the means of production and labour power must be maintained and reproduced otherwise human life would progressively disappear as the means of material existence declined. Thus simple reproduction involves reconstituting all the elements of production at a sufficient level to replace them as they wear out. Any surplus arising in production must be consumed and used to support activities that do not themselves yield a surplus, for otherwise this surplus could only be accumulated and used to buy additional means of production and labour power thus expanding production. This process can go on indefinitely as long as all the elements of production are reproduced on the same scale.

Expanded reproduction involves converting surplus value into additional capital, constant and/or variable. Instead of it being consumed it is *accumulated* to obtain more surplus value. Surplus value is thus transformed into additional capital by ploughing it back into production and the circuit of capital can be repeated on a larger scale:

$$M \rightarrow C \dots C' \rightarrow M' \rightarrow C' \dots C'' \rightarrow M'' \rightarrow C'' \dots C''' \rightarrow M'''$$

As production under capitalism is for exchange not use, and as capitalists, through ownership of the means of production, control the the production process and have access to the surplus produced, it is not in the least surprising that they should wish to increase this surplus through expanding production and thus increase their income in the process. This explains the incentive for production and the growth impulse that is an inherent characteristic of production for private profit. It also means that capitalist relations of production are reproduced i.e. the capital/labour relationship is reproduced, with workers selling their labour power to capitalists, thus workers 'continually consolidate the power which exploits them, whilst at the same time reproducing and perpetuating the conditions through which they themselves are exploited'.[17]

However, the capital accumulation process does not solely rest on the desire of capitalists to increase their wealth. There is an inner compulsion in the capitalist system to accumulate capital and expand production, because the system consists of autonomous competing capitals, and this competition is fought through reducing costs – the cheapening of commodities through reducing the labour time necessary for their production. Individual capitalists therefore have no choice but to aquire more elements of production in order to reduce costs *vis-à-vis* their competitors, for otherwise their costs will be higher and they will be beaten out of the market. These cost reductions can be achieved either through the economies of scale associated with production on an expanded scale, and/or through more efficient and advanced techniques of production.[18] If an individual capitalist does not use such techniques and his competitors do then clearly the commodities he produces will embody more labour time than is necessary and will produce less value. Thus there is a tendency to mechanisation which reduces the amount of labour time necessary to produce the wage and increases surplus labour time and the rate of surplus value. This progressively renders obsolete and uncompetitive the existing means of production, as well as allowing those capitalists who employ the more efficient machinery to produce more surplus value and accumulate more capital. This tendency is accelerated when the demand for products at current prices is satisfied and therefore further surplus value can only be realised by reducing costs, or entering new markets. Thus the capitalist system is inherently expansionist and growth orientated, a process only limited by barriers to the extraction of surplus value and capital accumulation.[19] The accumulation of capital reproduces both capitalist relations of production and the productive forces on an ever greater scale.[20]

The process of capital accumulation itself, however, leads to certain changes in the capitalist economy, the most notable of which are the effects on the competitive process; the effects on the labour force and the effects on the path of economic development.[21] As competition between producers is fought by reducing costs, capitalists feel the need to grow and expand as a force external to them over which they have little control. Each producer is in a constant struggle with his rivals to reduce costs, which involves the accumulation of capital. We have already seen how this leads to larger production units as the surplus is ploughed back and circuit of capital is reproduced on a larger scale. This source of capital accumulation is referred to as the *concentration* of capital, for it concentrates capital in fewer hands because many capitals will lose out in the process and either go to the wall or grow more slowly. This occurs because smaller capitals cannot benefit from scale economies or because capitals using less efficient methods of production create a smaller surplus and thus accumulate less. However, this is a relatively slow method of accumulating capital, a more rapid method is to combine together existing capitals.This is referred to as the *centralisation* of capital, for it gathers together and thus centralises already existing capital, rather than creating new capital. Again to the extent that scale economies are important these new combined capitals will have a cost advantage over their competitors and thus grow faster. The continual changes in methods of production brought about by capital accumulation, which increase productivity and reduce costs, also increase the minimum capital required to enter, and compete in, sectors where accumulation has taken hold. Thus inherent in the capital

accumulation process and the competition between capitals is a
tendency to monopoly i.e. the domination of sectors by a relatively
small number of large capitals.

The capital accumulation process is accompanied by the progressive
mechanisation of production which means that the same amount of
labour can produce a larger volume of commodities, so increasing
productivity and the rate of surplus value. Thus there is a tendency for
constant capital to replace variable capital, means of production replace
labour power, and for any given level of production of commodities to
progressively contain less variable capital. Thus the number of workers
employed by a capital of a given size tends to decline as new production methods are labour saving. This increase in the ratio C/V is referred
to as an increase in the *organic composition of capital* (O).

As for the effects of capital accumulation on the labour force, it is
implicit that as accumulation proceeds the demand for labour power
will increase as capitalists purchase more elements of production, both
means of production and labour power, in order to expand production.
Similarly if accumulation slackens[22] so will the demand for labour
power. However, as we have just seen there is no reason to suppose that
capitalists will increase their demand for labour power and means of
production equally, it is more likely that the demand for labour power
will increase less quickly than the growth of means of production.
Indeed, depending on the growth of output and the wage rate the
demand for labour power may actually fall. The wage rate is crucial.

First, if the price of labour power (the wage) is increased through
trade union or working class pressure this will increase its price above
its value. Secondly, if the demand for labour power approaches the
limits of available supplies, for example in periods of rapid expansion,
then its price will rise above its value. In both cases, the usual mechanism for commodities to bring price back down to value doesn't apply.
That is, the production of labour power cannot be increased to increase
supply and thus reduce its price; the law of value doesn't work with
labour power. What does happen however in order to counteract the
effect of the price of labour power exceeding its value and thus
reducing the rate of surplus value, is that the application of labour-
saving innovations will accelerate and the demand for labour power will
fall. The same will happen if wage increases exceed the growth of
productivity, in order to slacken the squeeze on surplus value. The
capitalist class may also through the state attempt to directly reduce
the price of labour power through so-called incomes policies i.e. freeze
or reduce real wages.

Thus there is a continuous expulsion of labour from production in the process of economic development, which added to the uncoordinated nature of technical change between sectors and over space, and the reduction in the demand for labour power when accumulation slackens, creates an *industrial reserve army* (IRA), a pool of unemployed labour power continually changing in size and composition. It is through the generation of the IRA that in many periods, wages are held in check; the domination of capital over labour is ensured, and capital accumulation can proceed unhindered. The competition of workers with each other, because there are not enough jobs for them all, acts so as to exert a downward pressure on wages. If accumulation slackens because of a reduction in the rate of surplus value or profit, then the demand for labour power will fall and the IRA will increase. This increases the competition for jobs and should lead to a fall in (real) wages, thus making production more profitable again and restoring the accumulation process. Thus the existence of the IRA is inherent in the capital accumulation process and functions so as to discipline labour (by regulating wages) and ensure capital's domination – as the existence or not of employment for workers lies outside their own control.

The effects of capital accumulation on the path of economic development are discussed in the next section.

6. The Breakdown of Capitalism – Theories of Economic Development and Crisis

Unlike orthodox economics which views capitalism as being capable of reproduction over time, either automatically and smoothly (supply creates its own demand) or with a little help from the state to manipulate demand, marxist political economy views reproduction under capitalism as endemically crisis-torn. Ultimately, it is argued, capital is a barrier to itself and reproduction is self-limiting under capitalist relations of production. It is through economic crises that capitalism will eventually collapse. Our concern here then is the economic development of capitalism and in particular the difficulties capitalism experiences in its expansion and development. The causes of these difficulties lie in the threats to profitability that develop in the capital accumulation process, because as we have seen, under capitalism production and reproduction will only take place if in so doing it expands the value of capital. It will only take place if it is profitable to do so. Thus it is declines in the rate of profit that cause crises in capitalism. These crises may be cyclical and hence short run (in which case potentially they can generate endogenously the conditions for recovery from the crisis) or secular and long run (in which case recovery cannot be endogenously assured), but they always arise out of the threats to profitability that arise in the accumulation process. These various causes are disproportionalities between the various production sectors; the exhaustion of the IRA or a change in the balance of class forces having similar effects to such exhaustion; realisation crises associated with overproduction; and a secular tendency for the rate of profit to fall due to changes in the organic composition of capital. The causes then are variously located in the production, distribution and circulation spheres and views differ over which is the *primary* cause of a fall in the rate of profit. It should be noted however that only the final one of these can propel capitalism to an eventual and inevitable collapse, the others are all potentially capable of resolution, though the social conflict they may cause does endanger the future of the system. Moreover, it is possible that the balance of the various causes is different in different epochs and even in different capitalist economies. Only specific concrete, historical study can identify the primary cause of any particular crisis.

6.1: The Possibility of Crisis

Before analysing the causes of crises, we must first define what we mean by a crisis and discover how it is that they can *possibly* arise in capitalism. Crises are disruptions in the accumulation process and are manifested in the under-use of existing human and physical resources, idle labour power and means of production, as well as in declining profitability. Thus the concrete outcome of crises are increases in unemployment and reductions in output, demonstrating once again how the relations of production restrict the development, or even the existing level, of productive forces. The possibility of such crises occurring arises out of the separation of purchase and sale, by money, that is associated with a market economy i.e. when production is for exchange. In such an economy it is obviously possible to sell a commodity without simultaneously buying one, and thus individuals may hoard the proceeds from the sale of a commodity rather than buy another one. Such a situation is impossible if money is not used as a medium of exchange, for in barter economies the exchange is simultaneously an act of purchase and sale and consequently supply necessarily creates its own demand. But if purchase and sale, demand and supply, are separated by money then it is possible for the aggregate of purchases, demand, to be less than the aggregate of sales, supply. Therefore, there may arise an *overproduction* of commodities, in the sense that they cannot be sold, and because the aim of production is to expand value, production will be held back as the value embodied in the commodities cannot be realised on the market. Note that this is an overproduction not of use values, but of exchange values and can, and does, therefore co-exist with unfilled human needs and wants. Under-used machinery and unemployed people co-exist with inadequate housing, insufficient energy and hungry stomachs, because it is not profitable to use the resources, and it is not profitable to fulfil the needs. In a society where production was for use not profit, such overproduction would be a cause for celebration rather than a cause of crisis. Crises occurring due to there being 'too much' produced rather than not enough to go round, again demonstrate the irrationality of the capitalist system. Moreover, such crises are barriers to further development and thus a barrier to capital itself in the search for profit through accumulation. Capital will therefore do everything in its power to overcome such obstacles.

6.2: Disproportionality Crises

Production under capitalism is essentially unco-ordinated and un-planned. Production is regulated by the law of value, and thus changes in the structure of demand for commodities should be transmitted to capitalists through changes in the prices of commodities, and the required adjustments in the output of the different sectors of the economy should be made in accordance with these to achieve a new structure of production related to the changed structure of demand. Thus *disproportionality* problems, the existence of excess supply or demand in different sectors, will arise to the extent that the law of value fails to bring about a rapid and smooth adjustment in the levels of output in different sectors. These failures arise out of capital and labour not being perfectly mobile, sectorally or spatially, and not responding 'perfectly' to changes in price, output and profit signals.[23] As a result excess output in one sector, causing reductions in output and employment, may become generalised as it begins to affect production in other sectors related to it. Moreover individual capitalists, rather than attempting to switch their capital to other sectors when faced with overproduction in their own, may react by reducing production to match the new demand, and thus effectively hoard money. The effect will be similar, but even more problematic as no capital switches sectors. Reductions in output, profit and employment will again spread through the economy because of the linkages and interdependencies between sectors, bringing in their trail overall reductions in demand as income levels fall and damaging 'business confidence' as profit levels fall. Therefore, because of the uncontrolled character of production under capitalism, imbalances between supply and demand of particular commodities can become generalised into crises for the whole economy.

6.3: Exhaustion of the Industrial Reserve Army

Historically there has been a tendency in capitalism for the supply of labour power to exceed the demand for it, hence the existence of unemployment or the IRA. However, and partly because of the existence of an IRA exerting a downward pressure on wages, production was highly profitable and thus the accumulation process proceeded rapidly, though irregularly, and over time with its increasing demand for labour power tended to exhaust the IRA in prolonged periods of rapid accumulation. As the IRA diminishes in extent the relative strength of capital and labour is modified and the bargaining position of the latter improves. Also the price of labour power is bid up on the market as capitalists compete more intensively for the insufficient number of workers. This increase in the strength of labour and their increased wages inevitably reduces the rate of exploitation and the rate of profit, leading to a contraction in capital accumulation and production. Thus there may be a tendency for the rate of accumulation to exceed that which can be sustained in the long run, because of a 'shortage' of labour power.[24] Capitalists react by introducing labour-saving techniques to reduce their demand for labour power and increase productivity.[25] As the IRA expands again as a result of the accumulation problems just outlined wage rates are forced back down.

Such a crisis is clearly cyclical[26] and contains the seeds of its recovery, though much depends on the strength of the working class. If they are strong enough to resist the reductions in real wages necessary for recovery, which will be encouraged through the expansion of the IRA or even direct state intervention through incomes policies or the restriction of trade union activities, then instead one such crisis could be capitalism's last.

6.4: Realisation Crises

In capitalism production is undertaken in order to expand value. However, to *realise* this value the commodities must be sold at appropriate prices, and thus realisation crises stem from overproduction of commodities in relation to the effective, market demand for them; an inability to realise the value contained in the commodities. This must be caused, as we have seen above, by some hoarding of money creating a deficiency of demand. It is unlikely that this will originate with workers for the value of their labour power is regulated around an historically specific 'minimum', and consequently large falls in their spending is unlikely. Capitalists, however, hoard money instead of purchasing constant and variable capital when profitability is threatened. Thus realisation crises are really the form or *appearance* that crises take, it is not the basic cause of a crisis. The cause lies, as we have seen earlier in this section, in reductions in the rate of profit.

6.5: The Tendency for the Rate of Profit to Fall

In this section we analyse the possibility that there may be a long term tendency for the rate of profit to fall. This is in contrast to the causes of crises so far identified, where falls in the rate of profit are neither inevitable nor secular features of the course of capitalist development. Here it is argued that a necessary feature of the accumulation process is a tendency for the rate of profit to fall, due to the changing balance of constant and variable capital in production, and therefore that the reproduction and development of capitalism is limited by itself.

We remember from section 4 that:

$$C = S/V \quad \text{and} \quad \Pi = \frac{S}{C + V}$$

and in section 5 we defined the organic composition of capital (O) as:

$$O = C/V.$$

Dividing the expression for the rate of profit (Π) through by V we have

$$\Pi = \frac{S/V}{C/V + 1} = \frac{E}{O + 1}.$$

Thus the rate of profit depends on the rate of exploitation, or rate of surplus value, *and* the organic composition of capital. It is clear that any increase in O will, other things remaining unchanged, reduce the rate of profit, threaten the accumulation process and bring about a crisis. As the only source of surplus value, and thus of profit, arises from the purchase of labour power it follows that a reduced reliance on labour power, that is an increased proportion of constant to variable

capital, will reduce the rate of profit. How likely is it that the proportion of constant to variable capital will increase in the process of capital
accumulation? With technical change, there is a continual replacement
of existing production techniques by progressively more advanced ones,
involving more constant capital per worker. This is the relative extraction of surplus value referred to in section 4, and arises out of competition forcing capitalists to increase productivity. It is reflected in the
increasing proportion of machines to workers employed in modern
industry. So, it would seem that the rate of profit is bound to fall
secularly and propel capitalism to progressively deeper crises in the
course of its history.[27]

   It is, however, not nearly so inevitable or so straight forward as this.
The rate of profit not only depends on O but also on E. It is most
unlikely that the rate of surplus value E would remain constant as the
organic composition of capital rises. This would mean that there was no
change in the proportion of surplus to necessary labour time in the
worker's day, and that therefore labour and capital had benefited
proportionately from the increased productivity, with real wages
increasing in proportion to it. Whilst this is possible, particularly in
periods of heavy demand for labour power and when the bargaining
position of labour is relatively strong, given the capitalists control over
the production process and the generation of the IRA, it is unlikely.
After all the rationale for altering the balance between constant and
variable capital was to *increase* profitability through increasing the rate
of surplus value. However as we will see in Chapter 5, because of the
competitive process, this rationale may well not bear fruit! There is
then a 'race' between E and O; only if the increase in the latter exceeds
the increase in the former will the rate of profit fall.[28]

   It can be argued however, that whilst there are no limits to the
possible increase in O there are limits to increasing E. As V falls in
relation to S the chances of increasing S further, by speed-ups, increasing the intensity of work and so on, decline. Logically one cannot
reduce to zero the proportion of a working day in which the worker
reproduces his own wage, and therefore there are limits to increasing E.

   This tendency for the rate of profit to fall should be seen as such. It
is not an iron law, an inevitable event that occurs regularly over time as
O progressively increases, but a tendency that demonstrates the ultimate limits to capitalism, and around which the struggle between
capital and labour revolves on a daily basis — productivity deals,
redundancies and so on. Moreover, there are a number of *counteracting
forces* that modify the tendencies which operate more or less at

different points in time and may allow periods of crisis-free growth. We
have already mentioned increases in the rate of exploitation, but also
important are some forces acting so as to depress the *value* of C, notwith-
standing its increasing *mass* relative to V. Such cheapening of the elements of constant capital might include capital saving technical change
through, for example, more efficient ways of extracting raw materials;
or state action to subsidise or provide direct research and development
activity; or even the export of capital and the acquisition, through
foreign trade, of raw materials cheaper than domestically.

6.6: Summing Up

Marxist political economy then locates crises in the capital accumulation process and the threats to profitability engendered in it. The
barriers to the development of the productive forces lie in the nature
of production under capitalism, and thus the abolition of the capitalist
mode of production is a prerequisite for the development of human
well being. This becomes all the more likely in crises as class antagonisms and the class struggle intensifies, as the contradictions and limits
of capitalist relations of production become more obvious. Crises in
capitalism are not due to scarcity but to overproduction; they are not
due to the inability of people to provide for themselves. They are due to
capitalist relations of production acting as a barrier to the further
development of productive forces.

7. Conclusions

We do not wish to summarise here the main points made in this
chapter; rather we content ourselves with some political implications
of our analysis and more particularly offer a few remarks on the problem of the relationship between economic change and social change,
and its political implications.

The class struggle is the central issue. Capitalist relations of production are inherently exploitive and the task is to change them.
Potentially revolutionary situations emerge in the development of the
capitalist mode of production. Whether these are seized depends on
the organisation and perspective of the working class and its organisations; union and party. Reactionary and reformist 'solutions' to
capitalism's problems posed from outside or inside the working class
have to be rejected, and analysis and action based on a marxist perspective promoted. This, amongst other things, implies that the struggle

lies primarily at the point of production and in the community rather than in parliament, and that in these struggles the common objective interests of working people in transforming society have to be demonstrated and realised.

However, social change and the establishment of a socialist society require much more than transforming capitalist relations of production and replacing the anarchy of the market by planning mechanisms basing production on need rather than profit. There is more to oppression in capitalism, and thus more to liberation, than economic phenomena. For if the transition to a socialist organisation of production, distribution and exchange were to occur without the transformation of social and personal relationships, new ways of living may not emerge: 'Revolution in the sense of the socialist transformation of economic life and social forms does not automatically entail changes in actual persons.'[29] Parallel to overthrowing capital, this implies throwing off the *psychological* repression of people under capitalism. There is a dialetic between the dynamics of economic change and the forces determining personality. Changes in the latter are not inevitable in the course of economic and social revolution and, moreover, changes here may hasten economic and social revolution itself. It is therefore important for there to be no dichotomy between the so-called political and personal dimensions of the revolutionary process. Otherwise the authoritarian personality fostered by class society and the patriarchal family, with its domination and oppression of women and children, will re-emerge in socialist society and reproduce authoritarian institutions and so frustrate the development of a socialist society. The collapse of the capitalist mode of production is a necessary, but not sufficient, condition for human liberation.

Further Reading

Harrison (1978) and Jalée (1977) are intelligible introductions to marxist political economy which take further the material covered here. Rather more advanced are Mandel (1973) and Kay (1979). Mandel (1968), Howard and King (1975) and Desai (1979) are more difficult, whilst Fine (1975) is an excellent introduction to Marx's *Capital*. Sweezy (1968) though difficult to obtain is still a classic. Hardach *et al.* (1978) cover the development of socialist economic ideas, MacLellan's (1975) little book introduces Marx's life and thought, whilst 'Rius' (1974) provides an amusing alternative. Sloan (1973) compares and contrasts marxist and orthodox approaches.

For an excellent critique of reformism see Harrison (1978).
Van Parijs (1979) provide a rigorous analysis of historical materialism.
On the controversies surrounding the falling rate of profit, as well as
those in contemporary marxist economic theory in general see Fine
and Harris (1976b). The debates are extended and refined in Fine and
Harris (1979).

For an analysis of the importance of psychological liberation see
Brown (1973) and for a further explanation of the relation between
economic and social revolution, and why it hasn't occurred in the
advanced capitalist nations, see Ollman (1978). Useful collections of
readings from Marx's writings are to be found in Howard and King
(1976), Freedman (1962) and Físcher (1973).

Notes

1. This chapter can therefore also be seen as an extension of the critique of
orthodox economics which was undertaken in the previous chapter.

2. See sections 3-5 of this chapter for an analysis of capitalist relations of
production and the role of profit as the guide to the system of production.

3. On the limits of capitalism see section 6 of this chapter, which deals with
how the productive forces are held back by the periodic crises inherent in capitalism. Thus the struggles between classes are likely to intensify in such periods.

4. See Chapter 7.

5. See section 7 for more on the relationship between economic and social
change.

6. I.e. not for consumption by the producer. Production is undertaken not for
the intrinsic 'use value' of the objects but rather for the objects' 'exchange value'.

7. It is not the place here to go into the history of 'primitive accumulation',
or the transition from SCP to capitalism, whereby one class accumulated wealth
and capital through 'conquest, enslavement and robbery'. (See Marx (1976),
Vol. 1, Chapters 26-33.) Nevertheless such a monopoly is clearly only possible
when the means of production become fairly complex and expensive, so that
large numbers of people are unable to purchase them i.e. factory production.

8. See section 4 below for more detail.

9. See section 5 below on this issue.

10. It should be noted however, that commodities of equal value do not always
have equal prices i.e. values do not always correspond to prices. This may occur,
in the short run as mentioned above, due to changes in the supply of, or demand
for, a commodity. For example, if the demand for beer rises relative to books the
price of beer will increase above its value, but the operation of the price system
(or law of value) will encourage new entrants into the beer industry and the proportionality between prices and the values will be restored. The operation of the
law of value, and its many deficiencies, is discussed in Chapter 7.

11. The *full* value of commodities does not however have to be realised for
production to occur. All that is required is an *expectation* of realising the value
of commodities. Indeed all that is actually required is an expectation of realising
more value than the value of the inputs i.e. M' can be less than C', their *full* value

does not have to be realised.

12. See sections 5 and 6 below on the accumulation of capital and its implications for capitalist development.

13. However as we will see in sections 5 and 6 below, if this surplus is reduced beyond a certain point or even eliminated it can have catastrophic implications for the accumulation process and thus for the capitalist economy.

14. These are different also in that profit is measured in money terms, surplus value in value terms. The surplus value is only *realised* when the commodities are sold.

15. It should be noted also that such technical change will itself cheapen commodities for example workers' means of subsistence, and thus reduce the value of labour power V and hence increase E.

16. It is worth noting in passing that surplus value is in reality a heterogenous fund of value and includes not only profit, but also rent and interest. We have been discussing the issue as if only industrial capital existed. The existence of, for example, commercial capital or interest-bearing capital, only affects the distribution of surplus value between capitalists. As they operate in the sphere of circulation no value can be added, though of course it is in this sphere that surplus value is realised, and it may produce surplus value indirectly by reducing the time and costs of circulation. See Fine (1975), Chapter 9.

17. Hardach *et al.* (1978), p. 21.

18. This enables capitalists to either reduce prices and expand the market, thus increasing the total realisable surplus, or retain present prices and increase the surplus on each unit of output.

19. See below and the next section on the barriers to capitalist reproduction.

20. This is of course one of the 'progressive' features of capitalism, for it develops the productive forces and hence the potential for material abundance, increased leisure, the abolition of the division of labour and hence for an abundant, classless, communist society. The key to unlocking the potential is the transformation of capitalist relations of production. See section 2 above.

21. On the last of these see the next section on crises.

22. See the next section for the conditions under which accumulation may slacken.

23. See Chapter 7 on the operation of the law of value in practice.

24. Unlike other commodities the supply of labour power cannot be increased in response to increased demand through changes in its price, except through immigration.

25. They may also react by exporting capital to where labour is cheaper.

26. Falling real wages is not the only reason for recovery from the cyclical down turn. The rate of profit will also increase because in the crisis many weaker capitalists go out of business.

27. See Chapter 5 for evidence on changes in the rate of profit and a more substantial analysis of the 'tendency for the rate of profit to fall'.

28. Though the rate will fall the absolute mass of profits will of course increase.

29. David Cooper quoted in Brown (1973), p. 21.

3 BIG BUSINESS

'The growing accumulation of capital implies its growing
concentration . . . capital becomes a strange, independent
social power, which stands opposed to Society' (Marx)

1. Introduction

As we saw in Chapter 2, to understand capitalism we have to begin with
the economic base of society and inevitably therefore, the organisation
of production is of central concern. Another major reason for studying
the organisation of production, is that it is in the process of production
that wealth is created. The overall level of *material* well being in society
depends heavily on the quantity, type and quality of goods and services
produced as well as on the methods used to produce them.[1]

There are four major characteristics of the *capitalist* mode of production:

(a) Production takes the form of production of commodities for sale on
the market viz. production is for exchange not use.
(b) The forces of production are sufficiently developed to be able to
generate a surplus.
(c) The means of production are monopolised and are the property of
capitalists. Those who do not own the means of production must sell
their labour power to those that do.
(d) There exist separate, autonomous capitals which compete with each
other in order to 'earn' profit.

Consequently the aim of production under capitalism is to continuously expand value through the generation of surplus value and its
accumulation. Production is for private profit. This does not only lead
to capitalists receiving unearned property income,[2] and the holding
back of the development of the forces of production,[3] but gives them
the control of major strategic decisions concerning the pattern of
growth and development of the economy, for example, in such areas as
investment levels and patterns of output, employment, production
techniques, and the location of economic activity as well as what to do
with the £24,000 million of profits 'earned' by UK companies in 1978.
Our concern in this chapter is with the organisation of production in

modern capitalism and how the dynamics of the accumulation and competitive processes generate the concentration and centralisation of capital, and hence an economy dominated by giant corporations.

There has been a tendency over time for the 'representative' firm to increase in size from the workshop, to the individual factory, to the multiplant firm, to the national corporation, to the multinational corporation.[4] Capitalism has thus evolved from an organisation of production where there was a *relatively* large number of small firms, each with a small share of individual markets and too small to influence the prices of the goods which they produced, to one where there is a small number of very large firms able to dominate individual markets, national economies and, increasingly, the entire capitalist world.[5] This phenomenon is not unique to the UK. Indeed in spite of the many differences between the capitalist nations of the world in terms of their size, political organisation and many other features, including government policies towards the growth of monopoly, this development is parallelled in nearly every one.[6] This would tend to suggest that there are forces inherent in the nature of capitalist development that make such developments inevitable.

The chapter proceeds as follows. First, we shall describe and analyse the level and growth of 'market concentration' in the UK (i.e. the domination of particular industries by a small number of large firms); secondly, we shall describe and analyse the level and growth of 'aggregate concentration' in the UK (i.e. the domination of the economy as a whole by a small number of large firms); and thirdly, we shall discuss the contributory factors determining these changes in the organisation of production. In the fourth section we shall analyse the processes *underlying* these changes in the organisation of production in terms of the processes of capital accumulation and competition inherent in the capitalist mode of production. In the final section of the chapter we provide a critique of the view that capitalist firms have become less interested in profits and the expansion of value and have become socially responsible because of the so-called 'divorce' of ownership from control.

2. The Growth of Market Concentration in the UK

There are a number of problems involved in analysing the level, and changes in the level, of concentration – in particular the problems associated with measures of concentration. The most common measure of concentration is the *concentration ratio*, that is the proportion of an industry accounted for by the largest, say four or five firms in it. This proportion can itself be measured in a variety of ways, including the sales revenue, assets, employment or profit shares accounted for by a certain number, or proportion of, firms in that industry. However, the extent of these shares are not invariant with the measure used, nor are they a measure of the entire size distribution of firms in that industry, as they say nothing about firms other than the largest, nor do they tell us anything about the relative size of the largest firms, i.e. the share of, say, sales of each individual firm. Other measures can be used that are based on the entire size distribution of firms, for example, Lorenz curves and Gini co-efficients, but apart from data difficulties, these measures are sensitive to the number of firms rather than their size, so that a change in the number of small firms in the industry would have a more than proportionate impact on the measure of concentration.[7] The evidence surveyed here uses solely concentration ratios and rarely goes beyond 1968 due to changes in the data base making temporal comparisons hazardous.

Figure 3.1 documents the extent of market concentration in 1968 and plots the percentage of sales of manufactured goods accounted for by industries with different degrees of concentration. Thus it shows that 30% of manufactured goods come from industries where five firms or less acount for at least 90% of that industry's sales, whilst nearly 50% come from industries where five firms account for at least 70% of that industry's sales. Nearly half of all sales of manufactured goods then are in markets where five firms or less control at least 70% of the market between them. Examples of these include cigarettes and tobacco (99.7), vehicles (91), electrical engineering (77), chemicals (92), food (70) and beers, wines and spirits (70). As has been noted elsewhere[8] just under a half of separately identifiable *product groups* (168 out of 340) had five firm sales concentration ratios of over 70% in 1968. Indeed, in the same year there were 156 commodities in which one firm alone controlled at least half the market.[9]

It is not just that concentration levels are generally so great however, the level of concentration in UK manufacturing has been increasing dramatically in recent years. For example, between 1963 and 1968, in 23 of the product groups referred to above the concentration ratio either *at least* doubled, or increased by 20% points, and whereas in 1958 26% of all manufactured sales were in industries with five firm concentration ratios of $> 75\%$, by 1968 this proportion had increased to 48%.[10]

Whilst the average five firm concentration ratio was 52% in 1935, it had increased to 69% in 1968 and in 1974 was estimated to be around 76%.[11] It has also been shown that for the 150 products for which comparisons in changing levels of concentration can be made between 1958 and 1968, that the average five firm concentration ratio has increased from 56% to 65%.[12]

Figure 3.1: Market Concentration in the UK — Five Firm Sales Concentration Ratios in 1968

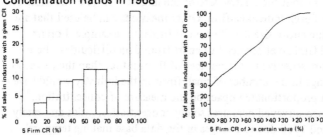

Source: Adapted from Aaronovitch and Sawyer (1975), Table 4.7, p. 98.

Further evidence on increased concentration relates to the declining number of firms operating in a given industry. For example, between 1957 and 1968 the number of firms, with assets over £1½ million and quoted on the Stock Exchange, declined by 63% in the drinks industry, 45% in chemicals, 41% in textiles and 54% in food. These figures are by no means exceptional instances, indeed the number of firms (with assets of more than £½m in 1961) in each industry declined by 30% on average over the period *due to merger activity alone*,[13] so that by 1968 there were only two industrial sectors in the UK where more than six companies accounted for 50% or more of that industry's net assets. All that we have said above refers only to manufacturing industry, and it remains for something to be said about the non-manufacturing sector of the economy. Data here are more difficult to obtain, but some useful material has been collected regarding concentration in the non-manufacturing sector.[14] For example, four of the clearing banks hold 92% of all bank deposits; five finance houses provide around 70% of all loans; five building societies hold 50% of all deposits, and four unit trusts manage 43% of all funds. Moreover, there is evidence to indicate that the degree of concentration is increasing, not only in the financial sector but in other non-manufacturing sectors too like agriculture, leisure services and retailing. We shall have a little more to say about concentration in non-manufacturing in section 4 of this chapter.

There are a number of reasons for believing that the extent and growth of the market concentration documented above is an understatement of the degree of concentration. First, the data above takes us only into 1968 and as the process of concentration is increasing, we may infer that by today the degree of concentration is considerably more than we have evidence to confirm.[15] Secondly, much of the data refers to widely defined industry groups. This will tend to underestimate the degree of concentration for any one product or market to the extent that the industry grouping used is not homogeneous. So for example, a firm may account for only 10% of the sales in an industry group as a whole but may have 50% or more of the market for a particular 'product'. A third reason why our evidence understates the true degree of concentration relates to how in the census of production (the source of most of the evidence we have referred to) a decision is made as to the ownership of firms. According to the census one enterprise owns another if it has more than 50% of the equity capital. However, as we shall see later in this chapter much less than this is often sufficient for *control* of the firm due to the dispersal of share ownership. Here again concentration will be underestimated, for what is classified as two or more separate firms may in fact be effectively owned and controlled by one firm. Fourthly, the implicit assumption is made in any analysis using census of production material that the UK constitutes the relevant market for the analysis of market concentration. However in some industries the market may be smaller than this, especially where transport costs account for a large proportion of the consumer price of a good. Consequently, 'spatial' monopolies may arise. Thus though a particular industry, say bricks or containers, may not seem to be highly concentrated, in the relevant market area it may be.

The final, and most important, reason why our evidence understates the concentration of industry in the UK is that modern industry is not organised on one product, one market or one industry lines. Modern industry is highly diversified and consequently any analysis of market concentration cannot isolate the full extent of the impact of the increasing concentration and monopolisation of industry in the economy as a whole. Hence we analyse the level and growth of aggregate concentration in the next section.

We now briefly examine developments in two particular industries with regard to the trends towards increased concentration.[16] Both industries are vitally important to society's welfare though in somewhat different ways viz. the brewing industry and the mass media. Table 3.1

shows the number of public houses owned by the six largest breweries
in the country, in 1960 and 1972.

Table 3.1: Number of Public Houses Owned by the 'Big 6' (Approxi-
mate Figures)

	1960	1972
Ind Coope/Allied Breweries	2,400	8,000
Bass Charrington	2,400	9,300
Courage	3,500	6,000
Scottish & Newcastle	1,700	1,700
Watneys	4,000	6,000
Whitbread	2,250	8,500
Total	16,600	29,500

Source: Hutt (1973), Chapter 6.

Thus they have, over the period, increased the number of houses
they own by around 2,000 per year on average. In 1960 they owned
24% of all public houses in Great Britain and by 1972 it was 56%;
though this figure is considerable greater in specific geographical areas
as many of us are well aware! This means that the public houses are tied
to purchasing the products of the brewery that owns them. Some of the
public houses are newly built, but by far the largest proportion of this
increase has come either through merger (e.g. Ind Coope and Allied
Breweries) or the takeover of small local breweries with their own outlets (e.g. Watneys' takeover of Trumans and Websters, or Whitbread's
takeover of Threllfalls). Whitbread, for example, have taken over 22
firms since 1961. Not only has the proportion of retail outlets owned
by the 'Big 6' increased so has their proportion of beer output. Indeed
two-thirds of all breweries operating in 1960 were not so doing in 1972.
On average 18 breweries closed every year, Whitbread alone taking over
21 between 1960 and 1969, 15 of which were closed. These 'Big 6'
now produce 80% of the brewing industry's output.

It is interesting to note that developments in the brewing industry
reflect developments in the economy in other ways. For example, these
firms are diversifying and are part of organisations not wholly based on
selling beer. For example Watneys are part of Grand Metropolitan
Hotels, and Courage are part of the Imperial Group. These trends in
mergers and diversification are treated in the next section.

The mass media are extremely important in contemporary society,

in that they are by far the major source of information about how
society functions and operates and yet they are dominated by private
capital and thus subject to similar processes as the rest of capital. We
content ourselves here with a few remarks about the newspaper industry. The newspaper industry exhibits similar tendencies to other industries with regard to the extent and growth of market concentration,
merger activity and diversification. For example, the five firm sales
concentration ratio for national daily newspapers is 86% and for
Sunday papers 88%. Indeed just four firms account for four out of
every five copies of national newspapers sold, and one company, Reed
International (which itself owns the International Publishing Corporation), accounts for 30% of all morning daily papers sold, 40% of all
Sunday papers sold and 30% of the sales of *all* papers including the
provincial press. The firms involved are increasingly diversified and
international. For example, IPC contributes only 30% to Reed's total
turnover and the Thomson Organisation, which obtains only 50% of its
turnover from newspaper publishing, owns more newspapers in North
America (*c*. 90) than in the UK (*c*. 50). A situation not unhelpful to
the firm in its dealings with the unions during the recent *Times*
publication suspension.

However, what is particularly important about the media is that we
are dealing with the concentration and control of *information* in the
hands of a few firms, information which helps to mould people's views
about the nature of reality in society. The amount of information they
make available, the selection of 'relevant' facts and issues, as well as
the framework for interpreting events, encourage a specific view of
reality. This ideological role acts so as to consolidate consensus, and
encourages the view that opposition to the status quo is illegitimate,
by concentrating on events *per se* and magnifying their immediate
consequences, rather than on their content, causes and significance
(e.g. strikes, demonstrations, terrorism and so on). A particularly
blatant example of this was the treatment of the NUPE industrial
action in the winter of 1978-79, which contributed considerably to the
return of a conservative government in 1979.[17] Debate in the newspapers, what there is of it, is limited to means rather than the ends, the
latter are taken for granted as being given and desirable. Those who
challenge these 'ends', those who seek to change the status quo, those
who adhere to alternative views of reality are branded 'extremists'
and their views (as opposed to their activities) ignored. Those who
control the means of communication therefore have considerable
power, particularly with regard to encouraging the consent/consensus

so necessary for stability in capitalist society. Given that, for example, newspapers are capitalist enterprises and that they are deeply dependent on advertising revenue for their existence, they are hardly likely to back labour against capital.

3. The Growth of Aggregate Concentration in the UK

Here we focus on concentration at the level of the economy as a whole rather than at the level of individual markets or industries. Consequently we are able to make more visible the actual extent of the concentration of monopoly power in the UK economy. Much of the power of a firm arises from its 'share' in the economy as a whole rather than in individual markets. This is as true for its bargaining power on the economic and political front as it is for its possibilities for survival and growth. We shall first present evidence on the extent of, and changes in the degree of, aggregate concentration, and then we will outline the consequences of the trends in concentration that we have documented and analysed in the previous section (at the market level) and in this action (at the economy level).

The extent and growth of concentration in the economy as a whole is summarised in Table 3.2. From the table we can see not only that concentration is increasing but is doing so at an increasing rate.

Table 3.2: Percentage Share of the Largest 100 Firms in Net Manufacturing Output 1909-1970

1909	1935	1949	1958	1963	1968	1970
16	24	21	32	37	42	46(est.)

Source: Aaronovitch and Sawyer (1975), Table 6.2, p. 117.

At the rates of change experienced in the 1960s and early 1970s, the largest 100 firms in the UK may well produce 80% of the nation's net manufacturing output by the 1990s.[18] Between 1949 and 1970 the top 100's share of output increased two-and-a-half times i.e. by 250%. Naturally even within the top 100 there is further concentration; although the top 100's share of net output was 42% in 1968, the top 50 accounted for 32% of the net output i.e. three times as much as the next largest 50 firms. Each of these largest 100 firms on average has 72 plants in the UK and employ more than 30,000 people.[19] Taking net manufacturing assets rather than output we find not only that concentration is higher, but also that it has been increasing at a faster rate than shown above. The proportion of the UK's manufacturing assets held by the largest 80 companies increased from 38% in 1957 to 70% in 1968, an annual growth rate of 7%.

If we focus our attention solely on quoted companies (which account for 85% of all manufacturing industry's profits) the extent of concentration becomes even more marked as the estimates in Table 3.3 show.

Table 3.3: Proportion of Sales of Quoted Manufacturing Companies Accounted for by the Largest 10, 25 and 100 Firms

	1957	1962	1968
10 firm C R **	24.6	na	27.1
25 firm C R*	36.7	43.0	46.3
100 firm C R*	58.3	64.3	73.2
100 firm C R**	60.1	na	74.9 (1969)

Source: *Aaronovitch and Sawyer (1975), Table 6.4, p. 119.
**Hannah and Kay (1977), Table 6.1, p. 86.

For example, three-quarters of manufacturing sales of quoted manufacturing firms in 1968 were accounted for by 100 firms.

Estimates of aggregate concentration updated to 1973 and 1976 have been prepared, though the data base only cover manufacturing firms with assets of over £2 million in 1969. These are set out in Table 3.4 and again demonstrate the high and increasing degree of dominance of the national economy by a small number of very large firms. What their size means in more concrete terms can be seen from a brief portrait of the 20 largest UK-based private firms.[20] Just 288 men (not people, there were no women) made up the boards of directors of these 20 firms which between them control 8,000 subsidiary companies.

Table 3.4: Changes in Aggregate Concentration 1969-1976

	1969	1973	1976
10 firm C R*	30.9	31.6	na
10 firm C R**	32.8	33.7	34.0
50 firm C R*	65.0	67.3	na
100 firm C R**	78.9	78.4	80.9

Source: Adapted from Hannah and Kay (1977), Tables 6.4 and 6.6, pp. 94, 96.
* Concentration ratios based on net assets.
** Concentration ratios based on market value.

The 20 firms had sales of more than £58,000 million in 1976 with pre-tax profits of more than £6,900 million. Their combined assets (at 1976 prices) were more than £30,000 million and they employed around 1,250,000 people.

The concomitant of the growth of giant firms, with enormous power and resources, has been the decline of small firms.[21] For example, in 1963 the 100 firms employing more than 10,000 people each, employed nearly one-third of the manufacturing workforce, whereas in 1935 firms of such size only employed 14%. Firms employing less than 500 people in 1963 employed only 29% of the manufacturing workforce compared to 49% by such firms in 1935. Whereas in 1935 there were 136,000 firms employing less than 200 people, by 1968 only 58,000 such firms existed.

What are some of the more immediate consequences of this growth of concentration in the UK economy?[22] The major consequence, already alluded to above, is the increased concentration of decision-making into the hands of fewer and fewer capitalists with regard to location, employment, investment, product changes and so on. This has the effect of increasing the domination of capital in at least three important ways: it reduces the extent of consumers' say in deciding what gets produced particularly in so far as such large corporations are able to influence wants through their artificial creation or stimulation; it increases capital's domination over labour power in the labour market; and it leads to the domination of particular areas by large multi-plant, often multinational organisations. Moreover, it is likely to exacerbate workers' feelings of alienation through the increasing necessity to work in large organisations, and to lead to increasingly hierarchical decision-making structures.

One further aspect of this growth of 'monopoly' power is such firms' ability to control prices and earn monopoly profits. Some of these can be used for the purpose of eliminating competition, including cross-subsidisation to eliminate potential rivals or 'price cut' firms, and heavy marketing expenditure (advertising, brand names, etc.) to act as a barrier to competition and to attempt to distinguish the firm's products from others. Monopolistic firms can also start 'price wars' so that smaller firms may be eliminated from the market. Thus it is likely that prices and profits in concentrated sectors of the economy will be higher than in more 'competitive' sectors. If this is so we may well ask what role prices and profits play in the capitalist system. They are intended to perform the function of allocating and distributing resources in accordance with consumers' wishes, for as consumer demands change so, under perfectly competitive conditions, will prices and profits in different sectors. Yet where major sectors of the economy are dominated by a high degree of monopoly, instead of reflecting this 'desirable' allocation of resources, they merely reflect monopoly power. Thus resources will tend to flow into these sectors for no other reason than the persistent presence of monopoly. It is unlikely, and certainly not necessarily true, that resources flowing in this way are reflecting a more efficient allocation of resources. We must add to these broad economic consequences of the growth of concentration the political consequences: an economic policy that does not secure the compliance or consent of 'Big Business' is likely to have little hope of success, for the reaction to many economic policy changes rests in the hands of the few powerful individuals and groups who own and control the giant corporations.

In the next section, we analyse the contributory causes of the growth of concentration, and in section 5 we explain how growth of, what we have so far referred to as, concentration at market and aggregate levels is an inevitable development of the existence and expansion of the capitalist mode of production.

4. Mergers and Concentration[23]

What then have been the main contributing causes to the rapid growth of concentration in the UK economy? The causes are threefold. First, the relatively faster rates of growth of output, assets and so on, experienced by the larger firms in the economy. Second, the liquidation/death of firms through being competed out of business. Third, and most important, is merger activity, causing the 'disappearance' of the merged/taken over firm. This, as we shall see, is the dominant cause of increased concentration at both the market and aggregate level. All three, however, are a result of the competitive process, where large firms grow faster, internally and externally, and have more chance of 'survival'.

Even in the 1950s mergers were occurring at an historically unprecedented rate except for the 1920s. For a typical manufacturing firm quoted on the Stock Exchange in 1954, the probability of 'dying' within six years (i.e. before 1960) was one in four, and its probability of dying through acquisition by another firm was one in five. But this process speeded up dramatically throughout the 1960s so that in 1964 the typical firm had a one in three chance of being taken over by 1970.[24] Thus throughout the 1960s and early 1970s the average annual death rate of UK quoted firms was around 4%-5% and this was almost *entirely* due to merger activity. For example, between 1966 and 1968 about 80% of deaths were due to merger[25] and between 1948 and 1972 half of all quoted firms were subject to merger activity in the period.[26] Between 1957 to 1968 38% of all quoted firms died through merger.[27] Spending on mergers rose to more than £2,500m in 1972 involving some 1200 companies – this was 15 times as much money as was spent during the whole of the 1950s on such activities, itself a period of almost unprecedented merger activity.

Table 3.5 sets out the pattern of spending on acquisitions by industrial and commercial companies from 1963 to 1978. It is noticeable that the level of merger activity rose again in the late 1970s.

Table 3.5: Merger Activity 1963-1978 as Measured by Expenditure on Acquiring Subsidiaries

Date	£m	Date	£m	Date	£m
1963	352	1968	1946	1973	1304
1964	505	1969	935	1974	508
1965	517	1970	1069	1975	291
1966	500	1971	911	1976	427
				1977	812
1967	822	1972	2532	1978	1104

Source: Updated from Secretary of State for Prices and Consumer Protection (1978), Table 1, p. 107, Appendix D.

The importance of expenditure on mergers can be gauged by expressing it as a percentage of investment in manufacturing.[28] It has increased from 17% in 1957/59 to 30% in 1963/65 to 58% in 1966/68, and reached 94% in 1968. The full impact of this merger activity on concentration is, of course, not fully represented in our analysis as for the most part our analysis excludes the 1970s.

There are a number of important features about mergers, apart from their dramatic growth and impact on concentration from the 1950s onwards, which we will now outline, that shed further light on the processes *underlying* this growth. We will analyse the processes in the next section.

First, the impact of merger activity is not evenly spread across different industries and so it contributes to increased concentration in certain sectors. For example, over the 1955 to 1968 period merger activity was particularly marked in the following industries: electrical engineering, textiles, drink, chemicals, vehicles, paper printing and publishing, and non-electrical engineering.

Secondly, mergers are becoming increasingly diversified (where one firm merges with another not producing the same commodities, but where the commodities are linked to the existing commodities produced) or conglomerate (where the commodities produced are dissimilar). In 1955 only 12% of all mergers, by value of assets involved, were of either of these two types, but by 1972 51% were.[29] Examples of conglomerates that have come about through merger activity in recent years include the Imperial Group which owns, inter alia, Ross Frozen Foods, Smedleys Tinned Foods, Unigate Foods, Gallaghers Tobacco and Courage Breweries; and ITT which owns Standard Telephone and Telegraph, Revlon cosmetics and Abbey Insurance, inter alia. Some idea of the growing importance of multiplant, multi-product, diversified and conglomerate firms can be gauged by noting that the average 'index' of diversification increased from 14.2% in 1958 to 19.3% in 1963, i.e. even before the merger boom of 1967 to 1973.[30]

Thirdly, it is the already large firms that are most active in mergers. The largest ten firms in the UK, in terms of assets, showed not only the highest rate of growth of all firms over the 1957 to 1968 period (they trebled their assets over this 12-year period), but were involved in more than one in seven of all mergers, thus consolidating their dominant position further. It is smaller firms, or those firms growing more slowly that tend to be most subject to mergers.

Fourthly, merger activity is increasingly important in other sectors of the economy than manufacturing; its impact is being felt in the distribution, property and finance sectors, especially since 1968. For example in 1973, for the first time, expenditure on acquisitions in distribution was greater than in manufacturing. Table 3.6 summarises the situation. The rapid growth of merger activity in other sectors than manufacturing is readily apparent, and is summarised in column 5.

Expenditure on mergers in manufacturing in 1966 was more than 350% of what it was in all other sectors combined, whilst by 1973 it was only 40% of what it was in all the other sectors combined. Thus mergers in finance, property and financial conglomerates are of rapidly increasing importance, spreading growth in concentration to other sectors than manufacturing and reducing the possibility of fully assessing the growth of concentration and monopoly power by individual markets or even sectors of the economy.

Table 3.6: Merger Activity by Sector 1966-1973

Year	1 Manufacturing	2 Distribution	3 Property	4 Finance	5 $\frac{1}{2+3+4}$	Total (1-4)
1966	399	59	10	42	3.6	510
1967	774	77	27	68	4.5	946
1968	1529	284	122	590	1.5	2525
1972	1292	967	126	406	0.9	2791
1973	457	498	263	308	0.4	1526

Source: Adapted from Aaronovitch and Sawyer (1975), Table 7.13, p. 145.

Finally its worth noting that between 1965 and 1973 only 2½% of mergers were referred to the monopolies and mergers commission. Indeed the Industrial Reorganisation Corporation's specific aim in the 1960s was to promote mergers in order to increase firms' competitiveness in international markets.

5. The Concentration and Centralisation of Capital

In orthodox economics the existence of a high degree of monopoly is often treated as a 'fringe' phenomenon — an 'imperfection', an 'aberration', from the norm of a competitive market economy. The impression is given that monopoly is a special case, a situation that can be dealt with through anti-monopoly legislation. However we have already seen that monopolistic markets are *not* special cases. The general situation is where increasingly a small number of large firms dominate individual markets, the economy as a whole and, as we shall see in a later chapter, the capitalist world as a whole. This does not imply that competition is eliminated, quite the opposite is the case. As we shall see competition and rivalry is intense between these large firms and it is the competitive process itself which generates them. Competition is reproduced on a higher scale.

In this section our concern is with the process through which this concentration occurs, a process that orthodox economics fails to treat adequately for it does not look dynamically at the forces of competition, it does not countenance that competition *inevitably* leads to concentration. We argue here that the development of concentration at the market and aggregate levels is a direct result of the accumulation process and the existence of separate private capitals competing to 'earn' profit. Thus it is the forces of accumulation and competition, endogenous and structural to the system, and not individual capitalists' malice or greed, that feed this process.

The aim of production under capitalism is to expand value ($M' > M$) by as much, and as quickly, as possible. This surplus value is accumulated by capitals so that the expansion of value can be renewed on a larger scale. This is forced on capitals because competition is fought by the cheapening of commodities, and there is therefore continuous rivalry between capitals to reduce costs of production by taking advantage of scale economies and more efficient and advanced production methods. There is, therefore, a competitive drive for accumulation and as the surpluses are ploughed back into the production process the size of capitals increase as production takes place on an expanded scale. Those capitals that accumulate more slowly and hence reduce costs less will be beaten out of the market and hence 'disappear' or at least grow more slowly. For both these reasons the average size of capitals and the degree of concentration increases. These ceaseless efforts to reduce costs relative to rivals/competitors are at the heart of the accumulation process. There is a further reason why this process encourages concentration. As the accumulation process proceeds the minimum size and capital requirements necessary to enter the market and compete effectively increases, thus providing a 'barrier to entry' to new or small capitals. As capitalism develops, the growth of constant capital relative to variable and the growth of fixed relative to circulating constant capital increases the average size of production units.

This slow, but ongoing, process of accumulation of capital through continually ploughing back the surplus into production and increasing the overall mass of capital is referred to as the *concentration of capital* and clearly demonstrates how competition leads to concentration as a direct result of the processes inherent in the capitalist mode of production. But this is not the only method by which individual capitals can accumulate more capital. A more rapid way is to gather together or combine *already existing capitals*, rather than create new capital. This process is referred to as the *centralisation of capital* and involves the expropriation of some capitalists by others, thereby centralising the ownership of capital and causing 'concentration'[31] to increase. Unlike the concentration of capital this process is not in principle limited by the rate of growth of markets; the firm itself does not have to grow. It can accumulate through external rather than internal growth and can accomplish instantly what may take years for concentration of capital to achieve. We have already seen in the previous section that this type

of capital accumulation through merger activity is the main determinant of the growth of giant firms, the decline of small firms and the
consequent growth in market and aggregate concentration, and so some
further comments on it are in order.

The accumulation process is competitive, both because markets and
profits are ultimately limited in size and because the advantages of size,
efficiency and so on are *relative* to the position of competing capitals.
Consequently rivalry is inherent in the relationship between capitals
with a ceaseless effort to eliminate and control rival capitals and thus
competition does not cease with the progressive concentration and
centralisation of capital, it simply reproduces it at a greater scale and
intensity. One method is through the concentration of capital, as
explained above, where costs are reduced relative to competitors, but
it can also be achieved more quickly in many cases through merger
which, like the concentration of capital, not only increases capital
accumulation, the possibility of reduced costs, and a likely reduction
in potential competition through restricting entry into the industry,
it also ipso facto reduces the number of competitors on the market (if
it is a horizontal merger) and hence the extent of such rivalry, and gives
increased control over output and price levels. It also makes collusion
and informal price fixing easier. It has other advantages too. It acts so
as to reduce excess capacity in an industry, which may have arisen
because of economic crises[32] (and hence declining markets for the
industry's output); or because of disproportionality problems (associated with changing consumer expenditure patterns or the imperfect
operation of the law of value); or because of unco-ordinated and
unplanned expansion of capacity (in times of expanding markets). Such
excess capacity puts on pressure to reduce prices and threatens profitability. In both declining and expanding conditions therefore there are
strong pressures to centralise capital. Such pressures have increased as
international competition and rivalry[33] has increased leading to further
pressure to reduce costs, and competitive pressures. But attempts to
reduce costs, limit competition (actual and potential) and reduce excess
capacity, are not the only reasons for the extent of merger activity. We
have already seen how important diversified and conglomerate mergers
have become. Such diversification of production through acquiring
another firm need not surprise us, for capital is not interested in
products but in profits, and thus which commodities to produce and
which markets to 'serve' are strategic decisions. Diversification is therefore one important strategy in overcoming the limits to accumulation
imposed by the slow (relative to accumulation) growth of particular

markets.[34] It may also act so as to stabilise profitability over time by reducing uncertainty and reliance on one, or a few, products and may further reduce rivalry through cross-subsidisation strategies or the denial of supplies or outlets to competitors, if the merger is of a vertical type.

6. Ownership and Control of Capital

It is often argued by orthodox economists and others that the motivation and goals of firms is no longer to attempt to 'maximise profits'. It is argued that modern large firms are increasingly controlled by professional managers whose interests are not the same as the capitalists who actually own the firms. This leads to the views that though resources may be concentrated power is not; large firms are more 'socially responsible' than hitherto; firms balance the interests of their owners with those of their employees, consumers, managers and society as a whole. Thus in the view of many, capitalism has been so transformed that we are, in the late Anthony Crosland's words, a 'post capitalist' society, hence neatly doing away with the need to abolish capitalism!

This type of argument challenges, and seeks to modify, the view that the central dynamic of capitalism is surplus value creation, accumulation and realisation. It argues that the goals of firms have changed. However, it rests on three propositions all of which have to hold for the argument to be sustained:

(1) There is a 'divorce' between ownership and control in large firms.
(2) The objectives of the owners and controllers of capital are different and divergent.
(3) The environment in which such firms operate allows them discretion to pursue different objectives than profitability.

It will be shown that all three of these propositions have been grossly overstated and that the goal of profitability remains paramount.

First, to what extent is there a divorce of ownership from control in large corporations? It has been shown[35] that this 'managerial revolution' where control is supposed to have been wrested from the owners of capital is patently untrue for many of the largest firms in the UK. Thirty-eight of the largest 120 firms have boards of directors which consists mainly of the owner, his family or his nominees. In these large number of cases there is no question of the divorce of ownership of the means of production from their control. In other cases there may indeed be a wide dispersion of share ownership giving rise to the *possibility* that owners do not have domination, but it is precisely this wide dispersion which means that ownership of only a small proportion of shares in a company is often required for effective, as opposed to nominal, control. What is more this dispersion is still limited within the hands of a relatively few people — 93% of all individually-owned securities and shares are held by 5.3% of the UK adult population.

A recent study[36] has analysed the ownership and control of Scottish-owned industry in Scotland in 1973/4. It was found that in 12% of all the companies, the board of directors had half or more of all ordinary shares, and in 45% of companies they held 30% or more of the ordinary shares. It was shown that one-third of all the companies were controlled by clearly recognisable groups with more than 50% of voting shares and that more than three-quarters of them were controlled by majority or minority[37] interests. Even in those companies with no 'identifiable' control, strong inter-relations were found between the various groups of owners through shareholdings, directorships and so on. So here again the appearance of no identifiable ownership is illusory — of the largest 68 Scottish companies 49 were interlocked through directorships.

Another study based on case studies of 20 of the largest UK firms and a less intensive study of the largest 250,[38] argues that ownership interests are very important and that the control of large firms by managements with little proprietary interests in them, has been over-played. Indeed 56% of the top 250 companies are 'owner controlled' on their criteria.

Secondly, do the owners and controllers of capital, where they are different, have different and divergent objectives? The pecuniary interests of managers/controllers and owners are in fact tightly linked. The former derive substantial income from the ownership of shares and the extent to which executive income is dependent on profit forges a community of interest between managers and owners. Though the *proportion* of shares held by managers may in some cases be small, this does not indicate a small value of such shares and a consequent lack of interest in profitability. For example, though in some large firms like Unilever, Imperial Group and ICI, board holdings may be less than even 1% of all shares, their value is considerable. In a study of six large UK firms where the average holding of directors was 0.17%, it was shown to represent an average market value of £15,000 at 1971 prices. There is then a unity of interest between top managers and owners, and a social unity too as the owners and controllers are all men of property. It is also the case that bonuses and incentives are linked to profitability, and that managers' motivations are a product of the moulding institutions of which they are a part.

Thirdly, even where there exists a divorce of ownership from control, and even if owners and controllers had different and divergent objectives, do firms have discretion to pursue other objectives than those that contribute to profitability? Is it possible to sacrifice profit when such objectives conflict with it? In many cases 'other' objectives like growth are not in conflict with the demands of profit, because growth is a function of profitability, both because internally generated funds are essential for expansion and because securing external funds from the Stock Exchange, banks and so on, are heavily dependent on profitable operation. Moreover, it is less profitable firms that are most at risk in the merger process, as well as in the process of the concentration of capital.

What if other objectives do conflict with profit? If the dominant group of shareholders disapprove of managers' actions, for example those that threaten profitability, they may well sell shares (for they are interested in income) which may well reduce their price and extent of capital gains, thus introducing the danger of takeover, or result in difficulties in obtaining external funds. Where large blocks of shares are held by institutions like pension funds, insurance companies and so on, their concern for long term profitability will reinforce such profit orientation. Again, the discipline of competition and the accumulation process ensures that those firms who sacrifice profits for other objectives will fall behind. Furthermore, profit remains the measure of success of corporate policies and if firms *did* have discretion and the owners and controllers *did* have different objectives, one would expect to find differences in managerial behaviour between owner and non-owner managed firms. It has been shown however, that for the USA at least, there are 'no fundamental differences in the level or stability of profit rates which might be attributable to management control'.[39] Also observable philanthropy, such as sponsorship of sport and so on, are undertaken not for reasons other than profitability, but as part of a marketing and public relations strategy which is designed to secure/ obtain the loyalty and affection of the public and employees and thus contribute to profitability. The potential gains of such activities are carefully assessed. Where 'social responsibility' conflicts with profitability, it is the former that is sacrificed.[40] Capitalism demands such behaviour.

In a sense then it is not overwhelmingly important whether there is a divorce of ownership from control and whether the owners and controllers of capital would prefer different goals, for the logic of accumulation and competition allows them little, if any, discretion. They must expand or die. We may conclude then that firms, within the constraints imposed by limited information, limited resources and perceptions of rivals' reactions indulge in a 'systematic temporal search for the highest practical profits',[41] or as one executive has put it to me 'attempt to maximise long run sustainable profits'. In this they are aided by modern business techniques from organisation and methods to market research and operational research, so that the impact of alternative corporate policies on profitability can be, as far as possible, rationally and efficiently calculated. Capitalism has changed its spots but has not had a change of heart. The coercive laws of accumulation and competition will survive as long as the capitalist mode of production survives.

Further Reading

For the 'original' discussion see Marx (1972) Chapter 27. Sloan (1973), Chapter 6 and Papandreou (1973) are useful general and theoretical analyses of the growth and impact of the concentration and centralisation of capital. See also Mandel (1975), Chapter 10 or (1968) Chapter 12. Aaronovitch and Sawyer (1975) is however the single most important work in this area from a theoretical, as well as empirical, viewpoint. Particularly relevant to our treatment are Chapters 1, 2, 6, 7, 8, 11 and 12. A useful summary is to be found in Nore and Green (1977), Chapter 5 which also contrasts marxist with orthodox accounts of the growth of concentration. Aaronovitch and Sawyer (1974) is an interesting empirical study of the aggregate concentration in the UK, whilst Friedman (1977), Chapter 3 charts the growth of monopoly power, arguing though that firms do have more discretion in their behaviour than previously. On the divorce of ownership and control and so on see Blackburn (1972), chapter 8 and Westergaard and Resler (1975), Section 3, Chapter 2. Scott (1979) is a thorough analysis of the corporation and its relation to contemporary capitalism in the UK.

Notes

1. The issue of for whom these goods and services are produced i.e. who gets what, is reserved for Chapter 4.

2. See again Chapter 4 4.

3. See Chapter 2, sections 5 and 6 and Chapter 5.

4. On the internationalisation of capital and the development of the multinational corporation see Chapter 6.

5. For example, many firms produce more than many countries. Measuring output as GNP for nations and gross sales for corporations, Unilever produced more in 1971 than the entire Portuguese or Irish economies.

6. On the growth of so called 'market' and 'aggregate concentration' see for example, in the USA Hunt and Sherman (1972), Chapter 18 and for Western Europe Jacquemin and de Jong (1977), Chapters 2 and 3.

7. For a review of the various measures of concentration, their advantages and deficiencies as well as other problems involved in this type of analysis see Utton (1970), Chapter 3, Aaronovitch and Sawyer (1975), Chapter 3 or Jacquemin and de Jong (1977), Chapter 2.

8. See Secretary of State for Prices and Consumer Protection (1978), p. 51 and Table 4, p. 52, Appendix A.

9. See Hansard, 6 April 1970.

10. For the 142 industry groups where comparisons are possible.

11. See Aaronovitch and Sawyer (1974).

12. See George (1975).

13. See Pickering (1974).

14. See Aaronovitch and Sawyer (1975), Chapter 5.

15. The justification for this view will become more apparent on reading the next two sections of the chapter.

16. The reader is referred for more detail on these industries to Hutt (1973) and Protz (1978) on brewing, and Murdock and Golding (1973 and 1977) on the media, on which the following remarks heavily rely.

17. This is just one example of the crude anti trade union bias in the media. For a critical perspective of the treatment of trade unions and industrial affairs by the media see Beharrel and Philo (1977).

18. See, for example, Hannah and Kay (1977), p. 114.

19. See Hannah and Kay (1977), Chapter 6.

20. See Labour Research (1978a), pp. 201-2 which also gives an interesting account of how omnipresent these firms are in our daily life.

21. See Prais (1976).

22. This issue is treated in greater depth in Sections 4 and 5.

23. The term merger is used to include *both* a transfer of control of a firm's resources to a controlling interest outside that original firm, sometimes referred to as a 'takeover' and a pooling of hitherto separate independent firms, sometimes referred to as a 'merger'.

24. See Singh (1975).

25. See Singh (1971).

26. See Hughes (1977).

27. See Hannah (1974).

28. Expenditure on acquiring controlling interests in subsidiaries by UK public quoted companies in manufacturing as a percentage of gross domestic fixed capital formation. Data from Hughes, quoted in George (1975).

29. See Gribbin (1974).

30. See Amey (1964) and Sawyer (1971). The index of diversification is the ratio of a firm's output in 'other industries' to its total output. Indeed 42 of the UK's largest firms operate in ten or more industry groups.

31. Concentration is used here in the same sense we have earlier used it, to mean the proportion of an industry's (or nation's) output, assets and so on controlled by a certain number of firms, and not in the sense of distinguishing concentration of capital from centralisation of capital.

32. See Chapter 5 on the causes of crises.
33. See Chapter 6.
34. The internationalisation of capital is another strategy, as we shall see in Chapter 6.
35. See Barrat Brown (1968).
36. See Scott and Hughes (1976).
37. That is, where between 10%-50% of the share ownership was in the hands of a clearly definable group.
38. See Nyman and Silbertson (1978).
39. Larner (1966) in a study of the 500 biggest non-financial corporations in 1963.
40. As the managing director of Gillette said on withdrawing from sponsorship of cricket's Gillette Cup in April 1980 'sponsorship is no longer cost effective for us because more than half the population do not associate the Gillette Cup with us'.
41. Earley, quoted in Baran and Sweezy (1968), pp. 36-7.

4 INEQUALITY – THE DISTRIBUTION OF WEALTH, INCOME AND POWER

'Property, Profit and Market -- the key institutions of a
Capitalist Society — retain their central place in social
arrangements and remain the prime determinants of
inequality' (Westergaard and Resler, 1975)

1. Introduction

Our concern in this chapter is with how the capitalist system, and in
particular capitalism in the United Kingdom, distributes the fruits of
society's productive efforts: the extent, and causes, of the unequal
distribution of 'rewards' between society's members. The determinants of inequality naturally relate to the basic institutions of a capitalist society — the private ownership of productive resources, and the
ability to transmit wealth accumulated through ownership to others;
the existence of wage labour and hence of the labour market; and the
activities of the state.

The chapter proceeds as follows. First, we outline our theory of
inequality. Secondly, we will consider the major features of the degree
of inequality in the distribution of wealth in the UK; changes in it over
time, its main determinants and the impact of the state. Thirdly, we
will examine the evidence on the distribution of income in the UK, and
the changes that have been taking place in it, prior to explaining the
causes of income inequality and to considering the impact of the state.
Then we will consider the distribution of power as an element of
inequality in capitalist societies, and finally we pay some attention to
aspects of inequality other than those of wealth, income and power;
so-called 'secondary' inequality, in particular education and health.

2. Class and Inequality – Elements of a Theory

Our objective in this section is to explain the *fundamental* causes of
inequality in a capitalist system. We are interested in the mechanisms
through which the fruits of production are distributed amongst those
who 'co-operate' in the production process and will argue that the

essential distributional feature is the existence of private ownership of the means of production. That is to say that *distributional* relations are structured by capitalist *production* relations. An essential characteristic of capitalist societies is that the means of production are privately owned, and this creates a class of society who, because of this ownership, are able to have first claim on the appropriation of any surplus gained in the process of production. The existence of private property gives capitalists this as a right, and simultaneously deprives the mass of society from access to the means of production which are monopolised by one class and must then sell their only remaining resource, their ability to work, in order to earn a livelihood. Thus those who cannot command a claim to income because of property ownership, must hire out their labour on the market in return for a wage, and in so doing provide capitalists with their income. Workers have no choice but to sell their ability to work, their labour power, in return for its exchange value, the wage. In return the capitalist has the right to put the worker to work as he sees fit, he obtains his use value, and ensures that he works more hours than is necessary to produce the wage, thus creating surplus value which is realised when capitalists sell the resulting commodities on the market. The surplus labour performed by workers thus forms the 'income' of the capitalist class.

Thus the relations of production under capitalism simultaneously create the existence of private capital and wage labour, and of two forms of income, profit and wages. The former arise solely out of ownership and are not a 'reward' for any productive activity. They arise from the particular form of production relations under capitalism and represent the surplus produced by workers but expropriated from them. These two major classes of society, capitalist and worker, are in conflict over the appropriation of the surplus and the struggle between them can therefore have an impact on the distribution of 'rewards' between capital and labour. This struggle takes the form of wage 'negotiations', productivity deals, conditions of employment and so on, and this objective conflict becomes clearer in periods of zero growth, at the level of an individual capital or in the economy as a whole. Where there is a 'zero sumgame' an increase in the surplus accruing to one class means less for the other. However there are strict limits to the success of such negotiations, over and above the unequal power of capital and labour, for if workers succeed in increasing their share of the surplus created, accumulation may falter or collapse as the surplus is eaten into and jobs will be threatened. Workers are therefore often faced with the choice, within the limits imposed by capitalism, of moderating wage

claims or facing unemployment. There are therefore considerable limits
on the extent to which inequality can be reduced under capitalism for
capitalists must be paid an 'acceptable' reward otherwise they will not
invest, undertake production or accumulate capital. Workers' earnings
on the labour market, from their sale of labour power to capitalists,
are thus ultimately governed by capital's goal of profitability.

This brief analysis of the fundamental cause of, and dimension of
economic inequality under capitalism contrasts strongly with orthodox
views of inequality in four important ways. First, orthodox approaches
argue that workers and capitalists receive an income proportional to
their 'contribution' to production. With regard to workers' income this
ignores the exploitation of labour that we have outlined above, and
with regard to capitalists' income, rests on a confusion over the
meaning of capital. Whilst capital goods are productive, ownership of
them is however not a productive activity. The capitalist is not productive but merely the capital goods that he owns. Secondly, inequality
in the orthodox approach is viewed as arising from inequality of *opportunity* in competing for different positions in society, a result of labour
market 'imperfections'. Equality of opportunity however is in no way
incompatible with capitalism, for such a meritocratic system merely
ensures that the most able and appropriate individuals are recruited for
particular positions thereby improving the 'efficiency' of the system.
Such equality of opportunity, for example for women and ethnic
minorities, whilst resisted by many in capitalist society actually implies
inequality of outcome and condition. Equal opportunities are in any
case generally only thought of in connection with the labour market,
for equality of opportunity in society generally would seem to imply
the abolition of inheritance. Thirdly, orthodox approaches to inequality, rather than adopting a class perspective, adopt a multi-
dimensional view wherein there is no one dominant source of inequality,
but a number, each as it were 'cross-cutting' each other where individuals are on different levels of the various dimensions. This implies
inequality is not functional to capitalist relations of production, a
proposition we seek to demonstrate *not* to be the case in the rest of this
chapter. A fourth contrast is that whilst marxist analysis stresses the
crucial importance of the key institutions in capitalist society in determining patterns of inequality, orthodox analysis argues that inequalities
arise out of differences between people (often argued to be innate) in
intellect, skill, application and so on. Once again we see that whereas
our approach sees individuals as being constrained/moulded and classified by society, orthodox analysis stresses individuals' decisions and

freedom of action independent of the organisation of the economic system.

3. The Distribution of Wealth

In this section we stress the role of private ownership of the means of production in the determination of inequality. We begin by describing the main characteristics of the present distribution of wealth in the UK and the changes that have taken place in this distribution over time, and then we survey the major causes of the patterns that we have observed. First, however, we must define what we mean by wealth. Broadly speaking wealth may be defined as a stock of assets, so that the distribution of wealth relates to the distribution of *ownership* of financial and physical assets. Thus wealth may be distinguished from income from wealth, about which we will have something to say in the next section, which refers to the *receipts* from the ownership of the assets. For measurement purposes it is usually defined as the value of assets of an individual minus his liabilities, often referred to as 'net worth'.[1]

The pattern of wealth distribution in the UK is not a peculiarly UK phenomenom rather it is a basic feature of all capitalist societies, though of course the degree of inequality observed does vary to some degree.[2] This implies that despite many institutional, cultural and policy differences between countries, the basic cause of inequality is common to them all i.e. an economic system based on capitalist relations of production. The Inland Revenue publish estimates of the distribution of wealth based on estate duty returns which is a major source of information on wealth distribution, because individuals, and not all individuals at that, are only required at death to reveal their net wealth holdings, for the purpose of filling in a return for estate duty payment. According to these estimates the distribution of wealth is becoming increasingly diffused and more equally distributed over time. For example their figures show a decline in the Gini co-efficient of concentration from 0.76 in 1960 to 0.65 in 1970.[3] However, the Inland Revenue data in its basic form is unreliable and inaccurate for a number of reasons.[4] First, the estimates cover less than half of the adult population for they are based on the estates on which duty was paid or probate needed in that year and in consequence more than half of those dying annually are excluded from the statistics. These exclusions of individuals, generally with zero or very small amounts of wealth, are thus ignored in the data and hence the degree of concentration is understated. Moreover this only gives us information about those dying in a particular year, so that to convert the data to an estimate of the distribution of wealth of the living requires the assumption that those who die in any year are a random sample of the living population, and moreover requires the use of the 'mortality multiplier' to achieve this estimate. Secondly, the wealth of those who are covered by the data is understated mainly because of the use of tax avoidance techniques by individuals, including the transfer of wealth as a 'gift' to others which is then exempt from duty,[5] and the holding of wealth in trusts. Thirdly, the figures relate to individuals rather than families or householders and thus family wealth is not aggregated.

However, after adjusting for these problems we can now outline in Table 4.1 the best estimates available of the changes in wealth distribution since 1938 and its present distribution.[6]

Table 4.1: The Distribution of Wealth in Britain 1938-1968
Percentage Share of Total Personal Wealth

Date	(1) Top 0.1%	(2) Top 1%	(3) Top 5%	(4) (3) - (2)
1938	27	55	78	23
1951	18	42	68	26
1955	16	41	66	25
1960	15	38	63	25
1968	11	31	56	25

Note: Estimates relate to the population aged 25 years and over.
Source: Atkinson (1975), Table 7.3, p. 134.

The differences between these estimates and those of the Inland Revenue may be illustrated by an example. In 1968 the share of the top 1%, according to Inland Revenue estimates, was 24% of total personal wealth, whilst the corrected estimate is 31%. We can see from the Table that the share of the top 5% of holders of personal wealth has been declining, though from column 4, we can see that the decline is confined almost wholly to the top 1%, the others in the top 5% have indeed slightly increased their share over the period. The share of the next richest 9% (after the richest 1%) has risen from 32% in 1938 to 40% in 1966, and was estimated to be 41% in 1974. The present day concentration of wealth is such then that 1% of the adult population have 31% of the total personal wealth. That is, just 400,000 people have a total holding between them of £29,000,000 the average holding being £70,000.[7] Indeed 10% of the population have 72% of the total personal wealth leaving just 28% for the remaining 90% of the adult population. By any standards this concentration is substantial. Indeed if the total personal wealth were divided equally among the adult population it would give an average of £6,000 per married couple in 1966, around £15,000 at 1980 prices.[8] Another important feature of the distribution of wealth is the form in which wealth is held. The fact is that the composition of assets varies enormously between groups of wealth holders. The less well off tend to hold wealth, if they have any at all, in the form of bank accounts or a private dwelling, whereas for the well off, the holding of wealth in the form of company securities forms a large proportion of their wealth holding. Thus the concentration of ownership of shares, that is the direct ownership of the means of production, is even more unequal than the distribution of wealth as a whole. It has been estimated that 81% of all personally owned stocks and shares are owned by 1% of the population.[9]

More recently[10] it has been estimated that in 1973 those whose net wealth was more than £200,000 (some 30,000 people owning between them net £19,000,000,000) own 37% of all quoted company shares, 39% of all other company securities, 31% of all government securities and 42% of all land. In consequence nearly 70% of their wealth holding was in ownership of the means of production or ownership of land. Those with a net wealth of more than £50,000, the top 3.5% of the population, held 90% of all personally owned shares and 96% of the land.[11] This may be compared with the asset structure of those whose wealth was less than £5,000. They held 1% of all company shares and 0.4% of all land. In consequence less than 2% of their wealth was in the form of company securities or land. Rather 38% was in the form of national savings and life policies, 25% in the form of dwellings and 20% in bank and building society deposits. It is true, however, that as a proportion of total shareholdings the personal ownership of shares is declining, whilst the holdings of insurance companies, pension funds and other financial institutions is increasing.[12] However personal ownership is still by far the major category of owners, and in any case the shares of the financial institutions are themselves owned by the same small number of people who own the personal shares in manufacturing.

Naturally wealth plays a vital role in maintaining investment, accumulation and production. Investors will not invest unless their capital is safe and the rate of return is 'adequate'. Consequently any sustained attempt to break it up or take it over would lead to a capital

strike and/or flight, and 'put off' foreign capital from investment in
the UK. As long as the nation's productive resources remain in private
hands, they must be 'rewarded'. An attack on wealth is an attack on
capital itself.

Attempts to reduce the inequality in the distribution of wealth in
the UK have occurred, primarily through taxation in the form of estate
duty. However, the revenue from estate duty was only about 0.3% of
the total personal wealth, that is less than 10% of the annual increase in
wealth. In any case avoidance of estate duty developed into an industry
in itself. It has been estimated[13] that the amount of duty avoided
through the transfer of wealth by gifts to other living persons alone
amounted to around £170,000,000 per year in the late 1960s. It has
also been estimated[14] that by 1969 estate duty might have expected to
yield three times as much as it did in fact yield. Indeed estate duty was
regarded as an essentially voluntary tax as its avoidance could be
achieved through 'gifts' before death and the placing of wealth into
trusts. The replacement of estate duty by a 'gifts' (capital transfer) tax
in 1974 is unlikely to make any significant impact on the concentration
of wealth. The tax rates are not penal and no greater than estate duty
rates, nor is the threshold at which it begins. If they were, if there was
a real attempt to increase dramatically the taxes on capital, then the
owners would refuse to invest. Any radical redistribution of wealth
would require the dissolution of private property itself, and thus
capitalism itself. Taxes merely aim to raise revenue and moderate some
of the effects of the concentration of private ownership, not to abolish
it.

What are the implications of the extremely unequal distribution of
wealth that we have documented, and what are the processes through
which the concentration of wealth is maintained? When we speak of the
distribution of wealth, we refer to how the wealth held by individuals
is distributed between those individuals. This implies that assets, especially productive assets, are privately individually owned. That is they
have property rights attached to them, that the individual concerned
has a legal claim over the ownership of assets. This is a function of the
legal code of society which is in no way sacrosanct for all time; the
means of production can exist in other forms than private property. It
is especially important to realise this because private ownership of the
means of production is at the heart of the inequality of the distribution
of wealth, and as we will see it is also at the heart of the inequality in
the distribution of income, power and overall rewards in society. Thus
any *radical* attack on the unequal distribution of wealth requires an

attack on the institutional arrangements that lead to that inequality, the basic institution being that of private property, private ownership of the means of production.

Given that private ownership exists in capitalist society, how does the concentration of wealth in the hands of a small proportion of the population persist? The roles played by 'accumulation' and 'inheritance' are central to the understanding of the dynamics of the unequal distribution of wealth. Accumulation, in this sense, refers to wealth gained from one's own income. This occurs when an individual saves and then invests these savings. One's ability to do this depends on one's surplus income over and above one's consumption needs, and those with higher incomes thus have a greater potential surplus and therefore greater opportunity to accumulate. As those on the highest incomes are likely to be the large owners of capital[15] the inequalities in wealth holdings, especially of productive assets, will widen under the market. Moreover the yield or return that one receives on wealth is crucial in accumulating further wealth during one's life span; thrift alone, without a high yield, is not important. For example[16] if an average individual saved 5% of his earnings between the ages of 25 and 65 and received a 3% cumulative rate of return, he would accumulate seven times his initial earnings by the age of 65. However if the rate of return were 10% he would accumulate 33 times his initial earnings. To enter the top 0.1% of wealth holders, the amount needed is 100 times average earnings.

Those people then who begin life with no inherited wealth are unlikely to have a large holding of capital by the end of their life, especially if their earnings are average. Even someone who earned three times average earnings (in 1979 this would be around £240 per week) and who saved one quarter of it, receiving a 3% rate of return, would never reach the top 0.1%. Moreover, of course, the more wealthy receive higher returns on their wealth holdings because of the structure of their assets. The wealth holdings of the bottom 90% consist largely of owner occupied houses, consumer durables and so on which do not yield an income as such whereas the assets of the top 10% of wealth holders are much more orientated towards higher yield, and partly because of this can generally gain even on the same assets. Even more important however as a source of capital gain is ownership of the means of production, especially the setting up of a business oneself, but also ordinary share ownership. In both cases it is the firm's accumulation of capital through the reinvestment of profits from the productive process that is the key, which itself results from the surplus value produced by the workers being appropriated and converted into new capital as the basis for future capital gains.

The second factor that is important in explaining the persistence of concentration of wealth is inheritance, that is the transmission of wealth between generations. As long as property can be transferred from parents to children then inequalities in the distribution of, inter alia, wealth in one generation will be transmitted to the next one. Any attempt to heavily regulate this under capitalism is impossible for it threatens the very heart of the system, that is the institutions of private property and the legal relations of ownership thereof. Without the abolition of these twin institutions even equality of opportunity is not guaranteed. Moreover it has been shown[17] that the importance of inheritance in amassing personal wealth has not declined since the 1920s and that twice as many of the top 0.1% of wealth holders are such by virtue of inheritance rather than accumulation i.e. unrelated to their own efforts.

Naturally the ownership of wealth confers many advantages on those who own it other than the wealth itself. First, the holding of wealth implies income from that source. Indeed the distribution of income from wealth is even more unequal than the distribution of wealth itself, so that property ownership has implications for the distribution of income too. When held in the form of shares, dividends are received as income, and capital gains are made. This income of course also brings other advantages such as increased security from risks, as well as from uncertainty about the future and gives increased 'freedom' of action in life style and so on. Secondly, there is the question of control. Ownership of company shares, which are disproportionately held by the very rich, carries with it control over privately owned productive resources and financial institutions – they can influence, not to say direct, the use to which capital is put. Note that with the kind of assets the less rich hold, bank deposits, insurance policies and so on, there is no such control over the use of their wealth. Thirdly, with ownership of property goes the right to sell property to others i.e. the right to transfer one's wealth to another person either inter vivos, or between generations.

Before leaving this section on wealth we must briefly refute an argument that is sometimes put forward about future trends in the distribution of wealth. The argument is that the degree of concentration of wealth has been declining and there is no reason to suppose that the process will not continue in the future without any further action to reduce the concentrations. There are two reasons why this argument is unsound. First, we have seen that the reductions in wealth concentration, when the available data is properly adjusted, have been marginal and indeed some of the most well off groups have even improved their relative position. In any case, the concentrations are so great that another 50 years at the rate of diminution in inequality that proceeded in the past 50 years would still leave the top 10% of wealth holders with something like 40% of the total personal wealth of the country — more than the bottom 90% of the population has between it today!

Secondly, short-run falls in the prices of stocks and shares will reduce temporarily the degree of inequality as they are disproportionately held by the most wealthy. Thus fluctuations in the distribution of wealth over short time periods does not necessarily indicate a change in the underlying concentration of wealth.

4. The Distribution of Income

In this section we begin by analysing the pattern of income distribution in the UK and the changes that have taken place in it since 1949.[18] Then we shall analyse the determinants of the degree of inequality that we have described, and finally we consider what impact the state has had on income inequality.

Table 4.2[19] outlines the major trends in pre-tax distribution of income in Britain for three broad income groups over the period 1949 to 1967.

Table 4.2: Pre-tax Distribution of Income in Britain 1949-1967

Date	Top 10%	Mid 60%	Bottom 30%
1949	33	54	13
1954	30	59	11
1959	29	61	10
1964	29	61	10
1967	28	62	10

Source: Atkinson (1975), Table 4.1, p. 51.

Table 4.3 furnishes us with more detail as well as some updating (see also Table 4.4). However, it is based on certain adjustments to the Inland Revenue figures, and uses the family expenditure survey for the year 1970/71. Consequently the two tables are not strictly comparable.[20] However both tables do relate to the pre-tax distribution of income and thus show the degree of inequality in incomes arising from market processes.

Table 4.3: The Pre-tax Distribution of Income in Britain 1954-1971

Date	Top 1%	2-5%	6-10%	11-40%	41-70%	Bottom 30%
1954/55	8.8	11.0	8.5	35.3	23.1	13.5
1959/60	7.9	10.8	8.7	35.5	23.7	13.4
1964/65	7.7	10.6	8.7	35.9	23.8	13.5
1967/68	7.0	10.4	8.8	36.5	24.2	13.2
1970/71	6.3	10.3	8.8	37.2	23.9	13.5
1971/72	6.1	10.3	8.9	37.4	24.1	13.2

Source: Harrison (1974) and Royal Commission on the Distribution of Income and Wealth (1975), *Report No. 1.*

It is clear from Tables 4.2 and 4.3 that the upper groups of income recipients receive more than a proportionate share of income. For example, from Table 4.3 we can see that in 1971/72 the top 1% of income recipients received more than 6% of all income, whilst the next top 4% received more than 10% and the bottom 30% only received 13.2% of the income. In 1973/74 the top 2% of tax units, some 591,000 received the same income between them as the bottom 28.6% of tax units, some 7,874,000.[21] The Gini co-efficient of inequality for 1967 is 0.37 i.e. the expected income difference between two income units chosen at random was 74% of the average income in that year. This broad pattern of income inequality is observable in all the advanced capitalist countries. Sawyer[22] has compared the pre-tax income distributions in 12 countries and found that in all cases the top 10% of income earners receive between 24% and 31% of pre-tax income and the bottom 10% between 1.2% and 2.9%. The degree of difference in other decile groups was even less. Once again this indicates that the basic features of income inequality are shared by all capitalist economies.

As for the changing degree of inequality, the top 10% of income recipients (see Table 4.2) reduced their share over the period by 5% points and at the other end of the scale the share of the bottom 30% of income recipients also declined. Indeed from Table 4.3 it is particularly clear that any redistribution over the period was almost wholly confined to the top 40% of income recipients. Moreover the degree of change for all groups, except perhaps for the top 1%, was very small.

The Gini co-efficient only fell from 0.39 to 0.37 over the period in question and moreover from the tables it would seem that most of the redistribution occurred in the 1950s. Between 1964 and 1972 the relative shares of the top and bottom 10% did not change at all, the top 10% still receiving nearly eight times as much as the bottom 10%. The relative shares of the top and bottom 25% did not change over the period either.[23] The structure of income inequality remained essentially the same in the 1970s as it did in the 1950s.

Additionally there are two major reasons why the above figures underestimate the degree of income inequality. First, the figures for personal income exclude capital gains which accrues to shareholders as a gain in the future; effectively it is a personal income of shareholders saved for them by companies. These capital gains amounted to, on average, £350 million per year between 1967 and 1969. Secondly, the data on which the above tables are based, are collected by the Inland Revenue for taxation purposes and in consequence 'non-taxable' income is not included in the figures. The main consideration here is that many 'fringe benefits' are often either tax free or not fully taxed, for example, company cars, subsidised mortgages, private medical care, school fees and so on. Now the quantitative importance of such non-taxable income rises disproportionately with income, and to the extent that it does so increases the degree of real income inequality that we have observed above. The extent and impact of these fringe benefits are difficult to quantify, but it has been estimated that in 1966 they were worth around 30% of income for those earning more than £7,000 per year, whilst in 1974 on average they added £3,000 to a £10,000 a year salary (30%) rising to £8,000 for a £20,000 per year salary (40%).[24] A survey conducted in 1975 also indicates that the percentage of gross salary accounted for by fringe benefits varied from 5% for manual workers to 29% for managing directors.[25] Inequality is understated for the additional reason that the self-employed tend to understate their real incomes.

In commenting on the unequal distribution of income that we have documented in the UK we have here little to say on poverty. There is good reason for this, because a preoccupation with an arbitarily defined group (for example those whose income falls below supplementary benefit levels) diverts attention from the larger *structure* of inequality in society within which poverty is embedded. Focusing below a certain level of income may divert attention from what is occurring above that line and the fact that the two are interdependent. Moreover it encourages the view in some people that poverty is the accumulated product of 'individual' deficiencies – laziness, lack of intelligence, lack of initiative and so on, and thus locates the problem as of the people's own making. Some of the *characteristics* of the poor are somehow viewed as the *causes* of poverty – old age, unemployment, physical and mental handicap, one parent families and so on.[26]

Before we move on to the determinants of income inequality, we must deal briefly with one further issue and that is the impact of inflation on inequality. This is clearly an important consideration given that the UK is at the time of writing, experiencing rates of inflation of around 20%. The pattern of expenditure of different income groups naturally varies, with low income families spending a relatively larger proportion of their limited income on, for example, fuel and food than do higher income families. Now, in the construction of the retail price index (cost of living index) the pattern of expenditure used is that of an 'average' family and as prices change at different rates on different commodities over time then the application of a single index to measure the inflation experieneed by families of different incomes is clearly, to say the least, inadequate. If the prices of those goods which constitute the bulk of low income groups' expenditure are increasing faster than other goods then changes in money incomes only, that is those that we've been describing above, will *underestimate* any changes in the degree of inequality. There is evidence that this is in fact the case. It has been shown[27] that between 1956 and 1966 an individual in the top 5% of the income distribution experienced, on average, a 38% increase in the price of goods purchased whilst an individual in the bottom 5% experienced a 44% increase, and this in a period where inflation was running at 2% to 3% per year. In 1975 alone inflation was running ¾% faster for low income families than for the average family.[28] Another recent study[29] has shown that over the period 1964 to 1972 changes in prices in the UK had a clear bias towards increasing inequality. Indeed between 1964 and 1970 the small reduction in money income inequality that occurred overstates the real inequality reduction by 13% to 15%. Furthermore the inegalitarian bias in price changes was even greater in 1970 to 1972. Thus increases in lower income groups' share of income may not mean the groups are increasing their share of *real* income.

We have already outlined in a previous section a theory of inequality but we give more flesh to this theory now by analysing the influence of different forms of income on inequality. There are basically three sources of income: income derived from ownership of assets and property; income derived from the labour market; and income derived from the state in the form of benefits. We treat each of these in turn.

Income derived from ownership of assets, from wealth, often referred to aptly as 'unearned income' is the major factor determining
income inequality. We have already seen in the section on the distribution of wealth that it is even more unequally distributed than the
distribution of income, and that income from wealth is likely to be
even more unequally distributed than the distribution of wealth itself,
because of the different structure of assets held by the most wealthy
compared to those with little wealth. Much of the wealth of the bulk of
the population is held in the form of owner occupied houses, consumer
durables and other personal assets which do not yield income, and
much of the rest is in a form that yields lower incomes than those of
the more wealthy groups in society, whose assets are constituted
largely by ownership of land and the means of production. Only 20%
of tax payers receive any income from wealth at all, 8% receive about
75% of this income whilst a mere 1% have 33% of it — receiving the
same amount that, after tax, the poorest 30% of the population receive
in all as their income! This is of course additional to the capital gains
that arise from holding wealth in the form of stocks and shares and
which can be realised through their sale. The contribution of 'unearned'
income then to income inequality is of paramount importance. If the
income yielded from private property were distributed equally to every
'married couple' it would be equivalent to 25% of gross average incomes. Such redistribution would of course fundamentally threaten
capitalism itself.

The second source of income is 'earned income', wages and salaries,
income derived from selling one's labour power to others. Essentially
the labour market operates on similar principles to other markets in a
capitalist economy. Labour power is a commodity like any other to be
bought and sold and its price, the wage, is its exchange value expressed
in money terms. It is the amount of money a capitalist must pay to
'persuade' workers to work during which process they perform surplus
labour for the capitalist thus producing surplus value. Whilst the relations between workers and capitalists seem free and equal at one level,
the level of markets, at another level, that of production, they are
coercive and unequal. Labour power once purchased is used, controlled
and dominated by capital. Thus wages reflect the relative power of capital and labour at any particular moment in time or any particular situation. This balance of power whilst being fundamentally loaded in
favour of capital, may shift somewhat under the operation of market
forces as excess demand for labour power develops, in general or in

particular, and the industrial reserve army, the extent of the excess supply of labour power, shrinks. This has the effect of reducing the degree of competition for jobs between workers and increasing the competition between capitalists for workers and may therefore cause wages to rise. Of course, labour is not passive in this unequal relationship at work, and exploitation is resisted through struggles in bargaining over wages, conditions of work and so on. This struggle is a permanent feature of relations of production in capitalism. There is a continuous conflict over the distribution of surplus value between capital and labour, for though the former has first claim to it, it is possible for workers through their collective organisations, depending on their strength, organisation and militancy, to claim some of the fruits of increased 'productivity'. However in situations where productivity is not increasing, or increasing slowly, successful attempts to increase wages beyond a certain point may threaten the accumulation process as the rate of surplus value falls. Hence workers are often faced with the choice of moderating wage claims or facing unemployment caused by a break in the accumulation process. Such are the 'choices' of a capitalist economy.

As we mentioned above the principles that operate at the level of markets are those of supply and demand. So that as far as occupational differences in wages are concerned, these will tend to reflect the supply of the relevant type of labour power relative to the demand for that particular 'type' of labour power. Relative scarcity, whether 'natural' or artificially imposed, therefore has a role to play in explaining occupational wage differentials. Such wage inequalities play a crucial role in capitalism, for work is a burden, something that *has* to be performed. Thus material incentives are required to motivate workers and attract and expel workers from different occupations and locations as patterns of commodity demand change. These are also required so as to persuade workers to acquire more or different skills, and perform certain functions. The division of labour under capitalism thus requires unequal rewards so that the labour market can operate and allocate labour to appropriate jobs. An important dimension of inequality generated through the labour market, is that which is required to separate the interests of 'managers' of capital from those of 'workers'. Capital controls the labour process through the agent of 'management', to discipline the workforce, co-ordinate production and preserve authority. This authority, responsibility and decision-making is then an important justification for unequal rewards. Coupled with the de-skilling of many elements of the labour force through the development of 'scientific management' and the application of technological change, this has created a widening of wage incomes.

Another factor which has contributed to inequalities of reward between occupations, is the fact that the labour market does not operate 'perfectly', in the sense that the mobility of labour, occupationally and spatially, is restricted. Labour markets are 'segmented' and overlaid with inequalities of opportunity. This restricts occupational choice and reduces the efficiency of the labour market in allocating labour in accordance with market price signals. This division of the labour market into groups or segments between which there is great difficulty in moving, has a number of important aspects, which we can only briefly mention here.[30] First, there is a primary labour market and a secondary labour market. The latter differs from the former in that wages are lower, promotion prospects are few, few skills or qualifications are required and labour turnover is high. Many workers in such jobs are ethnic minorities, youths or women. Secondly, overlapping this segmentation is another based on sex-, and to a lesser extent race-, typing of jobs. For example women are typed for 'serving' jobs like secretarial and waitress positions, a situation encouraged by the socialisation process from an early age and the undertaking of similar jobs in the home as girls develop to 'serve' men in a variety of ways.[31] Such divisions in the labour market not only operate against reducing wage inequalities through raising barriers to occupational mobility, but also through breaking down the unity of experience and purpose of workers and dividing them into distinct groups, it separates them from each other and enables the capitalist class to exploit sexual and racial differences between workers. Equally important in this context of dividing workers and thus reducing their cohesiveness and organisation, is the operation of internal labour markets or job ladders which stress differences between workers (with regard to skill, responsibility, manual v non-manual and so on) rather than their community of interest.

Finally, we may note that the distribution of earnings in the labour market between different occupational groups has in fact remained broadly constant since 1914, and that the distribution of earnings among manual workers has hardly changed since 1886.[32] In consequence we can say that the degree of inequality associated with the functioning of the labour market shows little evidence of a long term trend to diminish. The third major source of income, and the third factor that has an impact on the degree of income inequality, is the state.

5. The Impact of the State on Inequality[33]

In order to isolate the impact of the state on income inequality we must look at who benefits from the state and who pays for it. This involves analysing the incidence between income groups of taxes and benefits. Table 4.4, as a first approach to this, outlines the main features of the distribution of income in the UK between 1949 and 1973, and the impact of *direct* taxation on this distribution.[34]

Table 4.4: Percentage Share of Total Income Before and After Direct Taxes 1949-1973

Year	Top 10%		Mid 60%		Bottom 30%	
	pre	post	pre	post	pre	post
1949*	33.2	27.1	54.1	58.3	12.7	14.6
1954*	29.8	24.8	59.3	63.1	10.9	12.1
1959*	29.4	25.2	60.9	63.5	9.7	11.2
1964*	29.0	25.1	61.4	64.1	9.6	10.8
1967*	28.0	24.3	61.6	63.7	10.4	12.0
1971**	25.4	22.1	61.1	63.1	13.5	15.0
1973***	24.7	21.4	61.1	62.7	14.2	15.9
1977****	26.2	23.1	63.0	64.3	10.8	12.6

Note: The figures for 1971 and after are not strictly comparable, due to data source differences.

Sources: *Atkinson (1975), Table 4.1, p. 51.
** Harrison (1974).
***Royal Commission on the Distribution of Income and Wealth, *Report No. 1* (1975), Table 10.
*****Social Trends* (1980).

Clearly the impact of direct income taxes is to reduce the degree of inequality by reducing the share of the top 10% and increasing the share of, especially, the bottom 30% though the extent of the changes in income shares are not large enough to radically alter the distribution. The largest change over the whole time period is in fact only enough to increase the share of the bottom 30% by 1.7 percentage points. Moreover if we take the post-tax shares as a percentage of pre-tax shares, we can see that the income tax system has made negative progress over the time period. For example, in 1949 the share of the top 1% after income tax was 55% of its pre-tax level, yet this had risen to 67% by 1971. The top 5% also increased their post-tax share as a percentage of their pre-

tax share from 87% to 90% over the period, whilst the bottom 30%
saw their share decline from 114% of pre-tax income to 111%. Thus
direct taxation has been relaxing its grip on inequality, both at the
top and bottom of the income range. Though the direct tax system
does have some small impact on reducing income inequality, this
impact has progressively lessened since 1949. One cause of this is that
the low paid are increasingly being pushed into the tax bracket and
hence the burden of taxation is shifting towards them. For example,
in 1975 a person earning two-thirds of average earnings paid more than
10% of their income in tax, whereas in 1965 the same person would
have paid none. Indeed total deductions from pay as a proportion of
gross earnings have increased by nearly 300% for such workers between
1965 and 1975, whereas for the high paid it has increased by only 50%.

Now we move on to look at the impact of other forms of taxation
and benefit provision on income inequality. This is important because
direct taxation only accounts for about half of all tax revenue and
when indirect taxes are included we find that the tax system *as a
whole* has very little net impact on inequality: 'Families within a wide
range of income from nearly the lowest to nearly the highest, consti-
tuing in fact the great bulk of population, pay taxes at almost a uni-
form rate',[35] and 'to try to use taxation as a veneer on inegalitarian
society such as ours can only have disappointing results. Taxation cannot compensate for an unequal society'.[36] Westergaard[37] for example,
has shown how the tax system maintains inequality. In 1976, taking
households with two adults and between one to four children, taxes
took 36% of the 'original income' of the richest 10% and about the
same proportion from all other deciles except for the bottom 10%
where taxes took 44% of original income. Another recent study[38] has
analysed the impact of total taxes (including National Insurance contributions) on income distribution and as can be seen from Table 4.5 the
percentage of income paid in taxes is virtually the same for the richest
20% of households as the poorest 20%. Indeed in no decile group is the
difference between (1) and (2) more than 0.2% and in all decile groups
the percentage of income paid in taxes is virtually identical at around
33%. We may therefore reiterate our conclusion that taxation has no
real impact on the degree of inequality in the UK.

A further study[39] attempts to assess the impact not only of all
taxes, but also of state benefits which were possible to allocate by
income groups. This almost 'total' impact of the state was found to
reduce the Gini co-efficient of inequality by only 0.03 and this moreover assumed that the benefits of the National Health Service and state

education, inter alia, were *equally* distributed between families, whereas in fact in a class society different groups have a *differential* access to
publicly provided services. Moreover, no attempt was made to estimate
the distributive impact of the benefits from such public services as
roads, police protection, museums or local welfare services, the inclu-
sion of which, if it were possible, may well increase inequality rather
than reduce it.

Table 4.5: Distribution of Income Before and After Taxes and 'Tax
Rates'

Decile groups	(1) % share of gross income	(2) % share of income remaining after tax	Taxes paid as % of gross income
Top 10%	20.8	21.0	32.7
11-20%	13.6	13.6	33.4
81-90%	6.1	6.2	32.0
Bottom 10%	4.5	4.6	33.1

Note: Gross income includes all state cash benefits.

Source: Royal Commission on the Distribution of Income and Wealth (1978),
Report No. 4, Table 12.

We saw above that the income tax systen was relaxing its hold on
income inequality. What picture emerges if we include all taxes and
social service benefits that are allottable both direct and indirect?
Table 4.6 shows how inequality did in fact widen between 1961 and
1970. Another recent study[40] has shown that between 1961 and 1973
the impact of all taxes, cash benefits and allottable benefits in kind,
barely reduces inequality at all. The Gini co-efficient of inequality
declined only from 32.8 to 32.4 and if only cash benefits and direct
taxes are included the co-efficient did not change at all over the period.

Table 4.6: Income Inequality After all Taxes and Social Service
Benefits 1961-1970

	Lowest income of richest 20% ÷ highest income of poorest 20%			
	1961	1965	1968	1970
2 adults	214	197	209	238
2 adults and 2 children	182	178	178	180
All households	270	275	282	295

Source: Westergaard and Resler (1975), Table 3, p. 46.

We have demonstrated that the state has had at best only a small impact on income inequality in the UK. This raises the issue as to how capable is the state of reducing inequality in a capitalist society. After all, social democratic parties ostensibly pledged to a more equal society have formed governments in a number of advanced capitalist countries, including the UK since 1945 and yet the 'reforms' (sic) that have been introduced with regard to welfare, education, taxation, employment and so on seem to have had little effect. This is hardly surprising for such reforms still leave the means of production in private hands, and still leaves the economy organised on market principles. These are the *root* cause of inequality. However, such policies do have the effect of broadening the social base of recruitment to privileged positions in society, even though they do not attempt to equalise the rewards to these positions. This move towards equality of opportunity and a merit-ocratic society is compatible with capitalism, indeed it will improve its efficiency. Such reforms may be tolerated, providing they can be achieved within the capitalist framework. However, substantial redis-tribution, even if it were possible through taxation and social reform, must not go beyond the point where it impairs the working of the market system. Differentials, incentives, differential status and so on must be maintained for the system to work. Earnings *must* remain unequal to motivate people to change jobs and locations, to acquire new skills, to reward effort and responsibility, otherwise the relevant supplies of labour will not be forthcoming. Moreover, redistribution must not impair the profitability of capital. Yet the abolition of inequality is impossible without the abolition of the root causes of that inequality, capitalism itself — private ownership of the means of production and allocation and distribution of resources through the operation of markets. Taxation and benefit provision may marginally alter income inequality, they may mitigate some excessive inequalities, but they only deal with the symptoms of the problem and not with the root causes that produce the inequality.[41]

6. The Distribution of Power

We may provisionally define power as the ability of a person or group to realise objectives against the wishes of another person or group.[42] Often, a number of interdependent but conceptually distinct forms of power are defined, which include political power, cultural power and economic power. The last of these refers to control over the means of production, distribution and exchange and more generally to control over resources. We have seen evidence both in this chapter and in Chapter 3, that this economic power is highly concentrated in capitalist society. The inequalities in wealth and income distribution are a visible manifestation of the distribution of power, for they reflect the dominance of capital. The power of capital is demonstrated by the unquestioned priority that is given in capitalist societies, to capital accumulation and market determinants of the allocation, distribution and use of resources. We take the view that the ultimate basis of power, the dominant form of power, is economic; the ability to control the use of society's resources. It is ultimately from this source that other forms of power derive, both control of the political institutions,[43] that is in the ultimate case the resources of force, and in terms of cultural power, the control over the means of value creation, interpretation and maintenance, in other words the resources that create and transform society's values and norms which legitimise actions in society. It is this latter type of power that we have not yet dealt with and it is thus considered briefly here.[44]

The capitalist class is the dominant power in society, if by dominant power we mean those who control and benefit from the existing arrangements in society. As the fundamental source of this power is economic, they have access through ownership to one of the most powerful means of legitimation of values, the mass media, which purveys the broad values of this ruling capitalist class. However, this dominant value system which imposes their version of reality on the rest of society, has other sources which include the state, the Conservative Party, and the educational system, which encourage the acceptance by people at large of these capitalist values. Such values underpin the capitalist system and are accepted as part of the natural and eternal order of things by the mass of the population and, not surprisingly, by bourgeois social science. Their acceptance on this scale is essential for the capitalist economy to operate, and indeed as part of the 'superstructure' are an integral part of a capitalist society. Such core values include aspiration, individualism, materialism and an acceptance of the limits of social and economic policies and change, and a consensus view of society.

The acquiescence of large sections of the working class to the core values of capitalism increases the latter's legitimacy, its ability to create values, and enables it to 'punish' deviance and dissent from such values by 'extremists'. Moreover in so far as the leadership of working class parties, like the Labour Party, cease to espouse radical, alternative views of reality and endorse the values and institutions of the dominant class, workers' views of reality are likely to be further circumscribed. Thus working class interests may become increasingly unarticulated with an observable consensus emerging in society. Power includes the ability of groups to create and reinforce values and practices that limit the scope of debate to those issues which are relatively innocuous to the capitalist class. Thus control of the political agenda assumes crucial importance, as the very wants of the working class become increasingly shaped by the capitalist class. In some ways this is a supreme form of power, the ability to prevent conflict arising at all, by shaping the perceptions and preferences of individuals to accept their role in a capitalist society. Thus those subject to this 'cultural' power do not become aware of their real interests and do not become aware of objective reality. In such situations, without the help of a counter to this power, the economic power of capital is ensured. This book is one small contribution amongst many to counter the capitalist vision of reality becoming increasingly all pervasive in society and to attempt to present an alternative perspective on the workings of the capitalist system. Knowledge is a basis for Power.

7. Further Aspects of Inequality

It is clear from our discussion so far, that the distribution of income, wealth and power in contemporary Britain is highly unequal. We have also argued that these inequalities are structural to the workings of the capitalist system, and cannot be radically altered without fundamental changes in economy and society i.e. by abolishing the key institutions of capitalism. However there are other aspects of inequality that deserve some consideration here, as they directly impinge on the working and social lives of the bulk of working people and demonstrate in concrete terms what inequality and an unequal society really mean. These are often referred to as secondary inequalities because in order to understand their origins it is necessary to see them in relation to the primary dimension of inequality (i.e. class) as discussed above.

First, we deal with status. Status, honour and prestige are generally associated with the highly materially rewarded occupations and positions in capitalist society, indeed this relationship between economic class and status is necessary for if the distribution of social status and prestige failed to match the distribution of material rewards in society, the structured material inequality would be stripped of its normative

support. Wide differences in material advantages could not be justified
if the view was widely held that occupations were of equal social value,
or could be ranked in terms of social value very differently to the rank
order of material rewards by occupation. Thus the status order serves
so as to stabilise and legitimise inequality. How does this status ordering
arise? The social evaluation arises not from the moral evaluation of the
whole population, but from the moral judgements of those occupying
the dominant positions in the class structure, as Marx said: 'The ideas
of the ruling class are, in every epoch, the ruling ideas . . . the class
which has the means of production at its disposal, has control at the
same time over the means of mental production, so that thereby,
generally speaking, the ideas of those who lack the means of mental
production are subject to it. The ruling ideas are nothing more than the
ideal expression of the dominant material relationships.' We are back
once again to cultural power, its role here being that the prevailing
value system legitimises the existing inequality.

Secondly, we mention some aspects of inequality at work. As we
have already seen capitalists and workers stand in an unequal relationship to one another. Within the capitalist firm there is a hierarchy
where income and status differences are parallelled by other inequalities,
and class differences exist as a microcosm of society as a whole. For
example in 1970 90% of all male non-manual employees were covered
by employers' sick pay schemes, whilst 80% held occupational pension
schemes. The corresponding figures for manual workers were 65% and
50% respectively.[45] Class differences in conditions and terms of employment are legion. All manner of non-pecuniary advantages rise sharply
with income and status including the sick pay and pension schemes
mentioned above, career prospects, holidays, meal facilities, annual
increments as well as other less tangible but very real differences in
conditions of employment relating to security of employment, predict-
ability of income,[46] and safety and health of the working environment.
No less important are the differences in the intrinsic interest of the
work where, in general, high income occupations are characterised by
ability to exercise responsibility and power as well as the development
of the individual personality, scope for creativity and so on.

Thirdly, and finally, there are the inequalities in society which are
reflections of economic inequality. We briefly mention two here:
health and education. One might expect that as the allocation of health
resources is no longer dictated through market prices in the UK, and
as most health services are virtually 'free' and available according to
'need' rather than ability to pay, there would be no systematic inequality

in health care and provision. This is not the case[47] between classes or
spatially, even when the growing private health care sector is ignored.
One outcome is that the wide differences in mortality rates between
classes are widening further rather than narrowing. For many age
groups the death rates are twice as high amongst class 5 people than
class 1 people, and class differences in standardised mortality rates are
widening.[48] Life expectancy, infant mortality and proneness to most
diseases and illnesses also differ dramatically between classes.

As far as education[49] is concerned, again there are clear class variations in class size, resource provision and educational 'attainment' as
well as the wealthy being able to afford to exercise 'free choice' to
choose schools outside the state sector, hence giving rise to unequal
access to educational facilities. As far as the content of education is
concerned, it can be argued that much of it maintains and reproduces
inequality through the values and ideologies it promotes, and the
roles to which it implicitly assigns people from an early stage. Thirty
per cent of children of class 1 parents go to independent schools compared to 1% of classes 4, 5 and 6.[50] This is important for reasons in
addition to pupil/teacher ratios and so on, for a large proportion of
those people who hold major positions of power in society come from
such schools — 80% of High Court and Appeal Judges, 80% of bank
directors, 62% of top positions in the Civil Service, 68% of directors of
large industrial firms and so on. Yet such children only make up around
2.5% of the total school population.[51]

Other examples could be given of the reflection of substantial
income, wealth and power inequalities on individuals' overall life
chances and styles, including inequality in access to legal services and
decent housing. They all bear witness to the substantial and structural
inequality in UK society.

Further Reading

A useful collection of empirical material, and commentary on all
aspects of inequality in the UK can be found in Reid (1977). Labour
Research Department (1977) is a compact alternative. The most comprehensive and thorough empirical analysis of the distribution of
income and wealth is Royal Commission on the Distribution of Income
and Wealth (1975-9) various volumes. The first four of these are neatly
summarised in TUC (1976) and more comprehensively in Royal Commission on the Distribution of Income and Wealth (1980). Also useful

in this context are Blackburn in Urry and Wakeford (1973) and Kelsall and Kelsall (1974.)

The most useful single reference on the economics of inequality is Atkinson (1975). In particular, Chapters 2 and 4 deal with the main features of, and changes in, income and wealth distribution in the UK, whilst Chapters 7 and 8 concentrate on the determinants of wealth distribution. The latter is also comprehensively covered in Atkinson (1972).

Westergaard and Resler (1975) is a classic marxist analysis of inequality in the UK. Particularly relevant to our discussion above is Part 1. See Chapters 2 and 3 on income inequality, Chapters 5 and 6 on the labour market, and Chapter 7 on the impact of property ownership.

On the impact of the state on inequality, see Westergaard and Resler (1975), Part 1, Chapter 4 and Kincaid (1973), Chapter 6. More comprehensive from an empirical point of view is Field *et al.* (1977). For a more theoretical and explanatory perspective see Gough (1979), Ginsburg (1979), George and Wilding (1976 and Burden, Chapman and Stead (1981).

On power and its distribution see Lukes (1975) and Westergaard and Resler (1975), Part 3, Chapters 1 and 7. For comparative material on income distribution between capitalist economies see Sawyer (1976), and for material on socialist economies see Parkin (1971), Chapters 5 and 6 and Lane (1971).

Notes

1. See Atkinson (1975), Chapter 2.
2. On wealth distribution in the USA see Lampman (1959) which is also reprinted in Atkinson (1973) and Edwards *et al.* (1978).
3. The Gini co-efficient, in this context, is a measure of the degree of inequality in the distribution of wealth. It varies from a value of 0.0 (implying equality in wealth holdings – everyone having the same amount) to 1.0 (where all wealth was held by one member of the population).
4. For a more detailed account of the inaccuracies of the data and the methods of estimating wealth holdings see Atkinson (1975), pp. 121-32.
5. Providing the donor lives for seven years after the gift. With the introduction of a 'gifts tax' (Capital Transfer Tax) in the mid-1970s this particular loophole is now closed.
6. See Atkinson (1975) and Atkinson and Harrison (1978).
7. The figures are for 1968 at 1968 prices.
8. However it should be noted that the potential increase in production and wealth that would result from the abolition of capitalism, the freeing of productive forces from being held back by the capitalist relations of production, far exceeds any increase accruing through distributional changes.
9. Lydall and Tipping (1961).

10. Royal Commission on the Distribution of Income and Wealth (1975), *Report No. 1*.

11. Royal Commission on the Distribution of Income and Wealth (1978), *Report No. 4*, Table 25.

12. See Scott (1979), Chapter 3.

13. Horsman (1975).

14. Meacher (1971).

15. See the next section on income inequality and its causes.

16. This example is taken from Atkinson (1975), pp. 143-7.

17. Harbury and McMahon (1975.) For further analysis of inheritance see Harbury and Hitchens (1980).

18. On the distribution of income in other capitalist countries see the excellent review by Sawyer (1976). For more detailed analysis of the USA see Edwards *et al*. (1978).

19. These figures are based on Inland Revenue records of incomes for tax purposes, but the relevant table as far as I am aware, which used to be published in the National Income Blue Book, has not appeared since 1967.

20. For a discussion of the problems involved in the measurement of income inequality see Atkinson (1975), Chapter 3 or Sawyer (1976).

21. See TUC (1976), p. 15.

22. See Sawyer (1976).

23. See Royal Commission on the Distribution of Income and Wealth (1975), *Report No. 1*, Table 5.

24. See Royal Commission on the Distribution of Income and Wealth (1976), *Report No. 2*.

25. See the useful summary of the available data on the distribution of income provided by TUC (1976). In this particular case see p. 21.

26. Readers interested in poverty *per se*, are referred to the reports of the CPAG or the major recent study of poverty in the UK produced by Townsend (1979).

27. See Tipping (1970).

28. Low Pay Unit (1975).

29. Muellbauer (1974).

30. For further analysis see Reich *et al*. (1973) or Gordon (1972).

31. In the UK women make up around 40% of the working population and earn wages, on average, less than 75% of those of males. However it is appropriate to point out here that the inequality and oppression that women face is not solely the result of the capitalist mode of production. Women are 'doubly oppressed' both by capitalism and by patriarchy. Whilst the overthrow of capitalism is a *necessary* condition for the abolition of patriarchy, it is by no means a *sufficient* condition as changes in the mode of production in other nations demonstrate. See Mitchell (1971).

32. See Westergaard and Resler (1975), Part 2, Chapter 5.

33. On the theory of the capitalist state see Chapter 7, and to some extent Chapters 1 and 2.

34. As well as ignoring indirect taxes, it also ignores the problems of tax avoidance and evasion. Moreover transfer incomes (pensions, supplementary benefits and so on) are included in the pre-tax income figures and therefore especially for low income groups the pre-tax figures do include an element of state derived income. It is also worth noting here that only 6% of all tax revenue in the UK comes from taxes on corporate income.

35. See Nicholson quoted in Blackburn (1967).

36. Field *et al*. (1977), pp. 248-9.

37. See Westergaard (1978).

38. See Royal Commission on the Distribution of Income and Wealth (1978), *Report No. 4.*

39. See Nicholson in Wedderburn (1974).

40. Royal Commission on the Distribution of Income and Wealth (1975), *Report No. 1*, pp. 58ff. Redistribution is primarily horizontal rather than vertical. See, for example, Gough (1979), pp. 108-14.

41. See Chapter 7 for a further discussion of the nature of state welfare policies.

42. On the problems of defining power see the introduction to Urry and Wakeford (1973).

43. See Chapter 7, and Chapters 1 and 2.

44. For a more comprehensive treatment see Lukes (1975) and Westergaard and Resler (1975), Part 3.

45. Figures refer to adult full time workers.

46. Only about 65% of male manual workers earnings are accounted for by the basic wage and so variations in the availability of overtime and the possibility of short time working are real uncertainties.

47. See *Patterns of Inequality D302 Unit 13* (1975).

48. See Reid (1977), pp. 124-5.

49. See *Patterns of Inequality D302 Unit 13* (1975).

50. See Reid (1977), p. 181.

51. See Reid (1977), p. 184.

5 ECONOMIC CRISES, UNEMPLOYMENT AND INFLATION

'The real barrier of capitalist production is capital itself' (Marx)

1. Introduction

The process of capitalist development is inherently unbalanced, uneven and unstable. This is the case whether we are referring to sectoral, spatial or temporal development. In particular in their unending quest for expansion capitalist economies experience disruptions in the accumulation process which are manifested in fluctuations in the level of economic activity, and hence in the rate of growth of output, as well as in levels of utilisation of physical and labour resources; means of production and labour power.

This instability and its consequences of unused and wasted resources demonstrates capitalism's limited ability to satisfy human needs. People and machinery lie idle in a world of scarcity; unemployed resources co-exist with unmet needs. There are unemployed builders and yet people are homeless. Such unemployed, and underemployed, resources could be utilised to produce goods and services to satisfy social needs, but the organisation, and relations, of production under capitalism prevent this happening. The relations of production hold back the development of productive forces, and act as a brake to society's ability to satisfy people's material, social and cultural needs. For example, if the current level of unemployment in the UK[1] were reduced by half this could increase production by around £7,500 million; enough to increase spending on health and education by 50% or double old age pensions, or secure a 10% increase in real wages.[2] Another estimate of the total costs of the increase in unemployment to society between the years 1974 and 1977, including the loss of output, loss of tax revenue to the state, and the payment of various compensations, amounts to £20,000 million.[3] The inability of capitalism to smoothly reproduce and expand over time, and achieve stable growth, not only gives rise to a waste of resources, but is a threat to the existence and future of the system itself. Growth serves as a stabilising function for it serves to reduce potential conflict between classes over the division of the economic 'cake'. In periods of relatively stable and sustained growth, it is possible to spread the benefits between classes and regions and for

108

workers' organisations to win concessions from the capitalist class and
the state. When the cake is not getting any bigger, however, or if it is
getting smaller, the objective conflict of class interests becomes clearer
and may give rise to an intensification of the class struggle. However,
as we shall see, economic crises do perform a function for capital and
it is by no means certain that such crises herald the end of capitalism.
Such an era can only be ushered in by the collective strength of workers
in their struggles.

Whilst this chapter offers an explanation of the tendency to crisis
and instability in capitalist economies, it focuses on the contemporary
UK and on the central issues of inflation and, especially, unemployment. The analysis presented here naturally contrasts with Keynesian,[4]
as well as the fashionable neoclassical, explanations of the nature of
'the crisis' and the high levels of unemployment and inflation currently
being experienced in the UK.[5] Our marxist perspective stresses that
crises arise out of threats to profitability and that these threats are
inherent in the accumulation process. In capitalism production is for
private profit and hence threats to profitability threaten production
and employment, as the 'incentive' to produce, and the means to
produce, are reduced. Thus explanations of crises and unemployment
have to be related to the characteristics and dynamics of capitalist
economies. Naturally, the implications of such explanations are radically different from those of the Keynesian and neoclassical approaches.

The chapter proceeds as follows. In the next section a brief outline
of the recent employment and unemployment experience of the UK
economy is given. The key section of the chapter, section 3, analyses
the nature of economic crises and their effects on unemployment. It
also deals with the *restructuring* process, the attempts to restore profitability, and its impact on unemployment, in the light of which, there
then follows an outline of the prospects for employment in the UK
over the next few years. The final section, section 4, outlines the UK
experience of inflation and discusses its determinants, whilst insisting
that inflation is not the real crisis but rather an expression of the underlying crisis: the threat to profitability inherent in the accumulation
process, deep in the heart of the capitalist economy.

2. Unemployment: The UK Experience

The appearances of secular decline and cyclical crises are readily
apparent. The slow and uneven growth of output, the lack of

international 'competitiveness'[6] and especially, from our point of view,
the increase in unemployment, all bear witness as we shall see below to
the slackening of accumulation and the holding back of investment,
associated with fluctuating, low and declining profitability. For
example, between 1970 and 1976 output grew by only 13% and
indeed the annual average for 1973 to 1978 was -0.9%. Figure 5.1
shows the pattern of registered unemployment in the UK since 1948
whilst Table 5.1 shows more recent experiences in tabular form.

Figure 5.1: Average Annual Percentage Rates of Unemployment in
the UK 1949-1979

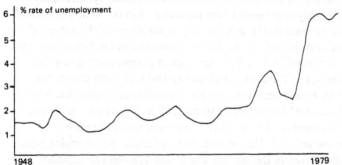

Source: Department of Employment (1971) and *Department of Employment
Gazette* (Various issues)

Table 5.1: Absolute Numbers (in '000) and Percentage Rate of
Unemployment in the UK 1972-1980

	%	Absolute Numbers
1972	4.2	971.5
1973	3.5	806.3
1974	2.7	627.5
1975	3.3	771.8
1976	5.5	1303.2
1977	6.0	1448.2
1978	6.4	1548.5
1979	6.0	1455.3
1980	6.1	1471.0

Source: *Department of Employment Gazette* (December 1979 and March 1980),
Table 106. The figures are seasonally unadjusted for January of each year and
include school leavers.

Two important features of the UK's unemployment experience are
immediately clear from these figures. First, there has been a secular
upward trend in average levels of unemployment, i.e. a tendency for
unemployment levels in recent years to increase at each successive
'boom' and each successive 'slump'. Secondly, the behaviour of unemployment is decidedly 'cyclical', with unemployment levels fluctuating over time. Again there has been a tendency for the size of these
fluctuations to widen. Unemployment has increased by around 300%
or by nearly 1,000,000 people between 1966 and 1978. At an observable level the main cause of this has been the declining number of jobs
in manufacturing industry. Between 1966 and 1979, manufacturing
employment declined by nearly 2,000,000 jobs; from nearly 9,000,000
to just over 7,000,000. Between 1970 and 1976 alone, over 960,000
jobs were lost — nearly one in eight.[7]

These figures relate to those who have *registered* as being unemployed. But many women, particularly in recession and slump, do not
register as being unemployed and the total figures therefore underestimate the 'true' level of unemployment.[8] Estimates put this 'hidden'
unemployment of women at around 230,000 in 1971.[9] Additionally,
large numbers of people are kept off the register through a variety of
temporary state measures. Such measures provided around 275,000
jobs at the end of 1978. Moreover these raw figures for total unemployment do not indicate the length of time, or duration, of unemployment.
In fact the length of time that people spend out of work is increasing as
Table 5.2 demonstrates. For example, whilst in 1965 48% of the unemployed had been out of work for more than eight weeks, by 1976
68% had been so. That is to say that in 1965 just less than 150,000
people had been out of work for eight weeks. The figure for 1976 was
nearly 900,000. It is worth noting too that unemployment varies considerably between different parts of the UK, an issue briefly taken up in
the next section. For example, in November 1979 regional unemployment rates varied from 3.5% in the south east of England to 11.1% in
Northern Ireland whilst even greater variations exist across the space
economy as a whole, from 2.1% in Guildford, to 12.3% in Liverpool,
and 23.1% in Strabane.[10]

The importance of unemployment lies not only in that it represents
a waste of resources, but that in a capitalist economy the vast majority
of people have only their labour power to sell in order to gain income
with which to purchase food, clothing, housing and other goods and
services. The means of production are owned by the capitalist class and
if they are unwilling to hire labour, or wish to reduce the numbers of

workers they employ, this puts workers' 'prosperity' immediately at risk. This threat continually hangs over workers, for they have little control over profitability and therefore over the labour market and the demand for labour power. The dictates of profitability continually attract and then expel workers, forcing them into periods of unemployment, changing their life styles, their skills and their location of work and home.[11] Moreover high rates of unemployment serve to strengthen the dominance of capital over labour, generating increased competition for jobs and threatening wages, conditions of work and job security.

Table 5.2: Percentage of Total Numbers Unemployed by Duration (in Weeks)

	<8	8-26	26-52	>52	Total Numbers Unemployed
1965	52	21	10	17	306,000
1970	45	25	12	18	574,000
1976	32	31	17	20	1,321,000

Source: Department of Employment (1977).

Unemployment is not suffered by all groups in society equally. Table 5.3 gives some information on unemployment by occupation, as well as numbers of people unemployed relative to vacancies in those occupations. The figures for registered unemployed refer to males only because of the unreliability of female registered unemployment figures (as noted above), whilst the vacancy figures, naturally, refer to both males and females.

Table 5.3: Unemployment and Vacancies by Occupation in GB December 1979 (Males Only)

	Unemployed	Vacancies
Managerial and professional	71,000	20,000
Clerical and related	70,000	27,000
Other non-manual	24,000	20,000
Craft and related	113,000	52,000
General labourers	364,000	9,000
Other manual	209,000	76,000

Source: *Department of Employment Gazette* (March 1980).

It is clear that the burden of unemployment falls most heavily on the unskilled and semi-skilled workers.

3. The Nature of Capitalist Crises – Accumulation, Restructuring and the Demand for Labour Power

In this section we firstly analyse the accumulation process and how this gives rise to crises, associated with declining profitability,[12] and the effects this has on the demand for labour power. Secondly, we analyse the restructuring process, a process designed to improve profitability, and its effects on the demand for labour power. Thirdly, we outline the spatially uneven nature of the accumulation, and especially restructuring, process. Finally, in the light of our analysis, we review the prospects for employment in the UK over the next few years.

3.1: Accumulation, Crisis and Employment

Capitalism, as we have seen in earlier chapters, is characterised by (a) the production of commodities, that is production is geared to sales on the market – to exchange, not use; (b) the capitalist class monopolising the means of production; and (c) the existence of competing capitalists. Thus production is for private profit, and capitalists are able to appropriate the surplus generated in production. They begin with a sum of money (M) with which they purchase means of production and labour power, to be put to work to produce new commodities in the expectation that when sold they will realise a sum of money (M′) which exceeds the value of the commodities originally purchased. This surplus $(M' - M)$ can be consumed by the capitalist or reinvested to buy more means of production and/or labour power, in the quest for further increasing the surplus. This *accumulation* of capital arises because (a) production is for private gain, and therefore it is in capitalists' own self interest to expand the surplus at his disposal, but also (b) because of competition between capitalists. This implies that if capitalists do not accumulate capital, or do so less quickly than their competitors, then they will be beaten out of the market by competitors who have lower costs of production associated with more efficient and advanced production techniques, and/or economies of scale. Clearly any barriers in the way of this accumulation process will result in capitalists refraining from buying further means of production and labour power and thus money will be hoarded. The expansion of production takes place only if it is expected to be profitable to do so. Thus the demand for labour power is a function of the accumulation process, and barriers to this process therefore threaten the demand for labour power.

However the demand for labour power may not increase in step with a smooth development of accumulation for two reasons. First, capitalists purchase *both* means of production and labour power. In certain conditions they will substitute the former for the latter, almost certainly reducing overall employment. This issue is dealt with in the section on restructuring below. Secondly, to the extent that the law of value works imperfectly, reductions in the demand for labour power in certain branches or areas will not necessarily imply its instantaneous transfer to expanding areas or branches. This is examined later in this section but it can be stated here that there are considerable barriers to 'perfect' mobility of labour between occupations and over space as a result of workers being more than 'units of labour' to be reallocated from one use to another according to the dictates of market prices and private profit. For these reasons then, even if accumulation proceeds unhindered, the demand for labour power may well not increase in line with it.

However, over and above these problems, there is the knowledge that accumulation far from being a smooth trouble-free process is in fact highly irregular because of threats to profitability. Moreover, such irregularities and threats to profitability (and therefore threats to employment and production) arise from, and develop out of, the nature of the accumulation process itself. Crises develop, characterised by idle and underused labour power and means of production. The *possibility* of such crises arises because of the separation of purchase and sale, by money, in an exchange economy. Individuals can sell without buying and thus hoard money. Each sale is not simultaneously a purchase, because production and exchange are orientated towards profit and the accumulation of capital, rather than for consumption. Commodities are only produced and sold for the purpose of buying *other* commodities. Consequently there is no reason why supply and demand must balance. Inadequate demand to clear the market, that is overproduction, can arise if production becomes unprofitable. Total purchases may be less than total supply. In such a case capitalists hoard money rather than purchasing means of production and labour power for unsold commodities exist and thus their production is held back. Crises are therefore made possible by sums of money being hoarded and not being used to buy other commodities. Thus arises the possibility of crises, but what *causes* it to happen? What are the threats to profitability that emerge in the accumulation process? How do disruptions and irregularities arise in the accumulation process? Crises may arise in three ways, and we deal with each in turn.

First, *disproportions* in the pattern of production may arise. Production and the division of labour are regulated by the law of value. Overproduction in one branch and underproduction in another should lead to changes in the profit rate in these branches and hence a reallocation of labour power and means of production between them, thus reestablishing proportionality between branches i.e. no over- or underproduction. However, there are many 'imperfections' in the law of value[13] which impede this process. The lack of conscious control, regulation and planning means that such disproportions occur regularly. Moreover, capitalists may not respond to overproduction of the branch's output relative to effective demand by switching capital to another branch but by reducing output and employment in the branch. This may especially occur if capitalists in the branch assume that the change in demand, and hence the overproduction, is temporary. But the cut back in production may become *generalised* as branches related to it are forced to reduce output and employment too. This is the situation at the time of writing in, for example, the motor car and steel industries where car components firms (from electrical components to tyres) and raw materials firms who supply such industries are also experiencing reduced output and jobs. As capitalism, nationally and internationally, becomes increasingly integrated and interdependent, within and between branches and over space, this speeds the transmission of disruptions and generalises them. If capitalists in one branch cut production, or fail to spend their profits, branches that supply them will experience similar problems as their markets in turn decline. Such transmissions of disruptions arising out of an original disproportion may be further exacerbated by downward multiplier effects caused by reduced workers' spending, now less of them are working, thus spreading difficulties to consumer goods industries, distributors and retailers. Such difficulties are particularly apparent in certain areas where the cutbacks in production and employment are most severe (for example, as a result of steel closures in parts of South Wales, and in North Wales and Corby). Further, capitalists' confidence (i.e. expectation of maintaining and increasing profits) overall may be damaged by these events thus leading to a holding back of investment and a reduction in output and employment. Hence a general crisis may ensue. Thus the unplanned, anarchic nature of production under capitalism *may* lead to crises to the extent that the law of value operates imperfectly.[14]

A second cause of crisis is that capital accumulation may proceed so quickly and consistently over a given period, that it exhausts the supply of labour power. In other words in a 'long boom' such as occurred generally in the UK in the 1950s and early 1960s, the growth of the demand for labour power may exceed increases in its supply and thus over time reduce levels of unemployment to a very low level. Over this period for example, despite considerable immigration of workers into the UK and major increases in the participation rate of women in the labour force, unemployment levels remained very low. Such a period of sustained high demand for labour power alters to some extent the relative strength and bargaining power of labour and capital. Competition for workers between capitalists forces wages up, or at least prevents them from falling, and unions are able (if not always willing!) to strengthen their bargaining position. The balance of the class struggle is modified and increases in real wages may exceed the growth of productivity, hence profits are bitten into and the level of accumulation cannot be sustained as profits fall. It is also sometimes argued that strong or increasing international competition prevents capitalists from passing wage increases on in higher prices and so profits are 'squeezed'.[15] This changed balance of class forces may mean that workers and their organisations are strong enough to resist attacks on real wages; attacks that are necessary for any recovery from such a crisis. Hence the class struggle and conflict over the surplus intensifies, and the crisis deepens. With commodities other than labour power, of course, an excess demand and hence higher prices would bring forth, eventually, an increase in supply thus bringing the market back to equilibrium with the pressure on prices being eased. The supply of labour power is different in that it is only partly influenced by such forces, for example immigrants and others previously not actively selling their labour power in the UK. It is unlikely to directly or quickly lead to an increase in the number of workers born![16]

Throughout much of the 1960s and 1970s there was an excess of earnings increases over the rate of price inflation, which exceeded the growth of productivity. This would tend to depress profit rates. For example the excess of earnings increases over those in the price level was 5.7% in 1970 and 6.3% in 1978,[17] well above the average increase in productivity. However, workers' organisations were *not* strong enough (or independent enough?) to resist cuts in real wages in 1976 and 1977.[18] Clearly however the bargaining position of workers plays an important role in affecting the instability of capitalist development. However it is by no means certain that British capital will not tilt the balance of power strongly in its favour again, thus once again emerging

from crisis at the direct expense of working people, for there are a
number of current developments objectively altering the balance of
class forces. These include the rapid and sustained growth of unemployment, the changing nature of state policies under the Conservative
government which are explicitly aimed at altering the balance of power
between capital and labour through 'employment' legislation, changes
in social policies and the strong emphasis given to market forces and
disciplines, and attempts by capital to further alter the balance of class
forces through for example changes in technology and the export of
capital. The ultimate outcome depends on the struggle over pay,
productivity and jobs.

A third cause of crisis, relates to the tendency for the organic composition of capital to rise in the course of the accumulation process,
thus giving rise to a *tendency* for the rate of profit to fall.[19] As competition between capitals is fought by decreasing costs of production,
existing production techniques are continually modified as accumulation proceeds. Those who fall behind in the accumulation process are
competed out of business. Hence competitive accumulation in search
of scale economies and more efficient techniques of production increases the proportion of means of production to labour power. This will
reduce the rate of profit, for only living labour can create surplus
value, and thus a reduced reliance on it must restrict the profit rate,
unless changes in the rate of exploitation outweigh its effect.[20] As a
result accumulation will slacken and reductions in production and
employment ensue.

It is important here to distinguish between different conceptions of
the composition of capital. The *technical* composition of capital, that
is to say the ratio of the mass of means of production to the mass of
workers, has clearly increased over time in the process of capitalist
development. This is, as pointed out above, a necessary outcome of
the competitive accumulation process associated with progressive
'mechanisation' of production. However, the *value* composition of
capital is the ratio of means of production to the mass of workers in
value terms. Now, if technical change is capital saving then the value
of the means of production may not increase as fast as their mass for,
due to increased productivity, their value per unit may be reduced.
Thus it would seem that the value composition may not increase in
line with the technical composition, because the value of the means of
production may increase less quickly than their physical amount.
However, there is no reason to suppose that there is any systematic
tendency for the value of producer goods to rise less quickly than the

value of wage goods, and hence no reason why the value composition should not move in the same direction as the technical composition, or at least not in the opposite direction.[21] Thus it would seem that the composition of capital *will* increase over time. In any case, it has been argued.[22] that the organic composition of capital abstracts from such changes, i.e. the values of producer and wage goods used are their 'old' ones. In which case the organic composition would move in direct proportion to the technical composition. Then forces operating to reduce the value of the means of production can be seen as one of the counteracting forces to the tendency of the rate of profit to fall.

Thus the organic composition of capital increases over time. Does this mean that the rate of profit falls inexorably over time?[23] No, it does not because the rate of profit depends not only on the organic composition of capital but on the rate of exploitation. Thus increases in the rate of exploitation, in large part brought about by changes in the composition of capital, may offset the tendency for the rate of profit to fall. Indeed this is one of the counteracting forces which may enable capitalist economies to enjoy periods of crisis-free growth, and demonstrates that the tendency of the rate of profit to fall is not a deterministic theory nor an empirical prediction. For naturally the rate of exploitation hangs crucially on the class struggle over the appropriation of the surplus, the balance of class forces at any particular time and the methods of state intervention. Empirical changes in the rate of profit depend on the relations between the tendency and the counteracting forces. The tendency is, rather, a *condition* of capitalism. It is a barrier to development and at the same time therefore a source of movement and change in the system. It is a dialectical process of growth, barrier, growth, barrier.[24] It is a barrier through which it is not impossible to pass but a barrier that gives rise to the need for restructuring, if it is to be overcome.

The *counteracting forces,*[25] particularly in so far as they may telescope in a particular period, may allow capitalist economies to enjoy periods of crisis-free growth, or even 'long booms'.[26] Such counteracting forces, in addition to increasing the rate of exploitation in various ways, include the export of capital to areas with higher profit rates;[27] state intervention to reduce the proportion of the value of constant capital that capital must pay (subsidies, grants and so on); foreign trade in the search for cheaper raw materials; the development of monopoly, giving capital more control over profit rates; and finally as noted above the capital saving nature of some technical change. Indeed the restructuring process with which we deal in the next section, can

be conceptualised as an attempt to mobilise these counter tendencies in
an attempt to improve profitability. It may be asked why capitalists
take actions, that is those which have the effect of increasing the
organic composition of capital, which causes a fall in the rate of profit?
The answer is that capitalists do not have a free choice in the matter,
they must continually adopt more advanced machinery or they will be
left behind in the competitive process. More interestingly, what is
rational for an individual capitalist is not rational for the system as a
whole. For in the short run, the increases in 'productivity' and reductions in costs over and above his competitors gives the individual
capitalist a temporary advantage over his rivals, and improves his profitability. However in the long run, as other competitors follow suit, this
advantage is eroded and the organic composition of capital has increased thus lowering the average rate of profit obtained.[28]

We have seen above that the ultimate cause of crises lies in the
threats to profitability that arise in the accumulation process. If profitability is threatened, or if capitalists 'expect' it to be threatened, then
they will hoard money instead of purchasing means of production and
labour power. The cause of crisis lies in the heart of capitalism and
therefore cannot be permanently overcome within the capitalist mode
of production. The economic base must be transformed in order to rid
society of economic crises.

Crises *appear* as crises of *realisation*, that is an inability to realise the
surplus value in commodities by selling them at appropriate prices.
Crises appear to be *caused* by, but are in reality only associated with
and only take the form of, a lack of demand for goods and services.
That is we observe growing unsold stocks of cars, stereo sets, steel,
furniture and so on. We observe firms closing down and cutting back
production because sales have declined or order books are empty. Overproduction of exchange values is therefore observed, but the deficiency
of demand *originates* in the hoarding of money by capitalists, because
profitability is threatened by the contradictions in the accumulation
process. It cannot therefore be solved by Keynesian type policies which
concentrate solely on realisation of surplus value; it first has to be
produced and accumulated. Indeed such policies may exacerbate the
problem under certain circumstances by increasing employment and thus
wages. As we shall see in the next section, there may be contradictions
between the conditions for the restoration of accumulation and those
for realisation. The former requires lower wages, the latter requires
higher wages to create purchasing power and markets. Hence the crucial
role played by international trade and foreign investment.[29]

To reiterate, the ultimate cause of crises is capitalists' unwillingness to purchase means of production and labour power when the rate of profit falls. It is changes in the rate of profit that dictate the level of economic activity and development in the economy. Table 5.4 gives some impression of the fall in the rate of profit in the UK over recent years.[30]

Table 5.4: The Rate of Profit in the UK 1951-1975

1951	1960	1970	1973	1975
8.3	3.7	3.9	3.5	3.0

Source: Harrison (1978), p. 143. Figures refer to the after tax profits of industrial and commercial companies as a percentage of capital employed.

Naturally these, as well as more detailed figures, do not show an inevitable year on year decline, because whether there occurs an actual fall in the profit rate depends on a number of factors as explained above, notably the response of capitalists to falls in profitability and the ensuing struggle over wages, productivity, job loss and so on. However the trend is in a downward direction and it may be that in recent years the forces acting to reduce the rate of profit have telescoped and some of the counteracting tendencies have weakened; in particular the lack of success of attempts to increase the rate of exploitation. The forces that seem to have telescoped are briefly as follows.

(a) Increases in the value of V (variable capital), associated with a tendency in the 'long boom' to absorb large amounts of labour power, has depleted the industrial reserve army, bidding up the price of labour and engineering a shift in the balance of power in the labour market between capital and labour. Workers' organisations have in some, but not all, of the ensuing time period been able to hold on to these gains because of their increased strength and militancy.

(b) Increases in the value of C (constant capital) have arisen because of upward pressure on the prices of energy and raw materials, caused by rapid accumulation.

(c) Increases in the organic composition of capital (the ratio of C to V) associated with the accumulation process, put pressure on the rate of profit as explained above. This is particularly associated with the restructuring of capital.

(d) The international nature of the current crisis causes realisation problems overseas as well as generalising and intensifying accumulation difficulties.

(e) The disproportions between sectors have become generalised because of the increasing interdependence between branches, regions and nations, as outlined above, and the 'imperfections' of the law of value have been increasing in product, labour and capital markets.

These taken together with the *relatively* slow restructuring of UK manufacturing capital, and hence relatively slow increase in productivity and therefore competitiveness, have caused real falls in the rate of profit. Hence money has been hoarded by capitalists, and the demand for labour power and the development of the means of production have been held back. Accumulation slackens, investment is held back by falling profitability and, thus, crisis. Manufacturing investment fell by £600m in real terms between 1970 and 1975, a fall of 55%,[31] and we have already seen that nearly 1,000,000 jobs were lost in manufacturing between 1970 and 1976. These are the immediate outcomes of the declining profitability of UK domestic capital, in consequence of which 'total demand' declines, realisation difficulties set in and spread. But they originate from, as we've seen, capitalists' failure to spend. They're caused by capitalists hoarding money.

Crises play an important role in capitalism, for it is through crises that the obstacles and barriers to further capital accumulation are overcome. In a crisis the conditions for profitable expansion and accumulation are re-established. Production is reorganised, weak capitals are weeded out, and workers are disciplined. Thus crises are generally overcome. Capital will do everything in its power to do so, for its power and its survival depend on it. Profitability must be restored. Moreover the social unrest associated with crisis has to be overcome. Crises 'bottom out' because the conditions for the renewal of accumulation arise from the *restructuring* of capital, in particular the scrapping of old techniques of production, the adoption of more productive ones, and the reduction of real wages. It is to this process of restructuring and its effects on employment, that we now turn.

3.2: Restructuring and Employment

As we shall see in this section it is not only economic crises that affect the level of employment. The restructuring process too is critical in determining the level of employment. In order to restore, or even maintain, profitability it is clearly necessary to restructure production in

order to reduce costs and increase productivity. In other words exploitation and surplus value extraction must be intensified, and the less
efficient and profitable capitals and, as we shall see, branches of capitals, must be eliminated. Capitalists must reduce the proportion or total
value produced that it pays workers as wages i.e. increase the unpaid
part of the working day, and hence increase the rate of surplus value
and profit. The rate of profit is given by $\frac{S}{C+V}$, and so the only method
of increasing profitability apart from increasing the rate of surplus
value (S/V) is to reduce the value of constant capital (C). This is achieved
through productivity improvements in industries that produce the
means of production, that is through increasing the rate of surplus
value. Thus the only way to restore profitability is through increasing
the rate of surplus value. As we shall see later in this section the state
may aid such a process, through subsidising the costs to capitalists of
the means of production and labour power, through grants, loans and
subsidies of various sorts. Moreover, it may actively seek to reduce real
wages and reduce the value of labour power through 'incomes' policies.
This could have a significant effect on the rate of surplus value. For
example in 1977 average earnings increased by 5.6% less than the rate
of inflation – a substantial cut in average real wages.[32] Of course, the
depth of crisis may itself reduce the value of labour power because of
rising unemployment, increased competition for jobs, and reduced
bargaining power of unions. These influences apart, it is only possible
to increase the rate of surplus value through two types of changes in
the organisation of production.

(a) Act directly on the amount of labour power employed by reducing
   the numbers of workers employed through (1) the closure of
   individual plants in a multiplant organisation. This would involve
   those with the lowest rate of profit, the least efficient production
   techniques and so on. It thus also gives rise to the centralisation of
   capital; or (2) reduce the number of workers employed at the
   individual plant level either through redundancies (as in (1) above)
   or changes in overall personnel policy, of which more later. On the
   whole these constitute a rather defensive strategy for capitals, and
   would seem to involve an adjustment to a smaller market demand.
   Both generally involve a reduction in labour costs and productive
   capacity, as well as reducing employment. They also involve increasing the rate of surplus value, by generally reducing manning levels
   and an intensification of labour.

(b) Act indirectly on the amount of labour employed by changing the techniques of production i.e. the type, and relative amount, of means of production in relation to labour power. This more aggressive, expansionist policy of increasing mechanisation of the production process, is designed to increase the rate of surplus value, through increased productivity (output per worker per given time period) and necessarily implies that the same number of workers can produce more output or, to put it another way, the same amount of output can be produced by fewer workers. Thus the demand for labour power will decline, unless output increases fast enough to compensate for the increased output per worker.

Thus, in concrete terms, the restructuring process involves a number of elements, which are currently experienced daily by workers throughout the economy and reports of which continually appear in the media viz. closures, rationalisations, cutbacks, speed ups, new machinery, relocations and so on. It involves the closures of individual plants and even firms (as, for example, Singer in Scotland and BSC in Shotton, North Wales in 1979/80); the contraction of individual plants and firms (as, for example, Vickers in Newcastle and Hoover in South Wales in 1979/80); increasing efficiency by changing production techniques, and intensifying the exploitation of labour (as, for example, in British Leyland or many textile and clothing firms). The impact on employment can be considerable. For example, the numbers employed in the steel industry in Wales in 1980 is well less than one third of what it was in 1976. In so far as the present government is 'disengaging' from industry and imposing the rule of the market, this restructuring process will intensify and the weakest and least efficient branches and firms will be forced 'to the wall'. However restructuring also involves the search for new areas of accumulation where profit rates are higher: the move into different branches of the economy, hence diversifying production, and overseas production, hence speeding up the internationalisation of capital.[33] As noted above, it may therefore be seen as an attempt to mobilise the counteracting forces to falls in the rate of profit. However as we saw in the previous section, whilst such restructuring may succeed in improving profitability for individual capitalists in the short run, in the long run because of increases in the organic composition of capital, it may lead to an overall lower average profit rate. Moreover the success of such measures also depends on being able to realise, as well as produce, the surplus value contained in the commodities. Thus the availability of profitable markets is crucial. Yet such restructuring may itself reduce the scope for realisation in the domestic economy and, also, if competitors have restructured more effectively, then profitability may not improve. Given the international nature of the present crisis and the degree of general overproduction and excess capacity, UK capital will have to restructure its capital dramatically to relieve competitive pressures.

Thus the outcomes of the restructuring process are not inevitable or predictable, both because of the competitive nature of the restructuring and the importance of overcoming realisation problems. But there is a more central reason why the outcome is not inevitable, why the rate of profit will not necessarily recover and why the crisis may not be climbed out of. The struggle by capital and the state to restructure production necessarily involves a *class struggle* over such 'reorganisation' and 'rationalisation' for it is an attempt to alter the balance of power between capital and labour in order to restore profitability once again. It involves making the working class bear the costs of, and pay for, the crisis that is not of their making. It involves increasing the surplus 'squeezed out' of workers during the working day; it involves dislocations in the pattern and location of employment, and very importantly, it may well involve a widespread and extensive loss of jobs. Thus in such periods the class struggle intensifies and much depends on who gets, and what proportion of, the benefits of the increased productivity, the increased potential surplus. In particular, the relatively weak position of UK domestic capital, and thus the need for major and substantial restructuring, makes the reconciliation of the opposing class interests, especially in a period of zero or negative growth, extremely difficult. That is unless the state attempts to directly reduce the power of the working class through changes in trade union legislation, for example with regard to picketing, closed shops, voting procedures, availability of social security benefits to strikers' families and so on. This type of action may well be required for with the decline in social stability engendered by the crisis and consequent restructuring, the authority and ideology of the capitalist class comes under pressure. However, such state actions may intensify the problem rather than resolving it. Much depends, as ever, on the response, organisation, and militancy of workers' organisations and the workers themselves.

What effect does restructuring have on the demand for labour power? This depends on the interaction between, and outcome of, the forces involved that we have identified above. But certainly, the attempts to increase the relative extract of surplus value (the process of investment in means of production which increases the amount of constant capital per worker) reduces the number of workers required for any given level of output, and consequently labour is continually expelled from the production process. Thus the relationship between output growth and productivity growth is central in determining changes in the demand for labour power, and hence levels of employment.[34] The potential for large increases in output is not great given the excess capacity and overproduction that exists; the competitive nature of restructuring; the international nature of the crisis and the contradiction between the conditions for successful accumulation and realisation.

Historically, productivity growth has exceeded output growth. For example, between 1960 and 1975 manufacturing output increased by 48% whilst manufacturing employment fell by 7%. A recent study[35] has shown that between 1954 and 1973 the average increase in productivity per year was 0.5% faster than the growth output. Moreover, the gap has been widening over time both in aggregate and between sectors, thus causing problems associated with the law of value. In crisis the reduction in employment will exceed the reduction in output, precisely because of the changing production techniques associated with restructuring, which increase productivity. Even though the growth of productivity in UK domestic capital has been slow by international standards, output growth was even slower – naturally the two are closely related. In terms of the demand for labour power then, we can expect restructuring to lead to its reduction. For example, given a rate of growth of productivity of 3.5% per year (the UK average for 1954 to 1973) and an increase in the size of the labour market by 1% per year, output growth must be more than 4.5% per annum in order to reduce unemployment at all; a rate of growth the UK economy has never achieved for more than one year. A rate less than this will reduce the demand for labour power and increase unemployment. We shall have more to say about the prospects for employment in the final section of this chapter.

Prior to this, and to analysing the spatially uneven effects of accumulation and restructuring in the next section, a few words are appropriate here on the role of the state in restructuring capital. Given the nature of the state[36] it is clear that the state serves to ensure the accumulation of capital and aid the restructuring process. We have already mentioned that the state may attempt to directly reduce labour costs through incomes policies. This can be achieved indirectly through socialising the costs of reproducing 'skilled' labour through state provided, or aided, training and retraining schemes. It may also attempt to socialise the costs of manufacturing and reproducing the means of production. This involves granting subsidies and tax relief of various sorts to capital, as well as directly undertaking or underwriting activities, the costs of which, individual capitals would be unable to meet because of cost, risk or length of lead times, e.g. nuclear power generation. Moreover, the state will attempt to regulate the relations between individual capitals taking into account the needs of capital in general, for example through the regulation of markets; a taking control of 'unprofitable' capitals and promoting combination of capitals and their restructuring. Thus the Industrial Reorganisation Corporation of the 1960s and the National Enterprise Board and the various Industry Schemes of the late 1970s were designed, in part, explicitly to restructure certain industries, without increasing capacity. For example, the Wool Textile Scheme designed to eliminate excess capacity in the industry and improve competitiveness, resulted in the closure of one in every ten firms in the industry and 3,600 redundancies. The industry still remains uncompetitive and is suffering continual job loss at the time of writing.

However, not all state activities contribute to the accumulation process. Some, as we shall see in Chapter 7, act as a drain on the generation of surplus value and the accumulation of capital. Hence in order to release surplus value to restore accumulation, certain state activities are likely to be cut back during a crisis, thus reducing the demand for labour power in the state sector. More importantly, the increasing fiscal burden on the state associated with the dynamics of late capitalist development and the impact this has on the accumulation process and inflationary pressures, gives rise to pressures on governments to reduce this burden, and thus cut back the overall level of the state's activities as well as restructure the state itself.[37] Particularly if this is associated, as it is at the time of writing, with parties in government that attempt to give freer rein to the law of value and the operation of 'free' market forces, the extension of state activities may be curtailed, with consequent effects on employment in the state sector.

3.3: Restructuring and Uneven Development[38]

Wide spatial variations in economic and social conditions are a general feature of capitalist economies. The differences in unemployment over space were indicated earlier in the chapter, and it is certainly the case that some areas have experienced more rapid economic decline and manufacturing job loss than others, whilst still others have experienced modest economic expansion and even manufacturing employment growth. These differences have little to do with the individual structure

of the area in terms of the 'types' of industries it possesses, and hence
the demand for the type of commodities produced in the area, and thus
employment.[39] Rather these differences are reflections of capital
accumulation, crises and restructuring. They are the spatial expression
of these processes operating at the national and international levels,
and result from the spatial allocation of stages of the production process in an attempt to increase or maintain profitability. Thus the spatial
impact of capital accumulation and restructuring generates uneven
development, but this bears little relationship to particular categories
of output.[40] Rather it reflects the spatial division of labour, and thus
the organisation of production in space, which focuses us in on the
organisational structure of firms, their competitive position and the
competitive position of their 'branches', as well as changes in these
variables over time associated with the processes of accumulation and
restructuring. These processes involve, as we've seen, the continual
concentration and centralisation of capital, the search for cheaper
labour power and more efficient production methods, and the tendency to crises. The effects of these are uneven over space because of
the spatial organisation of production within firms and the competitive
struggle between firms. The firms that decline and fail are not necessarily distributed over space in the same pattern as those that expand
and survive. Capitals continually readjust their demands for labour
power in the light of the prospects for profitability.

Thus the slackening of the accumulation process associated with
declining profitability and the consequent attempts to restructure
capital and improve profitability are unevenly felt over space. Their
effects are primarily felt by branches involved in production, *per se*,
where declines in profitability and output are first and most strongly
felt in terms of employment, and where the greatest scope lies for
reducing costs of production, increasing the rate of surplus value
extraction, and profitability. In a situation where the 100 largest UK
companies have an average of 72 branches each in the UK[41] the scope
for restructuring production activities between branches, altering the
techniques of production in them and changing their locations, is considerable. Thus those areas which are most dependent on routine production, rather than the 'head office' functions of finance, marketing,
administration, research and so on, are those which bear the brunt of
both a collapse in accumulation and consequent crises, and of competitive failure and consequent restructuring.

Moreover the centralisation and internationalisation of capital mean
that certain areas are increasingly dominated by giant, multiplant,

usually multinational, capitals. Thus there is a growth in external control[42] with the branches in an area being a relatively small part of the capital's spatial division of its activities and labour, and subject to their search, often global, for improved profitability in the light of their own performance and corporate strategies. Whilst capital as a whole continues to centralise, production activities on a national and international scale are decentralising in the continuing search for more profitable locations associated with a cheap, pliant labour power and often cheaper means of production because of state grants and subsidies. This increasing dependence of certain areas (and nations for that matter)[43] on large national and multinational companies, increases their integration into the world capitalist economy and increases the extent of, and speed at which, accumulation difficulties and consequent restructuring are transmitted to them. It also reduces the effectiveness of state attempts to control the economic development of the area.[44]

3.4: The Prospects for (Un)Employment

Changes in the level of unemployment are not only a function of the demand for labour power as we have analysed above, but also of the supply of labour power. The law of value does not operate perfectly with regard to the supply of labour power. With other commodities[45] an excess of supply over demand would, because of downward pressure on prices, lead to a reduction in its supply. However, workers must offer themselves for work in order to live[46] and a reduction in the number of jobs available or a reduction in wages will not lead to less workers wanting jobs. Indeed, as more and more workers lose their jobs and as real wages fall, other members of families who previously were not seeking work because they were supported by others who were working, will also begin to seek work.

The supply of labour power is increasing in the UK by about 100,00 to 200,000 per annum over the period 1976 to 1982. This is due to demographic factors and increases in the proportion of women seeking work.[47] Thus even if the demand for labour power were static, if there was no decline in the demand for labour power between 1976 and 1982 unemployment would reach 2,300,000 (or over 9%) by 1982. Or to put it another way, to reduce unemployment to 800,000 (or 3.5%) by 1982 the equivalent of 30,000 new jobs *net* have to be credited every month over the period.[48] Yet we have argued above that the demand for labour power is almost certain to fall in periods of crisis and rapid restructuring such as is currently being experienced. With registered unemployment hovering around 1,500,000 (or 6%) between

1977 and 1979 clearly the demand for labour power has not increased
by nearly enough. Between December 1976 and December 1977 less
than 3,000 new jobs per month were created – an amount equal to
less than 10% of the state's 'special measures' to keep unemployment
'under control'. Between December 1977 and December 1978 around
16,000 jobs per month were created. Again, less than half what was
'required' and less than the 'special measures'. And this was in a period
of relative boom, compared to the current situation, and relatively slow
restructuring. The prospects for employment are indeed bleak, as one
would expect from our analysis in this chapter.

With regard to employment in the *manufacturing* sector, between
the end of 1977 and the end of 1978 a further 65,000 jobs were lost,
and another 140,000 were lost in 1979.[49] Indeed a recent study[50] has
argued that even on the basis of optimistic assumptions about government policies, inflation, exchange rates and world trade growth, most
manufacturing sectors would experience job loss, and unemployment
would reach 2,300,000 (9.2%) in 1982. The industries which will
experience the biggest job losses are those with poor output prospects
but which are undergoing rapid restructuring, in search of higher
productivity, e.g. textiles, aerospace, shipbuilding and tobacco. However, even industries that are growing relatively quickly will still lose
jobs due to the pace of restructuring outrunning output and sales
growth e.g. chemicals, oil and drinks. With less optimistic assumptions
about productivity growth and demand, the job losses in manufacturing as well as overall unemployment would be higher still. The
above figures are based on productivity growth below the trend level
of the early 1970s. With more rapid competitive restructuring in an
attempt to reduce costs; continued, and growing, realisation problems
domestically and on a world scale; increases in world capacity in many
industries; and the locational behaviour of multinational companies
altering the international division of labour; the prospects for employment in manufacturing, particularly for workers in production *per se*,
is bleak indeed.

Additionally the impact of the so called 'new technology'[51] will
certainly reduce the demand for labour power in manufacturing. It has
the ability to reduce production costs and increase productivity by a
considerable extent. Whilst the increased productivity may lead, in
some cases, to reduced prices and thus larger markets, the gains are so
large that really dramatic increases in output are required to offset their
effects.[52] Indeed, despite extremely rapid growth of output and sales,
this has not stopped employment in computer manufacturing itself

from declining by nearly 20% between 1971 and 1977 and employment in electronic components from declining by more than 20% between 1974 and 1979.[53] Moreover the introduction, and development, of such technologies speeds up dramatically the obsolescence of existing machinery and renders uncompetitive capitals who do not adopt it. The reason for this is that the new technology is so superior to existing/ previous ones in terms of reliability, amount of energy input, extent of applicability and, most importantly, cheapness. The price of a micro-processor is currently only 0.01% of the price of a comparable computer in the late 1950s. Moreover they are applicable to almost any activity that involves the processing of information. This being the case, one would expect the rapid adoption and diffusion of this innovation which offers considerable scope for restructuring large sections of manufacturing industry.

The only possible scope for offsetting to some extent the declining employment opportunities in manufacturing is in the so called *services* sector. Here are found the only 'industries' to increase their employment between, for example, 1971 and 1977 viz. distribution; miscellaneous services; insurance, banking and finance; professional and scientific services and public administration. In the past the jobs lost in manufacturing have been absorbed, to a large extent, in the service sector. The reason why the service sector has grown so rapidly in terms of employment, is that productivity growth here has been slow at a time of rapidly increasing output and 'demand' for them. There has been no technological revolution here comparable to the processes of change in manufacturing and this has meant that services have become increasingly more expensive to provide compared to manufactured goods, and costs have escalated considerably. This technological lag has meant that employment has grown rapidly here, but *especially* in the state sector; it is increasingly straining organisations' ability to increase productivity. Thus the advent of microtechnology offering such significant potential cost saving, and state policies on public expenditure, implies a likely revolution in many parts of the services sector, with considerable implications for employment. The automation of offices is a central issue here, for much office work consists of acquiring, storing, presenting and distributing information and such 'jobs' are much more cheaply done through word and data processors. Again unless there is considerable scope for rapid output growth, employment will fall. Indeed one study[54] has shown that insurance, banking and finance is the sector that will be most affected by microtechnology with the possibility of shedding 500,000 jobs (over 40%) between 1977 and 1992.

Indeed service sector growth *is* now slowing down, largely because of productivity advances. For example it grew only half as fast between 1974 and 1976 as it did between 1971 and 1974, and in total the growth has now virtually ceased. The other reason for this, we will deal with in a moment. We have noted that there are doubts about whether the insurance, banking and finance sector will continue to be a source of newly created jobs in the future. The distribution sector is even more unlikely, for here though total employment is increasing it is due entirely to the growth of part-time jobs. Full-time employment is declining. Between 1971 and 1975 full-time employment in retailing fell by 150,000.

However by far the largest source of employment opportunities has been in professional and scientific services, and public administration. The great bulk of jobs in this area are in the state sector. For example between 1966 and 1977 the number of jobs in professional and scientific services increased by 300% or 2,100,000 jobs, primarily in health and education. This is unlikely to continue due to current public expenditure policies and more generally because of the so called 'fiscal crisis' of the state.[55] Indeed between 1978 and 1979 there was no increase in employment in professional and scientific services or public administration. Major struggles are coming in the services sector, particularly in the state sector, over the future of employment. Moreover, the more rein is given to the law of value, by reducing state intervention in areas like industrial subsidies, exchange controls, international trade and spatial policies, the more rapid will be the employment changes associated with crises and restructuring. It is worth briefly noting here, because of its crucial importance for workers' strategies in resisting job loss, that reductions in employment are by no means solely a function of closures, or even redundancies. Many other strategies are open to capitals, and the state, for reducing employment. For example, they need not replace those who retire, those who are dismissed or those who quit voluntarily to go to other jobs.[56] Thus the overall recruitment and personnel policy is of vital importance, Resistance solely to redundancies will not stem job loss. For example, redundancies as a proportion of total discharges in an industry rarely exceeds 10%. It is important to ensure that voluntary discharges are replaced, if employment is to be protected. This applies especially to the state sector.

In conclusion then it seems that, within the confines of a capitalist mode of production, unemployment will continue to rise unevenly over both time and space. Whilst there exist vast unmet needs in society, increasing numbers of workers are idle. Once again we see how capital stands in the way of the further development of society.

4. Inflation in the UK

Inflation refers to an increase in the general, or average, level of prices in an economy. Table 5.5 illustrates how the UK economy has not experienced stability of prices in recent years but, on the contrary, has experience increases in the general level of prices. Indeed it can be seen that not only have prices increased year on year but that the rate of increase of prices, the rate of inflation, has been significantly higher in recent years. Indeed if we go back to 1949, we find that in only two years prior to 1969 did the rate of inflation exceed 5%. Inflation is in fact a phenomenon of post-1945 capitalism and in common with the other issues that we have analysed in this book, is a phenomenon not peculiar to the UK, but is a characteristic of advanced capitalist economies in general. What the above figures imply is that the purchasing power of money is declining. For example £1 in 1970 was only worth 37p in 1978 because of the increase in prices over the period. In other words for a worker to have, on average, the same purchasing power, that is the same *real* income, in 1978 as in 1970, he/she would require an income nearly three times as great.

Table 5.5: Annual Rate of Changes of Retail Prices in the UK 1968-1979 (%)

1968	4.7	1974	16.1
1969	5.4	1975	24.2
1970	6.4	1976	16.5
1971	9.4	1977	15.8
1972	7.1	1978	8.2
1973	9.2	1979	18.4

Source: *Department of Employment Gazette* (various issues).

Why is inflation a 'problem'? At one level it breeds fear and uncertainty about the future, not least because people cannot be sure of retaining, let alone increasing, their real income by obtaining an increased money income equal to the increase in the level of prices. If there were no inflation, of course, capitalists would have to pay reduced money wages in order to reduce workers' real income – a much more difficult task to achieve than giving workers seemingly large money increases which do not keep pace with inflation, and thus still reduce their real income. All else being equal, if capitalists can keep workers' wage increases below the level of inflation, this will redistribute income away from workers to capitalists and improve the rate of profit. This is, of course, the aim of incomes (wages) policies. Moreover, inflation redistributes income in arbitrary ways as well. We have already seen in the previous chapter that inflation has tended to fall heavily on poorer groups in society, but it also redistributes income from the weak to the strong. Those on fixed incomes (pensioners, the sick, students, the unemployed and so on), as well as those working in unprofitable, poorly unionised and organised industries and occupations, stand less change of bargaining their way to retaining their real income and purchasing power than well organised groups of workers working in profitable industries.

Inflation can also be a severe problem for capital; for if the prices of commodities produced in the UK are increasing faster than the prices of commodities produced in other countries, then the competitiveness of capital in the UK is threatened, putting pressure therefore on profitability, sales, output and eventually employment. When aggregated up this means that the UK economy may slide into crisis as profitability falters, output and growth slow down and unemployment rises. The threat occurs both in export markets and domestically too, as commodities from capitals in other nations become relatively cheaper and are increasingly purchased by people and capitals both in the UK and abroad. Moreover, as a result the balance of payments may suffer causing further macro-economic difficulties.[57]

In moving on to attempt to explain the process of inflation, it is important to distinguish between 'once and for all' price changes that increase prices but do not operate continuously, from those that do, even though such once and for all price increases may, through expectations of the future, give a twist to the inflationary process. Such 'triggers' include for example a devaluation or downward float of the £ (as in the 1967 devaluation and 1971 float) thus increasing the prices of imported commodities; an increase in imported commodity prices (as in the 400% increase in oil prices in 1973/4); or an increase in indirect taxes (as in the VAT increase of 1979).

Inflation can only occur if the money supply expands faster than output. Money is the medium through which exchange occurs, it is the means of payment for commodities. If the total means of payment, the amount of money in an economy, grows faster than the growth of commodities available for exchange, then there will arise an 'excessive' demand for these commodities and there will therefore be pressure on their prices to rise. However what has to be understood, in order to *explain* inflation, is how and why the money supply increases in this way. What causes the growth of the money supply to outrun the growth of output? In analysing this question, it will become clear that inflation is in reality only the expression, the symptom of the real crisis of capitalism i.e. the threat of recession, slump and economic crisis. Inflation can in principle be controlled either through state intervention in the labour market or through control of the money supply, but this would exacerbate the real problem which the existence of inflation partly conceals and mitigates. For example by keeping the money supply increase to less than the increase in prices capitals will not be able to pay wage increases equal to the increase in prices unless made up by productivity increases. Thus inflation is controlled essentially by bankrupting capitals or at least by causing severe profitability and liquidity problems for those who pay wage increases 'out of line'. In the economy as a whole, as there is simply not enough money to pay all the workers in a situation of wage increases exceeding money supply increases by more than the rate of productivity growth, unemployment will rise and production will be held back, and capital and the state will hope that this will moderate wage demands and 'squeeze' inflation out of the economy.

The state plays a central role in the inflationary process for in attempting to maintain conditions for profitable accumulation and realisation of surplus value, as well as in its other roles,[58] it has not only grown considerably in size but sacrificed principles of 'sound finance' by indulging in deficit financing i.e. where expenditure out-runs revenue. The gap is made up by borrowing, and in so far as this is done through banks this increases the money supply, by expanding the banks' credit base and allowing them to expand credit. Thus long periods of time in which the state has warded off realisation problems through deficit financing, and has tried to regulate the accumulation process, tends to lead to the generalisation of inflation. The expenditure involved in trying to keep the system afloat, generates new problems. The costs of the long post-war boom and the growing role of the state associated with it are now being borne. There is no guarantee that the increased money supply will lead to increases in output for though it plays a key role in sustaining the demand for commodities through, for example consumer credit, it may not generate capital accumulation if capitalists do not expect such accumulation and subsequent realisation to be profitable. Thus there may be 'too much' credit, in the sense that the expansion of credit may exceed the expansion of accumulation and production, for the advance of credit cannot guarantee that the growth of output or surplus produced from its use will be adequate to repay the loan. In such a case the expansion of the supply of credit will exceed the expansion of production.[59] Also many of the workers in the state sector do not directly create value. The results of their labour are not commodities sold on the market yet they enter commodity markets like everyone else with money to exchange for commodities. Thus money purchasing power is injected into circulation without any corresponding commodities.[60] Buying power is created but there is no corresponding commodities on the market to absorb it.

The state plays a vital role in fostering inflation through attempting to maintain the accumulation of capital and the realisation of the surplus value generated, but the conflict over the distribution of this surplus value also must be crucially important in determining the rate of inflation. This conflict is endemic to capitalism. All value is created by labour but is able to be appropriate by capital by virtue of its ownership of the means of production. However, there is a continuous struggle (negotiation?) between capital and labour over wages, conditions of work, speed of work and so on, and it is possible for labour to bite into the rate of surplus value and profit. With the higher levels of employment and the growth of real wages associated with the long boom there were a series of reformist Labour governments; trade unions grew in numbers, strength and organisation; and most importantly the consciousness of workers strengthened and grew. As a result of this shift in the balance of power in the labour market, periods of crisis, higher unemployment and surplus labour have not, on the whole, led to a reduction in real wages. The automatic regulatory function of the size of the industrial reserve army on wages had been modified by the refusal of workers to shoulder the burden of capitalist crises. Whether this increased strength, organisation and militancy can survive a sustained period of 1,500,000 to 2,000,000 registered unemployed, even deeper crises and direct attacks by the state on trade unions, remains to be seen. But certainly in the past 10 to 15 years especially it has been possible at times for workers to gain real wage increases which exceeded the growth of productivity and have put pressure on the rate of profit.[61] Naturally it is possible for *both* real wages and the rate of profit to rise if wage increases do not exceed productivity

growth, but when the latter is small and workers are strong, capital and
the state may not be able to ensure that the rate of profit does not fall.
The value of a commodity is made up, we remember, of C, V and S.
Thus a wage increase will cause V to increase and, if all other conditions
of production remain unchanged, the value of the commodity will rise
and so will its price which is the monetary expression of value. However, this price increase need not arise if there is a corresponding fall in
surplus value and profit. Thus inflation is an expression of the class
struggle, the struggle over surplus value. Capitalists can fend off
declining profitability by raising prices. This is made possible for them
by the growth of monopoly power.[62] Thus chronic inflation can result
from the intensification of class conflict in an era of monopolistic
capitalism. It postpones the real crises and is a way of reconciling,
temporarily, the conflict between capital and labour. The real crisis is
the threat to profitability, but this threat can be temporarily diffused
by raising prices.

However, it can only be a temporary respite, because despite the
growth of monopoly and the ability to control prices that is associated
with it, a sustained period of inflation threatens the international competitiveness of UK capital, by raising the prices of UK manufactured
commodities relative to those manufactured elsewhere. Moreover less
monopolistic sectors of the economy will clearly suffer as they are less
able to raise prices, without losing markets and thus profits. Consequently at the time of writing the Conservative government is pursuing a variety of policies to reduce the rate of inflation. This necessarily intensifies class conflict and the irreconcilable demands of capital
and labour are laid bare. The only escape for capital, if inflation is
'conquered', is a rapid restructuring to improve profitability – a process
which itself increases the antagonism between classes, as it is an attempt
to shift the balance of power more in favour of capital.[63]

Thus inflation is only the expression of crisis. The real crisis lies in
the threat of a slump, induced by a fall in profitability. The inflation
problem is centrally connected with the process of capital accumulation
and the state's attempts to regulate it, and cope with its effects. It is
the attempts by capital and the state to stave off the threats to profitability in a period of intensifying class conflict, that generate inflation.
It can only be solved by breaking the collective power of the labour
movement in a period of deep crisis and fundamental restructuring.

Further Reading

For an outline of the theory of the tendency for the rate of profit to fall see Fine (1975) Chapter 8, and for a critical review of it see Howard and King (1975) Chapter 6. For an excellent review of the variants of marxist theories of crisis see Alcalcy, Shaikh and Weisskopf, all in URPE (1978) and Bell and Wright in Scwartz (1977). The debates around the falling rate of profit are reviewed in Fine and Harris (1976b) and Fine and Harris (1979), whilst Glyn and Sutcliffe (1972) analyse the development of crises in the UK economy in recent years through a 'profits squeeze' approach. Harrison (1978), whilst adopting a particular explanation of the current crisis, is one of the few analyses of it: see particularly Chapters 6 and 7. Gamble and Walton (1976) in Chapter 4 review the present crisis in the UK in terms of the theory of the falling rate of profit, whilst Mandel (1978) takes a more world wide perspective. On the 'counteracting forces' see Sweezy (1968), Chapter 6 or Gamble and Walton (1976) pp. 132-4. See Hobsbawn (1969) for a longer run analysis of the decline of British capital.

For an exposition of Keynesian and neoclassical view of crisis see OECD (1977) and for an exposition and marxist critique of them see Kay (1979), Chapter 8, Nore and Green (1977) Chapter 11, and Green and Nore (1979), Chapter 7.

On restructuring, the easily available published literature is rather thin, but see Fine and Harris (1975 and 1976). On uneven development, see Carney *et al.* (1980). For an analysis of the relations between inflation and crises see Rowthorn (1977), whilst a survey of marxist theories of inflation is provided by Harvey (1977) and inflation in the UK is analysed by Gamble and Walton (1976): see especially Chapters 1, 4, 5 and 6.

Notes

1. At the time of writing, February 1980, registered unemployment is around 1,500,000.
2. Figures adapted from Glyn (1979).
3. See Burghes and Field (1977).
4. With regard to unemployment, for example, the Keynesian approach stresses problems associated with deficiencies of aggregate demand and hence confines itself to problems of 'realisation' and under spending in aggregate without probing the underlying causes of this problem. It does however recognise that an unregulated capitalist economy cannot guarantee 'full employment'. The neoclassical approach essentially argues that the cause of increased

unemployment lies on the supply side i.e. that, crudely put, it is the workers' fault. It is due to increased 'voluntary' (sic) unemployment (due to a changing relationship between levels of unemployment and social security benefits and wage levels, which has reduced the 'incentive' to work); to wages having risen 'too fast', and to increases in the 'supply of labour', especially due to increased female participation rates. The policy prescriptions of this approach are transparently reactionary where workers face the threat of reduced social security provision and reduced wages, with women workers facing the additional threat of resuming their 'traditional' place in the home; looking after men and children and reproducing labour power!

5. It should be noted, once again, that the problems of unemployment and inflation are not unique to the UK. They afflict virtually the whole advanced capitalist world though, for reasons outlined later in the chapter, the problem is more severe in the UK. Currently, unemployment in the OECD countries as a whole totals more than 17,000,000. For a review of orthodox explanations of the increase in unemployment see OECD (1977) and my review of it, Campbell (1978b).

6. See Chapter 6,

7. CSO (1972) and (1976) and *Department of Employment Gazette* (November 1979). Figures are for Great Britain.

8. Many married women are not eligible for unemployment benefit, and therefore may not register though they are 'seeking work'.

9. Census of Population (1971).

10. *Department of Employment Gazette* (December 1979).

11. See Braverman (1974) for an excellent discussion of the impact of the continuous transformation of the processes of production on the work force, its skills and allocation between occupations and industries.

12. It is worth noting that other writers than marxists have posed a tendency for the rate of profit to fall (e.g. Ricardo (1951)). But such writers have based these tendencies on 'natural' laws, in Ricardo's case to do with population growth and the 'niggardliness' of nature, rather than on barriers to development associated with specifically capitalist relations of production. We are concerned here, therefore, with the difficulties, that *capitalism* experiences in its reproduction and growth.

13. See Chapter 7.

14. At the time of writing, February 1980, the major 'cut backs' in the UK steel and certain industries, could conceivably provoke a more general 'crisis'.

15. See for example Glyn and Sutcliffe (1972).

16. Though it may seem remarkable to some orthodox economists, the decision if, when and how many children to have is not entirely determined by changes in current wage levels.

17. CSO, *Economic Trends* (November 1979), Tables 40 and 42.

18. CSO, *Economic Trends* (November 1979), Tables 40 and 42.

19. See Chapter 2, section 6 for an outline of the theory of the tendency of the rate of profit to fall.

20. See Chapter 2, section 6 for a formal statement of how a rising organic composition of capital may lead to a fall in the rate of profit. Note it is the *rate*, not *mass*, of profit that falls. The rate is defined in terms of a proportion of the total capital advanced, the mass of profits is simply its total amount.

21. There is no reason why productivity improvements would only affect the means of production sector of the economy and not the consumption goods sector, and thus no reason why the value of C would fall, as a result of such changes, any faster than the value of V.

22. See Fine and Harris (1979), Chapter 4 and, on its implications for a theory of crisis, Chapter 5.

23. If it were so, the rate of profit in the early days of capitalism must have been literally, fantastic, if it has been falling for around 200 years.

24. See Lebowitz (1976).

25. For a review of these see Sweezy (1968) or Gamble and Walton (1976), pp. 132-4.

26. See Mandel (1978).

27. See Chapter 6.

28. Provided that the counteracting forces are no stronger than previously.

29. See Chapter 6. Exports of commodities (à la Luxembourg) and export of capital (à la Lenin) offer temporary respite from such contradictions between accumulation and realisation needs.

30. A useful summary of the studies of the declining profitability of UK capital is to be found in Gamble and Walton (1976), pp. 137-40.

31. Net fixed investment in manufacturing, *Economic Trends* (various years).

32. Calculated from *Economic Trends* (November 1979), Tables 40 and 42.

33. See Chapters 3 and 6 respectively, on these processes.

34. Thus $L_r = O_r - P_r$ for any branch or spatial unit.

   where r = the rate of growth

   and L = demand for labour power

   O = output growth

   P = productivity growth (output per worker employed).

35. Wragg and Robertson (1978).

36. See Chapter 7 on the theory of the state.

37. For a development of these ideas see Chapter 7.

38. A more comprehensive study of the ideas in this section is to be found in Campbell (1979) and the theoretical framework is summarised in Carney *et al.* (1980). See also Massey (1979), Broadbent (1977) and Campbell (1978a).

39. The industrial structure argument is of course the crude orthodox explanation of urban and regional problems i.e. specialising in so called 'declining industries'. Our view has been confirmed by a wide variety of studies using so-called components of growth analysis. See, for example, Allen and Campbell (1976) or Dennis (1978).

40. I.e. Standard Industrial Classification or Minimum List Heading groupings of commodities.

41. Hannah and Kay (1977).

42. I.e. where ultimate ownership and control of decision-making lies outside the area in question.

43. See Chapter 6.

44. In addition to the reasons above, this is because of the smallness of internal linkages, the outflow of non-wage income, and the locational flexibility of such capitals. See Holland (1976).

45. Under perfectly competitive conditions.

46. In order to receive unemployment benefit potential workers must be able and willing to take a job.

47. Currently only around 55% of women of working age, work or seek work compared to around 95% of men. If the constraints on women's freedom to work were reduced further, for example by compulsory creche provision at all work places, greater nursery provision and changes in male attitudes towards women's role in families, the supply of labour would increase much more quickly than this. This is *one* reason why the removal of such constraints is unlikely in the coming few years.

48. See for example, Manpower Services Commission (1977).

49. *Department of Employment Gazette* (February 1980).

50. Lindley (1978).

51. Microchips in general, and microprocessors in particular. See, for example, Sherman and Jenkins (1979) and Counter Information Services (1979).

52. See, for example, the PA investigation into the impact of technical change on employment in manufacturing in Manpower Services Commission (1977).

53. NEDO Sector Working Party reports. Part of this loss is due to the fact that the 'chips' themselves are increasingly produced in low labour cost nations.

54. See Sherman and Jenkins (1979).

55. See Chapter 7.

56. The actual change in employment is equal to the number of engagements *minus* the total number of discharges, which consists of voluntary discharges, redundancies, dismissals and retirements.

57. See Chapter 6 on international perspectives with regard to trade and the balance of payments.

58. See Chapter 7 for a full analysis of the state.

59. See Fine in Green and Nore (1979).

60. See Kay (1979), Chapter 8.

61. See section 3.1 earlier in the chapter.

62. See Chapter 3.

63. See section 3.2 earlier in the chapter.

6 INTERNATIONAL PERSPECTIVES – TRADE, MULTINATIONAL CORPORATIONS AND THE EEC

1. Introduction

Production under capitalism is for exchange not use. Privately-owned capitals compete with each other in the continual search for profit. Hence as we've seen[1] the capitalist system is inherently expansionist and growth orientated, with the accumulation of capital reproducing capitalist relations of production and developing the productive forces on an ever increasing scale. Capital thus continually presses outwards into new sectors and new areas and such a search for profit knows no international boundaries. Capital will expand wherever it is profitable to do so. Thus capital has a tendency to increasingly embrace more of the world and create a world economy dominated by capital, thus reproducing capitalist relations of production and exchange on an international scale.[2] Thus our analysis of the international aspects of capitalist development, and their effects on capitalism in the UK develops from an analysis of the process of capital accumulation, the barriers it meets in its expansion, and the attempts to restore or maintain profitability through breaking down such barriers. The drive for international expansion is the drive for the extraction, accumulation and realisation of surplus value and moreover represents a central mechanism for attempting to overcome the crises inherent in this process.[3] There is, in many circumstances, a contradiction between the conditions that are appropriate for the accumulation of surplus value and those for its realisation, and thus there is a quest to increasingly 'separate' accumulation from realisation by searching abroad for more favourable conditions for the production of surplus value and/or for its realisation on the market. Domestically the accumulation process comes up against the limits of market realisation owing to the very source of accumulation i.e. the profit expropriated from workers. Workers not only have to create profit but they also have to purchase the commodities produced, and in periods of restructuring conditions favourable to the former are not favourable to the latter, for if wages are held down there are likely to be realisation problems whereas if they are allowed to rise there are likely to be accumulation difficulties.

Three introductory comments are worth noting before proceeding in

141

more detail to analyse the role and effects of the international expansion of capitalism. First, this increasing integration of capitalist economies through links at the levels of production and exchange, means that individual nations are increasingly interdependent and hence instabilities and crises, when they occur, are more readily transmitted than hitherto throughout the capitalist world. Secondly, as conditions for profitable accumulation and realisation change, whether due to changes in transportation and communications; the relative growth and decline of different economies; changes in international differences in the value of labour power, or whatever, then the location of production and sales outlets will change. Thus capitalist economies experience continual changes and adjustments, relative expansion and relative decline, as a result of the search by capital for the extraction, accumulation and realisation of surplus value. Thirdly, this international expansion of capital which, it is to be remembered, is a requirement of the capitalist mode of production, is fraught with difficulties not the least of which is the increasing amount of the world economy that is *not* integrated into the capitalist world economy. For example, the Soviet Union, Eastern Europe, many so-called 'underdeveloped' economies, and some Islamic states lie at least partially outside the capitalist system and as such constitute barriers to the successful expansion of capital. Inevitably therefore capital and capitalist states have a strong interest in seeing such economies more tightly integrated into the capitalist world market and in helping to prevent other economies from loosening their ties with it.

Implicit in this process of international expansion and the consequent increasing integration into a world market is the rivalry between competing capitals and their nation states. Underlying the periodic 'international' problems of balance of payments deficits, devaluations and competitive floating of currencies, liquidity crises, protectionism, depleted reserves and loans from the International Monetary Fund (IMF) that are often treated as a separate set of problems with separate and identifiable causes and solutions, is the struggle between American, Japanese and various European capitals for markets and sources of capital accumulation. They are some of the observable forms of the unfolding of the dynamics of capitalist development on a world scale. The UK is a highly 'open' economy, very dependent on international trade and international capital movements, and thus highly sensitive to instability in the world capitalist economy. Hence the 'international' institutions set up to govern and regulate international economic relations like the IMF and the General Agreement on Tariffs and Trade

(GATT) operate as constraints on the actions of the UK state in relation to international trade and monetary policies. (Witness the UK
position in 1976 when a deteriorating exchange rate and reserves position 'forced' borrowing from the IMF conditional on deflationary
monetary policies and cuts in public expenditure.) Such institutions
were largely set up by the USA after the Second World War and dictated
the general thrust of their policies in regulating world trade and investment. This in turn reflected the supremacy in economic and political
terms of the USA economy after the war. However the regeneration of
the war-damaged economies of Europe and Japan in the last 30 years
has increased competition and rivalry between these capitals and in
consequence has led to instability of international monetary arrangements as the dollar has declined and other currencies, reflecting their
nations' increased economic strength, have become stronger. Thus
stable currencies, the hallmark of the 1945 to 1971 period, have
become difficult to maintain and realignment has proceeded. The rapid
increase in oil prices in the late 1970s required further exchange rate
changes and there is a danger for capital of nations resorting to protectionism, controls on capital flows and deflationary policies to 'correct'
balance of payments deficits, and thus reducing the growth in the
volume of world trade and foreign investment on which capital depends
to expand.

The chapter proceeds as follows. In the following section the role of
international trade in the process of capitalist development is explained,
and the UK's balance of payments[4] problem is outlined. In section 3
the internationalisation of capital itself, as opposed to the export and
import of commodities, is analysed and the impact of multinational
corporations (MNCs) on the UK is subjected to scrutiny. In the final
section, we explain the rationale of the European Economic Community (EEC), its relationship to the internationalisation of capital and
attempt to assess its long term impact on the UK economy.

2. International Trade and the UK Balance of Payments

As noted above, a marxist analysis of international trade specifies its
role in helping to sustain the accumulation of capital and its realisation
on the market. Clearly international trade involves the buying and
selling, the exporting and importing, of commodities across national
boundaries and arises in a similar way to any trade. As a result of
specialisation in production and the division of labour, the exchange of

commodities is required. There is no reason why such trade must only
occur within a nation because production is for exchange, for profit
not for use, and thus profitable markets are sought out whatever their
location. Naturally there are barriers to trade associated with distance
and transport costs, but these are progressively reduced as economic
development proceeds and the productive forces expand. Hence nationally and then progressively internationally trade develops and markets
are linked and integrated as capital continuously, albeit unevenly,
expands.

Thus the need to extend and expand markets in order to find new
sources of demand is a vital driving force in the expansion of international trade. This need arises not only from capitalists' desire to
increase the surplus at their disposal but because of the continual
threat of crises of overproduction, associated with the accumulation
process wherein productive capacity tends to increase faster than the
expansion of markets.[5] Hence the quest for overseas markets, so that
surplus value that has been accumulated can be fully realised, and so
that reductions in the rate of profit can be avoided and allow the scale
of production to continue to expand. Moreover, profitability and output may be expanded still further as a result of sales overseas, for in
such markets there may be competition with commodities produced
under less advanced technical conditions, for example in the importing
nation itself, and hence temporary surplus profits can be made prior to
the technical conditions of production becoming more widespread.
Indeed in some cases the sources of overseas 'demand' may be in pre-
capitalist modes of production in which case the exports may destroy
the existing economic formation and result in the absorption of the
economy into the capitalist mode of production.

However, the need to develop markets on an international scale to
absorb increased output is felt by all capitals as they expand, and international expansion of markets is conducted under conditions of competition and rivalry and thus, ultimately, less efficient or advanced
capitals will lose out in the battle for markets. It should not surprise
us then that 40% of UK international trade is carried out by just 30
firms. A few giant capitals dominate trade in the same way as they do
the economy as a whole.[6] If 'inefficiency' is a general characteristic of a
particular nation's capitals, it will mean that their share of export markets may grow only slowly or even decline, and that the penetration of
imports into the domestic economy may increase thus threatening the
rate of profit and hence output and employment in the home nation
unless the capitals can be restructured successfully, which again is a

process undertaken in competitive and rivalrous conditions, nationally and internationally.

However, international trade occurs not only as a result of the quest for new markets to absorb increasing domestic output and to overcome limited domestic consumption power (i.e. realisation problems), but also to speed up the accumulation of capital and to overcome accumulation difficulties. As we saw in the previous chapter, competition is fought by decreasing costs and one way of decreasing costs is through international trade. It is possible that elements of constant capital and some of the means of subsistence for workers can be obtained more cheaply overseas than domestically thus increasing the rate of profit and the rate of surplus value. Moreover threats to profitability that emerge in the accumulation process may be overcome, and thus reductions in the rate of profit offset, by this cheapening of C and V. Raw materials, fuel and foodstuffs are all examples of how trade may either increase the rate of profit, or stave off its fall, by improving the competitive position of capitals who import commodities rather than purchase domestically produced alternatives. Thus international trade can be seen as a counteracting force to the tendency for the rate of profit to fall. Needless to say, therefore, large increases in the price of such commodities as has recently been experienced will conversely put pressure on the rate of profit.

Thus international trade exists not only as a consequence of the expansion of markets, but also as a condition for continuing capital accumulation. Threats therefore to the expansion of international trade from for example protectionism, international monetary problems and the slow growth of world demand threaten the expansion of capital and thus its very existence. Capitalist states, as well as capital itself, may therefore, under such circumstances take steps on a supranational level to try to combat such tendencies. Given the need to expand markets overseas in order to overcome, or at least stave off, accumulation difficulties it is worth briefly considering whether domestic UK capital has been restricted in this process, and thus pressure put on profit rates as a result of competition with foreign capital. For internationally like domestically the least efficient and advanced capitals are eventually beaten out of the market unless they are heavily subsidised by the state.

The weakness of UK's domestic capital in terms of its lack of international competitiveness, caused by relatively low productivity growth and relatively high domestic inflation giving rise to high prices, is aptly reflected in the UK's chronic balance of payments deficit. Because of UK capitals lack of competitiveness it loses out in export markets and enables foreign capital to make major inroads into the UK domestic market. Clearly this restricts the growth of domestic output, employment and wages. The UK's share of world exports of manufacturing, for example, declined from 26% in 1950 to 9% in 1978. Table 6.1 outlines the UK's balance of payments on visible trade from 1962 to 1979[7] i.e. the export and import of commodities.

Table 6.1: The UK Balance of Payments on Visible Trade 1962-1979 (£million)

1962	1963	1964	1965	1966	1967	1968	1969	1970
-102	-80	-519	-237	-73	-557	-659	-143	-9
1971	1972	1973	1974	1975	1976	1977	1978	1979
+285	-685	-2383	-5221	-3195	-3592	-1709	-1175	-3312

Source: *Annual Abstract of Statistics* (1980).

In only one year has the UK experienced a surplus on visible trade, and the deficit has increased greatly since 1972 despite the effects of North Sea oil. It is important to make the point that nations as such do not trade with each other, it is capitals that trade with each other,[8] and thus the international trade performance outlined in Table 6.1 reflects the competitive position, and the deteriorating competitive position, of UK domestic capital. It is thus a symptom of the decline of UK capital. It is worth noting in passing that over one-third of the UK's visible trade is with the EEC and that the UK deficit on visible trade with the EEC currently amounts to over £2,000 million.[9]

UK capital has therefore failed in facing the rigours of international competition and because of the consequential industrial decline, people in the UK have experienced a series of 'policies' to attempt to 'correct' the balance of payments, as well as to improve industrial competitiveness, a problem which is seen as a constraint on the achievement of other government economic objectives (stable prices, economic growth and so on). For example, the £ was devalued in 1967 thus increasing import prices and domestic inflation; the £ was floated (sic) in 1972 and declined in value by a further 40% between 1971 and 1976; a loan from the IMF was agreed in 1976 to protect the £ from declining further, which was 'conditional' on policies of monetary restraint, public expenditure cuts and deflation.[10] None of these policies tackle the fundamental problem of UK capital's *underlying* competitive weakness and yet they all squeeze living standards and, temporarily, boost the profitability of capital without increasing investment significantly. Once again working people pay for capital's crisis. With the decline of UK domestic capital, as the less efficient capitals go to the wall under competitive pressures, jobs are lost. Continuous structural change and restructuring occurs under the workings of the law of value on an international scale, as capital continually seeks out more profitable branches and areas of activity and withdraws from the less profitable. These pressures intensify to the extent that barriers to international trade are reduced, for example in the EEC. Moreover 'freer' international trade is required for the development of the MNCs with their integrated production process spread across national boundaries. Indeed the export and import of capital is increasingly taking over from international trade as the main form of expansion of capital. Again this progressive freeing of the mobility of capital across national boundaries further intensifies competitive pressures, as well as giving rise to new problems. It is to the development of MNCs that we now turn.

3. The Multinational Corporation (MNC)[11]

In this section, we outline first some of the chief characteristics of MNCs and present some information on the scale of activities, and the importance of both foreign-owned MNCs in the UK and UK-based MNCs abroad. Secondly, we attempt to explain the dramatic growth of MNC activity in terms of the accumulation of capital and the competition between capitals. Finally we attempt to explain the consequences for the UK of both the activities of UK-based MNCs and those of foreign-based MNCs with subsidiaries in the UK.

3.1: Characteristics

We define an MNC as an enterprise that owns and controls assets in more than one nation. Thus we are concerned with foreign direct investment, where not only financial flows of capital are involved but also the control of branches of the capital and the locus of strategic decision-making. The nations in which MNC subsidiaries operate are referred to as 'host' nations, whilst the nation from which they originate are referred to as the 'home' nation.

The first point to note about MNCs is their sheer size. If all the nations and corporations in the world are ranked according to their size, as measured by output, then of the top 100 'outputs' in the world

54 are corporations.[12] For example, the gross sales of a corporation like Ford exceeds the GNP of, for example, Austria, Greece, Ireland or Portugal and ITT is about the same 'size' as Chile. Moreover they are growing more quickly than national economies and as such are increasing their relative as well as absolute size. Between 1957 and 1967 the largest 200 firms in the capitalist world grew by 1% per year faster than the capitalist economies as a whole, whilst their output in host nations is increasing twice as fast as world national income.[13] Such is their size that three-quarters of world trade in manufacturing is undertaken by MNCs and indeed 84% of UK's visible exports comes from MNCs. Secondly, MNCs originate predominantly from just four countries: USA, UK, West Germany and France. These four account for over 75% of all MNCs. They are also truly *multi* national. For example, 92% of MNCs in the UK have subsidiaries in more than 12 countries.[14] Other important characteristics, as we shall see later, are that they are particularly dominant in industries that are technologically advanced and monopolistic, and that they are often highly vertically integrated. It is worth noting too that the establishment of subsidiaries abroad is not always to supply the markets of the host country, but often is for export to third countries or to export back to the nation of the parent company.

Now let us be more specific and turn our attention to the scale of activities of foreign MNCs located in the UK.[15] Between 13% and 20% of UK manufacturing output is in the hands of foreign-owned corporations, and between 65% and 78% of this is attributable to USA corporations. These latter have been increasing their share of total manufacturing output by ¾% per year, and account for around a quarter of UK manufacturing exports and investment. In total there are over 3000 subsidiaries of MNCs operating in the UK employing over one million people. As indicated above these activities are not evenly spread across all industries but are particularly dominant in chemicals, vehicles, non-electrical engineering, electrical engineering and metals. In particular the crucial strategic area of oil and gas from the North Sea is dominated by MNCs. Two indications of this are that about two-thirds of the profits estimated to come from North Sea oil will go abroad, and 77% of natural gas production is owned by foreign MNCs. Table 6.2 gives some indication of the extent of direct foreign investment in the UK[16] as well as UK direct foreign investment.

It clearly demonstrates that the UK is a net exporter of direct foreign investment and that this trend is increasing. Indeed the UK has more than 7,000 subsidiaries abroad, with a total 'book value' of around £14,700 million. The 30 leading UK based MNCs identified in a recent report[17] produced nearly as much abroad as at home, an amount more than four times the value of their exports from the UK. Overseas investment is primarily undertaken by a small number of corporations with subsidiaries throughout the world.[18] This overseas investment is increasingly located in the advanced capitalists nations, as can be seen from Table 6.3.

Table 6.2: Foreign Direct Investment in the UK and UK Foreign Direct Investment (£million)

	1967	1972	1975	1977
Direct Investment — into UK*	+170	+405	+525	+1151
Direct Investment — out of UK*	-281	-737	-1094	-1899
Total	-111	-332	-569	-748

*Department of Trade Inquiry into overseas direct investment — excludes oil and insurance.

Source: *Annual Abstract of Statistics* (1979), Tables 13.10 and 13.11.

Table 6.3: Distribution of Accumulated UK Foreign Investment

	1930	1972
Developed Nations	53	72
Underdeveloped Nations	47	28

Source: Fine (1979), Table 7.3, p. 181.

Indeed between 1962 and 1974 the total of UK investment overseas increased by 268% in the developed nations compared to 74% in the underdeveloped nations. It is worth noting that in the same time period UK investment in the EEC countries increased by over 700%.[19] Direct investment abroad as a proportion of domestic investment was 27% in 1971 and 37% in 1975.

Having sketched the statistical background to the nature and extent of MNCs at home and overseas, which we trust will be a useful back-cloth for analysing the consequences of the activities of MNCs in the next section but one, we turn now to an explanation of their growth and importance.

3.2: Why Go Multinational?

The capitalist mode of production consists primarily of autonomous competing capitals searching for private profit. Capital must expand or die, for competition is fought through reducing costs and consequently capital must be accumulated to take advantage of scale economies and/ or introduce more efficient and advanced methods of production. There is no reason why the accumulation of capital, and the concentration and centralisation of capital which it implies, should be hindered by arbitrary political boundaries of nation states. The search for reduced costs, higher rates of exploitation or indeed markets knows no geographical boundaries. Thus the internationalisation of capital and the expansion of capitals on a world scale is a geographical expression of the process of capital accumulation and the concomitant concentration and centralisation of capital. The continuous restructuring of capital that is required to compete on a national and international scale requires a global search for profitable investment opportunities, and indeed for the markets so that the accumulated capital can be fully realised. The progressive development of the forces of production implies that national economies are an inadequate basis for continued profitable accumulation. The massive amounts of capital needed and the large volume of output required to minimise costs in many industries require a world market to be safeguarded and expanded and a worldwide division of labour to seek out specific locations advantageous to specific phases of the production process. Thus competition and rivalry between large capitals are reproduced on a world scale.

Thus the internationalisation of capital can be viewed as an attempt to maintain or stave off falls in the rate of profit caused by barriers to domestic accumulation. Capital can be accumulated overseas. This possibility arises because rates of exploitation differ between nations more than within nations, as a result of the relative immobility of labour internationally and the existence of barriers to international capital mobility being greater than those which exist within nations. Hence increases in the rate of exploitation and the rate of profit can be sought out through foreign direct investment.[20] In particular changes in the international division of labour arises as firms extend over national boundaries, as they seek out cheap, relatively unskilled and poorly organised labour to undertake routine production jobs whilst higher level jobs remain centralised. Thus the production process within the firm can be split up internationally to take advantage of the particular characteristics of different locations and the different characteristics of labour power. In this way both the absolute and relative extraction of surplus value can be increased over what it would have been had accumulation proceeded domestically, and capitals involved

in this process become highly vertically integrated with the production
of commodities embracing the labour power of different nations.

This type of expansion is a relatively recent phenomenon. In earlier
times the export of capital was primarily designed to cheapen the
constant and variable capital inputs to domestic manufacturing and as
such was primarily involved in the extraction and processing of raw
materials and basic foodstuffs, whereas today it is part of the manufacturing activities themselves which are being 'exported'. Moreover
extensive expansion overseas requires an already large mass of accumulated capital to be available for investment, as well as sophisticated
transportation and communication systems, not only to transport
cheaply the commodities, or part commodities, between points of
production and from points of production to markets, but also to enable centralised control by 'head office' of the worldwide operations.

There are two other related reasons which help to explain the recent
dramatic growth of MNCs. We referred in the introduction to this
chapter to the conflicting conditions for the accumulation and realisation of surplus value. As a result of the 'long boom' not only has the
industrial reserve army, until recently, been considerably depleted and
thus the regulation of the price of labour power been checked, but the
growing strength, organisation and militancy of many working class
organisations in many advanced nations has also checked the fall in
real wages that normally accompanies a significant increase in the
industrial reserve army. Hence the greater incentive to exploit 'cheap'
sources of labour power in other nations, particularly those with weak
working class organisations, authoritarian governments, or those where
workers have not been able to achieve wage increases in line with
productivity increases, and therefore where rates of exploitation may
be rising. Thus overseas expansion may aid the accumulation of capital.
It may also, however, help to secure markets for the expanded production made possible. With the development of customs unions,[21] notably
in our context the EEC, and the possibility of the growth of protectionism, particularly in periods of economic crises, markets can be protected by actually producing for such markets 'behind' the trade barriers,
and accordingly either market prices reduced or profitability increased.[22] This may also help to restrict competition from host country
rivals and to more effectively compete with other multinational rivals
in the same markets. As we shall see when we come now to analyse the
consequences of MNCs' activities for home and host actions, there are
also additional 'advantages' to be gained from being a MNC with regard
to sustaining continued profitable world wide capital accumulation.

3.3: Consequences for 'Home' and 'Host' Nations[23]

What are the consequences for the UK of the net outflow of foreign
direct investment that the UK experiences, as we saw from Table 6.2?
The increasing net outward flow is clearly indicative of the higher profit
rates to be obtained outside the UK. Capital is moving abroad, at a
quickening rate, to take advantage of the higher rates of exploitation
and the lower values of labour power that exist overseas. This rapid
growth is partly attributable to freedom of movement of capital
allowed under EEC regulations, which the UK has 'enjoyed' since
joining in 1973, and is likely to quicken further since the abolition of
all exchange controls in 1979. This offers the chance of overcoming to
some extent domestic accumulation barriers and thus increases the
profit rate of UK capital. Not only does the profit rate improve compared to what it would have been had investment been undertaken
domestically, but it also improves the overall profit rate for UK capital
by reducing pressure on the domestic labour market and thus on wages,
through reducing the domestic rate of accumulation below what it
would otherwise have been. It also slows down the rise in the domestic
organic composition of capital.

Thus the central consequence *for capital* is that it improves the
profitability of capital and hence counteracts the tendency for the rate
of profit to fall, and with it counteracts the tendency to economic
crisis. It is thus part of the process of restructuring. In this sense the
consequences are beneficial but whether the continued reproduction of
capitalist relations of production in the UK are beneficial *for working
people* is another matter! The immediate consequence for working
people is that it reduces the demand for labour power below what it
would have been had the production taken place in the UK rather than
overseas. Effectively jobs are being 'exported' as UK-based capitals
expand production and employment abroad whilst reducing employment in the UK. UK output and investment suffer too. Moreover, the
balance of payments on visible trade will suffer as a result of the export
of commodities being less than it would have been had the production
been undertaken domestically and the output exported.[24] However,
because the UK is a net *exporter* of direct investment it is unlikely that
the overall balance of payments effect will be negative. Net *importers*
of direct investment usually suffer such an effect, as the outflow of
profits, interests and dividends from most nations can often exceed the
inflow of foreign investment. Certainly the UK and the USA received
nearly twice as much in investment income from underdeveloped countries between 1964 and 1968 than the inflow of foreign investment to

them from the same countries.[25] Throughout the 1970s the UK experienced a net positive balance on interest, profits and dividends[26] and this exceeded the net outflow of direct investment creating a positive balance of payments effect on this count.[27]

What however are the consequences of the activities of the significant amount of foreign-based MNCs in the UK? As an important host nation to some of the world's largest MNCs, does the 'foreign' ownership of 13% to 20% of manufacturing activity matter? Does it make any difference that foreign capital rather than domestic capital is in control of large sections of manufacturing industry? There are in fact several ways in which the existence of foreign ownership poses additional problems.

Most obviously there is the problem of 'external control' where ultimate ownership and control lies outside the UK and indeed branches within the UK constitute a small part of the MNCs' global activities. Thus UK branches often have little say in, for example, investment planning and locational strategy though they are much affected by it. Strategic decisions are usually made by the parent company on the basis of a global search for profit. This locational flexibility is the source of a number of problems with which we will deal presently, but in the present context it implies that if the conditions that led to the original establishment of branches in the UK change for any reason, the long term prospects for such branches are uncertain. Naturally, all else being equal, MNCs will locate branches where controls over their activities are least, and/or where conditions are most favourable. Thus changes in profits, taxes or in state inducements and regulations or even changes in government and the power of working class organisation may prompt reconsideration of existing and future investment and location plans. Thus their range of corporate policy options is somewhat wider than those of domestic capital.

Related to this problem is the reduced power of the state to control MNC operations. For example a left government would find it very difficult to nationalise branches of MNCs because of the problems of capital flight, and the high degree of vertical integration and hence intra-company trade that exists across national boundaries. Their economic power thus confers on them considerable political influence, for though they are in a strategic position with regard to the development of the national economy (because of their size, extent and sectors in which they operate), governments have relatively little control over them, if they wish to secure their continued presence in the economy. They may thus considerably influence, if not dictate, policy in certain

circumstances. They may also blunt the effectiveness of state interventions in other areas of the economy than industrial policy.
Murray[28] has argued that they can blunt state monetary policies
through having access to funds not easily influenced by domestic policy
e.g. internally generated surplus in both home and a variety of host
countries, as well as international capital markets like the eurodollar
market. They may also limit the effectiveness of balance of payments
policies through, for example, speculation in financial transactions to
minimise losses as a result of exchange rate changes. It is possible for
them to indulge in 'leading and lagging' in the payment for imports
and exports which may increase instability in a fixed exchange rate
regime. Moreover, because of their high degree of vertical integration
UK branches may account for only a small part of intra-company
activities and thus a change in the exchange rate may have little effect
on the price of their final product because the sterling component of
the final product is small.

More important perhaps is the type of activity which MNCs undertake in the host nation. Much of it is routine production activities,
rarely are central control and head office functions like finance,
marketing and research and development, decentralised to the same
extent. These branch plants then are those that are most sensitive to
attempts to reduce costs and restructure operations, for it is here that
the costs of labour power are central to the corporations' competitive
position. They are thus subjected to continuous readjustments in the
demand for labour power as the competitive position of the corporation changes, as it restructures its activities and searches continually for
lower cost locations on a global scale. The regular reporting of branch
closures and redundancies in branches of MNCs like those at Singer,
Talbot and Massey Ferguson all in Scotland in 1979, bears witness to
the instability of such employment.

Another major problem is that of 'transfer pricing'. Because of the
considerable vertical integration of most MNCs, which incidentally
also implies relatively low domestic 'linkages' and spread effects, there
is considerable *intra-company* but *international* trading. Transfer
pricing refers to the pricing of transactions between branches of companies and, because MNCs are vertically integrated across national
boundaries, such transfer prices give rise to international remittances.
Because the trade is intra-company there is no necessity to apply 'market' prices to such transactions and consequently there exists the possibility of using them to help secure corporate objectives. As 33% of all
manufacturing exports from the UK consist of intra-company trade, and

as 55% of the exports of American MNCs from the UK are intra-company shipments[29] there is clearly considerable scope for their use. What advantages can MNCs derive from the judicious adjustment of transfer prices? They can be used to disguise profit repatriations, by-pass exchange controls, reduce 'world' tax liabilities and resist pay demands or 'justify' closures or restructuring of branches by making individual branches appear unprofitable.[30] The, by now, infamous case of the Swiss-based Hoffman La Roche illustrates the possibilities. Through overcharging its UK branch for the cost of selling it the ingredients to manufacture the drugs Valium and Librium it was able to remit considerable 'profits' from its UK branch back to Switzerland. Whilst these ingredients perhaps had a market value of £9.20 per kilo, the UK branch paid between £437 to £979 per kilo for them. This was 'overpricing' to the tune of some 5,000%! Not only does this reduce the amount of profits declared in the UK it also represents an increase in the value of UK imports. A recent study[31] has also shown how royalty and licence fees paid to parent companies by foreign subsidiaries as compensation for technology transfer can also be used to reduce tax liabilities. Such fees are not inconsiderable. In 1974 the total fees paid by American subsidiaries in the EEC to their parent companies amounted to more than £400 million. The study demonstrates that American MNCs had a high propensity to repatriate royalties in response to high 'foreign' tax rates and that 25% of total royalty remittances constituted 'overpricing'. The revenue loss to the UK as a result of this activity amounted to nearly £5 million in 1968.

One final important consequence of the growth of MNCs has been the alteration in the balance of power between capital and labour that they induce. Because of their multibranch, multinational character and because of their size and locational flexibility, their bargaining strength in relation to their employees and their union organisations is generally greater than in domestic corporations. They can play off groups of workers and branches against each other on an international scale in order to secure agreement in negotiations on pay, productivity or restructuring operations.

4. The European Economic Community (EEC)

Given then that the internationalisation of capital has led to the increasing territorial non coincidence between the organisation of capital and the nation state, and that therefore the 'political' organisation of the capitalist world differs increasingly from its economic organisation, it is pertinent to ask whether this territorial expansion of capitalist production requires a parallel expansion of state functions on a supra- national scale? We have already seen that the process of the international- isation of capital has rendered the state increasingly inadequate to 'manage' the economy and thus regulate the profitable accumulation of capital. In the light of this we consider whether the EEC represents the beginnings of the dismantling of the power of the nation state in Europe in response to the internationalisation of capital and the intensification of competition on an international scale. Then we consider what are the chief characteristics and economic 'logic' of the EEC in relation to this process as well as what effect membership of the EEC is likely to have on the UK economy.

It is important to recall our materialist perspective which argues that, primarily, developments and changes in political structures arise from developments and changes in economic structures. Thus we would regard the major changes in the international economic system that we have discussed above as the central determinants in the development of the EEC. In response to accumulation and realisation difficulties 'at home' capital has attempted to break the barriers imposed by the politi- cal organisation of the world into nation states. The tendency for the rate of profit to fall leads progressively to the extension of the sphere of capitals beyond 'their' national boundaries. However, the powers of the nation state in defending accumulation and profitability, promoting, restructuring and regulating markets[32] are undermined as the extent of internationalisation of capital proceeds. Hence the quest for a supra- national state body to undertake such activity. We shall return to this point in the next paragraph. Moreover, as international competition and rivalry between MNCs intensifies, in particular between the USA, Western Europe and Japan, ways have to be sought to 'protect' domes- tically based capital and secure for it a competitive edge over foreign- based capital. Again, the creation of a European market and the removal of barriers to trade and capital movements, is designed to improve the competitiveness of capital by allowing the law of value to operating freely between 'member' states. In this way weaker capitals are eliminated through 'freer' competition and production is switched from high to low cost capitals, there is greater scope for scale economies and 'incentive' to reduce costs of production. The gains from the re- structuring cannot, however, be fully realised unless all obstacles and barriers to the free operation of the law of value are removed, and this involves the removal of discriminating tax and subsidy systems between nations as well as differential industrial and other policies. Thus the degree of economic integration required is considerable and as 'progress' is made towards full economic integration, the necessity for a supra-national state with sovereignty in matters of economic policy increases. Needless to say, however, it is the nations with the 'stronger' capitals that are likely to be those who press for greater and speedier integration and the removal of barriers to more rapid accumulation.

With regard to capitals' requirements for the state to continue to perform certain functions for it as it expands overseas, there are four alternative possible arrangements with regard to the relations between international capital and the state.[33] First, the nation state can under-take territorial expansion itself through colonisation or occupation. Clearly there are severe 'political' problems associated with such action, not the least of which is the risk of this escalating into inter imperialist wars and the annexation of the world into a few antagonistic power blocs. A second alternative is for the foreign state to perform the necessary functions, though this arrangement, if done under pressure from the domestic state, raises the issue of neocolonial relationships. Even if foreign states are willing to perform the functions of their own accord there is the possibility of partiality and discrimination against foreign capital *vis-à-vis* domestic capital either in subsidies, state purchasing or even in the protection of private property rights. Nationalist governments have been known to nationalise foreign-owned capital! Thirdly, existing state bodies in co-operation with each other may undertake the appropriate functions. Such co-operation is often difficult to achieve on a long term basis and may not survive the intensification of rivalry associated with a prolonged or deep economic crisis. In some ways the position of the more recent members of the EEC, including the UK, may be seen in this light. Finally, there may be a quest for a more permanent and more highly integrated and supra-national economic and political union.

As capitals develop the international division of labour, with increa-singly integrated production processes, where different branches per-form different functions and produce different parts of the final com-modity, intra-company trade increases and free trade and freedom of movement of capital become more important still for them. As sugges-ted above this ultimately requires a set of common policies between states on for example industrial policy, taxation policy, monetary policy and currency alignments. Moreover, as economic crises and international rivalry intensifies capital will increasingly depend on the exercise of state power. However there are legitimation problems arising from the thrust towards economic and political integration in nations where domestic capital is fundamentally uncompetitive, for social cohesion can be threatened by the internal strains that arise as the new competitive market conditions are 'adjusted' to, and sectors of industry and geographical areas experience the decline of their industry.

We now turn to a consideration of the economic philosophy of economic integration in the EEC and its impact on the UK economy.[34] There are various stages or degrees of integration, and though the EEC has proceeded a long way towards the highest stages of economic integration, it has still some considerable way to go before attaining full economic, and thus likely political, union with the 'surrender' of national state 'sovereignty' in economic policy making to a 'supra-national authority'. It is helpful in analysing the rationale and effects of economic integration in the EEC to distinguish between the various stages, and so we will proceed by identifying and explaining these stages and at each point indicate the likely effects of them on the UK.

The EEC is a 'customs union'. This involves the abolition of all tariff and quota barriers to international trade between the members of the union, whilst applying a 'common external tariff' on commodities entering the union from outside it. Thus the protection afforded to domestic capital by such barriers is removed and competition between capitals located in different nations is intensified. Hence more efficient capitals are likely to expand more quickly, and less efficient capitals decline more quickly, than in a more 'protected' market. Shifts in the international pattern of production and hence employment will ensue and the amount of internationally traded commodities will expand. This free trade not only reduces output and employment below what it would have been in nations dependent on less efficient and advanced capitals but also places a balance of payments burden on such nations whose imports expand faster than exports. The extent of the UK's visible balance of trade deficit with the rest of the EEC is demonstrated in Table 6.4. Clearly the UK has experienced a deterioration in its visible trade balance with the EEC since joining in 1973 and is in a deficit which considerably exceeds that with the rest of the world. Moreover, this burden has also led in part to governments pursuing more contractionist policies in order to stem the flow of imports than it would otherwise have done in the light of a 'better' balance of payments.

Three final points are worth making briefly before proceeding to analyse the further stages in the process of economic integration. First, though the creation of a customs union, in effect a free trade area with a CET generates conditions for more profitable capital accumulation, it is only the more efficient and advanced capitals, and the national economies in which they are located, which gain from this process.

Table 6.4: UK Visible Balance of Trade with the EEC 1970-1979
(£million)

Year	1970	1973	1976	1978	1979
Imports	2486	5291	11526	16584	20896
Exports	2405	4105	9304	14103	17885
Balance	-- 81	−1186	−2222	− 2481	− 3011

Source: CSO, *Monthly Digest of Statistics* (various dates).

Weaker, less competitive, capital suffers as do the areas in which they are located. Secondly, the CET affords 'protection' for capital in general in the union against 'foreign' competition, though the very existence of this tariff wall is an encouragement to non union MNCs to locate production behind the wall within the EEC should they require access to EEC markets. This encourages foreign direct investment rather than trade between the EEC and its rivals. Thirdly, the free trade does not apply to agricultural commodities as we shall see in a moment, and thus agriculture remains highly protected.

The next stage of integration is the formation of a 'common market' which involves the freeing of the movement of labour and capital. Consequently capital will be free to locate its activities in accordance with variations in production costs between member nations, thus allowing them to restructure their operations and seek out more profitable investment opportunities. This is a considerable encouragement to the expansion of MNC activities involving as it does, the abolition of exchange controls. Thus capital is allowed to flow away from nations with less profitable opportunities, for example the UK, thus affecting output and employment in the home nation and encouraging their cumulative relative decline. This freedom of movement also constrains the ability of nations like the UK to pursue locational controls on MNCs in so far as their locational flexibility is increased.

A further stage in the integration process is the setting up of 'common' policies which are applicable to all member states, for example, with regard to agriculture, transport, industry and competition. This involves harmonising hitherto different state policies and is a further step in removing nation states' 'sovereignty' in forming economic policy. These have the effect of removing non tariff barriers to trade and competition by preventing individual nation states from pursuing policies that discriminate in favour of capital located in their nation, for example with regard to subsidies and industrial interventions.[35] These are additional to the constraints imposed on nation states through being members of a customs union and common market, where the ability to erect tariffs or impose controls on capital movement, *vis-à-vis* other member states, is removed. Thus we can see how the economic functions of the nation state are gradually transferred to a supranational body.

Moreover, the development of common policies clearly necessitates the ability of the supranational body to raise revenue to implement such policies. Hence the existence of a 'community budget' which raises revenue through the income from the CET, as well as VAT contributions from member states and 'agricultural levies' — taxes on the import of foodstuffs into the EEC which help to 'protect' agriculture. It is the UK's net contribution to this budget which is causing so much concern at the time of writing,[36] though as we've seen the effects of membership of the EEC on the UK economy are of a much wider nature.

It is apposite to say a few words here about the Common Agricultural Policy (CAP) as it is the major common policy that has so far emerged in the EEC and as it constitutes nearly 75% of all EEC expenditure. Unlike manufacturing activity, agriculture is heavily protected from free trade and competition. The combination of taxes on the import of agricultural commodities and the price support scheme, has not only led to the 'artificial' raising of food prices in the UK as low cost imports from outside the EEC are replaced by higher cost sources from within, but also to the constant outstripping of consumption by production and hence the existence of various mountains and lakes of agricultural commodities. There is no free market philosophy here as there is with regard to manufacturing.

The highest stage of economic integration involves the move to economic and monetary union (EMU) and the integration of macroeconomic policies, thus allowing the management of the European economy by a supranational authority and the final 'surrender' of nation states sovereignty in economic policy. EMU involves both monetary and fiscal integration. This ultimately involves a common taxation system; the locking in of individual nation's exchange rates to each other and therefore in effect a common currency which would presumably be under the control of a European-wide central bank, which would control the supply and price of money; and a central budget. Thus macro-economic policy would, ultimately, be fully integrated with supranational control of the balance of payments, policies towards inflation, growth and employment. Naturally this implies that the UK would no longer control its economy through domestic policies, and in effect the UK would become a region bearing much the same relationship to the EEC as Northern Ireland does to the UK at present. This would pose severe problems for a capitalist economy so relatively weak as the UK, particularly because, as has been argued above, the process of integration is likely to exacerbate the relative economic decline of the UK both because of the intensification of competitive and free market forces and because of the increasing inability of the UK nation state to pursue independent discriminatory policies. This latter would apply to a left government committed to, say, the Alternative Economic Strategy, whose main policies are in direct contravention of the philosophy of the EEC as enshrined in the Treaty of Rome e.g. import controls, the planning of investment, nationalisation and more direct state intervention.

Currently the EEC has reached the stage of a 'common market' as well as developing a range of common policies and making some steps towards EMU. Whether this degree of co-operation and integration can survive the developing economic crises remains to be seen. What is clear is that it will be working people who bear the brunt of the crisis and the restructuring required in attempts to overcome it.

Further Reading

On the development of the world market see Mandel (1975), Chapter 2 and on the balance of payments see Harris in Nore and Green (1977), Chapter 8. For a discussion of contemporary international monetary problems, not dealt with here, see Gamble and Walton (1976), Chapter 5. For a brief theoretical review of the geographical expansion of capitalism in general see Howard and King (1975), Chapter 7.

The material on MNCs is daunting. For a general survey of MNCs in world development see UN (1973) or Lall (1974), which is also a useful reference on transfer pricing, whilst Mandel (1975), Chapters 3 and 10, deals with the Marxist analysis of the internationalisation of capital. Radice (1975) is a useful collection of readings on the MNC, and Barratt Brown (1974), Chapters 3 and 9 is also valuable. For statistical information on the growth and extent of MNCs see Labour

Research (1974) or better still Labour Party (1977). Both of these review the problems MNCs pose for the UK economy. Murray (1971) also reviews the effects of MNCs on the economy and on state management, whilst Hughes in Urry and Wakeford (1973) reviews American investment in the UK. Lall and Streeten (1977), whilst being primarily concerned with MNCs in underdeveloped nations contains three useful general chapters (1, 2 and 3) on MNCs' characteristics and behaviour. Finally, Hood and Young (1979) is a comprehensive orthodox analysis of MNCs.

On the internationalisation of capital and the nation state, two readings in Radice (1975) are very useful — Murray (Chapter 5) and Rowthorn (Chapter 8). Both Fine and Harris (1979), Chapter 9 and Hardach *et al.* (1978), Chapters 3 and 5 discuss the relationship between the internationaliastion of capital and the nation state, and the possible development of supranational authorities. However, Holloway (1976) is the best single review of this in the context of the EEC. Currie (1979) is one of the few accessible reviews from a broad left perspective of the effects of membership of the EEC on the UK; see also Holland (1980). Holland (1976) discusses some of the implications of membership and the growth of large MNCs on regional development. For a conventional analysis of the EEC and its policies see Swann (1978) or Coffey (1979).

Notes

1. See Chapter 2, section 5 and Chapter 5.
2. Needless to say many peoples of the world have either rejected or overthrown the expansion of capital. This has prevented capital from expanding to every corner of the globe, and as we shall see this poses severe problems for capital.
3. See Chapter 5.
4. We are concerned here only with the balance of payments on current account. The effect of capital flows is analysed in section 3.
5. See Chapter 5.
6. See Chapter 3 on the competitive process and its outcomes.
7. This visible trade deficit has however in many years been offset by a surplus on invisible trade (services of banking, insurance etc. as well as profits from overseas operation of UK capital and government transfers), so that the balance of payments on current account as a whole is not permanently in deficit. On overseas investment see section 3 of this chapter.
8. In fact trade is increasingly not between capitals but *within* them. See section 3.
9. See section 4.
10. More recently the £ has increased in value due to the existence of North Sea oil and government monetary policies. Naturally this further reduces the competitiveness of UK domestic capital.
11. MNCs are also sometimes referred to as international firms or transnational corporations.

12. See Levinson (1971).

13. See Rowthorn and Hymer (1971).

14. See Buckley and Casson (1976).

15. Much of this material is taken from Labour Party (1977), Dunning (1973) and Labour Research (1973).

16. It should be noted that this excludes oil and insurance.

17. See Labour Research (1978b).

18. Just 50 MNCs account for 80% of all overseas investment.

19. See Casson (1979).

20. The internationalisation of capital will, of course, as it proceeds in itself act so as to reduce international differences in profit rates. There are then limits to the extent to which 'going multinational' can act as a counteracting force to declining profitability.

21. See section 4 of this chapter.

22. Transport costs will also be reduced.

23. As we shall see in this section it is dangerous to speak of the consequences for nations, when in reality they are divided into opposing classes with opposing interests. Wherever possible we shall identify the recipients of the 'costs and benefits' of MNC activity.

24. Of course not all the output would have been exported as some of the overseas production will actually be destined for the UK market. In this case, however, the balance of payments on visible trade will still suffer due to increased imports.

25. See Lall and Streeten (1977).

26. The balance between interest, profits and dividends flowing into the UK from overseas direct investment and the interest profits and dividends flowing out of the UK form direct investment in the UK.

27. For example in 1977 the former amounted to −£748m, whilst the latter amounted to +£979m. Data from *Annual Abstract of Statistics* (1979), Table 13.11.

28. See Murray (1975).

29. See Labour Party (1977), Table 2.

30. Naturally because such operations are internal to the corporation, the existence let along the extent, of such activities rarely becomes public knowledge.

31. See Kopits (1976).

32. See Chapter 7 on the role of the capitalist state.

33. Fro an extended analysis, see Murray in Radice (1975).

34. It ought to be noted that though the UK joined the EEC in 1973, 15 years after it had been formed, it did not become a full member, and therefore subject to the full gamut of EEC regulations, until 1978.

35. This also applies to discrimination in state purchasing behaviour between domestic and foreign capitals.

36. The net contribution is the excess of revenue contributed to the budget from the UK less the expenditure received from it, for example from the regional and social funds as well as from the Common Agricultural Policy.

7 THE STATE

1. Introduction

The state is a major institution in contemporary capitalist society. In the UK state expenditure currently amounts to some 50% of GNP. Most people in their daily lives are deeply affected by the state's actions, not least because government policies reach into most spheres of economic and social activity, and affect us as workers, consumers and taxpayers. Indeed more than one worker in four now works in the state sector. Moreover all of us, at one time or another, are recipients of the various services provided by the state, from education and health provision to unemployment benefit and old age pensions, and from social welfare provision to the activities of the police. Indeed many reformists argue that the activities and growth of the state have somehow transformed capitalism, and that socialism can be achieved through the ballot box. It is said too that we live in a democracy. For these reasons and also because of interest in, and concern over, cuts in the provision of state services, an analysis of the state is of crucial importance. Just as importantly the state's activities have a significant effect on the process of economic development, and as we shall see these activities are in turn structured by the problems that capitalist economies experience in their development.

We begin this chapter with an analysis of the deficiencies of free market processes in the allocation of resources. This is important not only because orthodox theories of the state seek to explain state intervention in terms of market 'failures' and as such, as we shall see, contain some partial truths, but also because market processes are a central feature of capitalist economies and consequently their critique constitutes another element in our analysis of capitalism in the UK.[1] In the next section we outline a marxist perspective on the nature of the state and briefly consider how it differs from orthodox views.[2] In section 4, we extend the analysis of section 3 in explaining the growth of the state and its functions in capitalist society. In section 5 we go on to consider the contradictions in the growth of the state and whether such growth has helped or hindered the capital accumulation process and thus economic development under the capitalist mode of production. This leads us to an analysis of the so-called 'fiscal crisis' of the state and the attempts to cut and restructure state expenditure. In the final section

we undertake a more specific study and, drawing together the features
of the foregoing analysis, consider the Welfare State in the UK.

2. The Market System and State Intervention

All societies require mechanisms to ensure that commodities are produced in broad accordance with the 'requirements' of the population[3]
and, derived from this, that the necessary resources required for their
production are allocated to the appropriate sectors of production.
Production also has to be co-ordinated so that the correct amounts
of one commodity which are necessary for the production of another
are available. In other words gluts and shortages have to be avoided. In
a world of scarce resources it makes little sense to waste them in
producing excessive amounts of some commodities whilst others are
underprovided. Thus there has to be some mechanism or set of principles on the basis of which resources are allocated. In a capitalist
society, where there is no overall direction, co-ordination or plan, what
mechanism is used to decide what gets produced and by whom?[4]

In capitalism production is undertaken, as we have seen, by privately
owned capitals whose objective is to earn profit; production is for
exchange, for sale on the market at a price. It is through these markets
that the co-ordination of economic activity is achieved. For each commodity there exists suppliers (capitalist firms) who produce it, and
prospective purchasers (workers and capitalists) who require it. If, for
example, the total amount of a commodity that is produced exceeds
the amount that is actually bought, then in order to 'clear' the market,
the price of this commodity will fall until the total output is sold. This
not only clears the 'glut' but also acts as a 'signal' to suppliers (capitalist
firms) to reduce production of this commodity, because at the lower
price it will be less profitable to produce it than previously.[5] Indeed
some capitalist firms may move out of the industry in order to reduce
production and are stimulated to do so by lower profits in this sector
and, by now, relatively higher profits in other sectors. They will move
into sectors where potential demand exceeds output, and where therefore prices are being forced upwards and with them the profits of
capitalist firms in that sector. This movement will have the effect of
increasing output and supply in the sector, eliminating the shortage,
and thus pushing prices and profits down.[6]

Hence, changes in demand and supply lead to changes in market
prices which clear gluts and shortages from markets, and ensure that

the total amount of a commodity that is produced is exactly equal to
that which is required. This occurs because changes in relative prices
and relative profits (between sectors) induces capitalists to expand or
contract production, as appropriate, and switch sectors in accordance
with differences in profit levels. It is because capitalists act in their own
self interest that this 'invisible hand' of the market mechanism works so
as to allocate resources between sectors in accordance with the dictates
of 'consumers'. Workers too will be expelled from, and attracted to,
different sectors as capitalist firms alter their demand for labour power,
in accordance with changes in the sector's output, prices and profits.
For workers work in order to earn money, and their self interest will
direct them away from some sectors and towards others in accordance
with changes in the demand for labour power and the effect that this
has on the price of labour power, the wage.

So the mechanism is automatic, self-regulating and invisible. Without
central direction or plan, millions of decisions are co-ordinated and
resources flow between sectors in accordance with the dictates of consumers. As relative prices and profits change they signal production and
the resources, both means of production and labour power required for
such production, into the appropriate sectors. Economic motives of self
interest are supreme. Workers must work to live, and capitalists must be
profitable to survive. In such circumstances their behaviour is governed
by a mechanism over which neither has any collective control, but one
that does at least serve the crucial function of allocating resources
effectively.

Or does it? The market mechanism can only operate in the way described if certain 'ideal' conditions obtain.[7] These can be summarised as:

(a) the existence of perfectly competitive markets;
(b) perfect resource mobility;
(c) perfect information or knowledge.

To the extent that these conditions do not exist then there will be
inefficiencies in resource allocation. *Perfect competition* refers to a
situation where there are a very large number of capitals (producers) in
the market competing with each other, as well as a large number of
buyers. Thus no one capital is large enough to influence the price of the
commodity produced, which is thus determined by the market forces
outlined above. Each capital is therefore a price 'taker'. Moreover, there
must be no 'barriers to entry' in the market, so that new capitals can
easily and freely enter if profits rise above the average for the economy

as a whole. This implies that there are no scale economies for otherwise this would act as a barrier to new capitals, in the form of a production cost disadvantage. In reality however perfect competition does not exist but rather, as we have seen in a previous chapter, most markets are dominated by a small number of large capitals[8] who do have an influence over price, do possess scale economies and therefore, in these as well as other ways, do impose barriers to entry. Hence new capitals cannot readily enter such markets.

Perfect mobility of resources refers to a situation where both labour power and capital are not restricted in any way, over space or between sectors and uses, from moving in response to price and profit signals. Now much capital is 'sunk' and cannot instantaneously be put to different uses, whilst labour power, due to family ties, geographical distance and other social and psychological barriers, is not perfectly spatially mobile. Occupationally too, there are barriers with regard to skill and training differences between workers which take time to acquire. Thus to the extent that resources are not perfectly mobile, price and profit signals may not be acted on to the extent necessary.

Perfect information refers to a situation where individual capitalists, workers and 'consumers' have complete and accurate knowledge about all the opportunities available to them. To the extent that information is not perfect, naturally individuals will not necessarily be able to respond to market signals. They may not know of their existence. This is particularly so of consumers and constitutes a severe problem, for if consumers are ignorant in the sense that they do not have complete and accurate knowledge and if they do not act in a completely rational manner, their observed preferences in the market cannot be relied upon to dictate the uses to which resources are put. Clearly this is asking a lot of consumers in a society where a bewildering array of commodities, many only very slightly different from others, is produced and offered for sale, and where their technical complexity may be only understandable to a few. But there are deeper problems here. What if consumers' preferences are not independently formulated? In a society where 'big business' has come to dominate and where there is a tendency for overproduction, is it not possible that capital has the power and motive to promote demand through advertising, and the promotion of social values more generally, which reinforce material acquisitiveness? If preferences are to a large extent moulded in this way then preferences are a function of the existing social order rather than individually generated, unconstrained, free choices. In such a situation are individual consumers necessarily the best judges of their own interests? The rational, maxi-

mising, isolated, individual choosing freely from a range of commodities
which have been produced as a result of consumers' wishes is hardly an
accurate description of reality.

One further problem with the operation of the market mechanism,
with regard to its responsiveness to consumers needs, is that such needs
are only registered in the market and therefore only met if they appear
as 'votes' in the market. In other words preferences/needs/demands are
only relevant to the market mechanism if they are backed by money,
by the ability to pay for the commodity needed. The aim of production
is, we remember, not to satisfy needs but to earn profit. Needs that are
not backed by money are irrelevant. Hence the unequal distribution of
purchasing power that we documented in Chapter 4 implies an unequal
say in the market, for some people have many more votes than others.
In this way the pattern of output does not reflect the pattern of 'needs'.

Clearly therefore the ideal conditions do not exist in reality, and in
consequence markets fail to operate perfectly and thus fail to generate
an efficient allocation of resources or one that entirely corresponds to
consumer needs. However they do none the less work, albeit in a
highly imperfect manner, to ensure a workable balance between the
pattern of output and the pattern of purchases.[9] This in itself is partly
achieved through state interventions in many areas designed to iron out
these inefficiencies and increase competition, resource and information
flows.[10] However, even if it were possible to remove all the above imperfections in the working of the market mechanism and thus establish
the ideal conditions the market mechanism could still not operate as the
sole one in organising and co-ordinating economic activity for markets
are unsuitable for the provision of two types of commodities.

First, they are unsuitable to provide commodities for which no price
can be charged, so-called 'public goods'. Clearly if no price can be
charged, no profits can be made and there is no incentive for private
capitals to undertake their production and sale. Such commodities are
those which when provided, the satisfaction or benefits to be derived
from them, are diffuse i.e. are available to a large number of individuals
in society, or even society as a whole. Once provided to one individual,
they are also available to others. Unlike with commodities that can be
provided through the market, those who don't pay the price in purchasing them are *not* excluded from consuming them and can thus gain
benefit from such commodities whilst not paying for them. Unless then
people can be excluded from benefiting from a commodity the market
cannot provide them, because private capitals have no way of forcing
everyone to pay for the commodity, nor can they exclude anyone who

didn't pay from benefiting from it. Hence they must be publicly provided by the state, who alone can force all to pay through the taxation system. Examples include national defence, police services, street lighting, roads and so on.[11]

Secondly there are many commodities, the production and consumption of which, generate *externalities*, that is costs and benefits to producers and consumers, other than those which accrue to the individual producer or consumer involved. In a capitalist economy these costs and benefits are *not* reflected in market prices, for individual capitals or consumers do not have to pay from them. They only take into account, in making decisions, the cost and benefits that accrue to them as individual capitals or consumers. Whilst commodities which generate these externalities, negative and positive, *can* be provided through the market, to do so would involve considerable misallocation of resources for the prices charged would reflect only the private, not social,[12] costs and benefits of their provision and consumption. Thus, under the market, commodities which generate external costs would be overprovided and those which generate external benefits would be underprovided. Production is for private profit and consumption is for private gain, so consequently such external effects are ignored. Commodities which exhibit such characteristics include health and education provision as well as commodities which in their production generate visual, air, water and noise pollution.[13] As one can argue that the production and consumption of a very wide range of commodities imposes/confers costs/benefits on 'third parties', the potential scope for state intervention here is considerable.

We have seen in this section that the market mechanism is deficient as a means of allocating resources in a large number of ways. This has implications for the orthodox theory of state intervention. Broadly speaking, the orthodox argument is that whilst the market operates reasonably effectively in general, there remain areas where state intervention may improve the allocation of resources. This is particularly so in the case of 'public goods'; intervention is required, in this case state provision, only when the market cannot operate. The presumption remains against state intervention. With regard to commodities which generate externalities, where *external costs* are generated the implication is that market prices should be adjusted, through taxes and subsidies, to more closely reflect social rather than private costs and benefits. Markets and private provision are not replaced, the 'arithmetic' is altered and markets continue to operate.[14] With regard to where *external benefits* arise, such commodities may be subsidised, again to

more closely align private with social benefits, or may be directly provided by the state at less than market prices, or even 'free', in order to
encourage their consumption.

As to the failure to establish the 'ideal conditions' for the operation
of markets the implication is that the state should intervene to make
markets more competitive, to improve resource mobility and to improve
information flows. In other words the market should be lubricated and
the assumptions of market model recreated in the real world. The market is therefore a normative ideal towards which state policies may push
the economic system. A wide range of state policies reflect this perspective.[15] The main differences between liberals and social democrats
with regard to their views as to the degree of state intervention relates
to their estimation as to the extent of the problems posed above as well
as to their belief of how far state intervention is itself desirable in a
capitalist economy, to achieve their economic and social objectives.[16]

This analysis whilst offering a starting point for the analysis of state
intervention in capitalist economies is by no means the whole story.
State intervention is required to do more than improve resource allocation and the operation of markets as we shall see. Moreover, the state
itself is not subject to scrutiny, nor is its relationship to the capitalist
economy or the balance of class forces in society. The state, in the
above, is seen largely as a 'black box' intervening in the economy, from
outside as it were, in a rational way to correct market failings. It is to an
understanding of the state and its relationship to the central elements
of a capitalist economy and society, that we now turn.

3. The State in Capitalist Society: A Marxist Perspective[17]

In this section we present a brief outline of the basis of a marxist view of
the state which is embellished in the remaining sections of the chapter.
Societies are characterised essentially through their mode of production, and capitalist societies are thus characterised through the level of
development of the productive forces and, in particular, the relations
of production[18] i.e. the way in which production is organised and the
relationship between people in this process. In capitalist society these
relations take the form of private ownership of the means of production
and the existence of wage labour. The mass of the population do not
own means of production and must therefore sell their ability to work,
their labour power, to those who do. Thus capitalist society is a class
society. This is the basis on which society is constructed. The way in

which production is organised determines the *general* character of other institutions in society. There thus corresponds to each mode of a production a superstructure of institutions, of political and social forms, which includes the state. Thus a marxist theory of the state must take as its starting point the analysis of the capitalist mode of production and the relations between the state and the capitalist mode of production – the nature of the state *in* a class society. However the relationship between the state and the capitalist mode of production is a dialectical one. Whilst the former can only be understood in relation to the latter, the connections and relationships between them are important. The state is more than an epiphenomenon of a class society. Conflicts in class society, and in particular the class struggle, may require state action to reduce such class antagonisms, through the 'granting' of concessions. The collective power of the labour movement can alter the balance of class forces in society and can influence state policies, in the same view as it can wring concessions out of capital. To suggest otherwise is to consign the struggles of the labour movement to the scrapheap of history.

Thus the state is not *determined* by the capitalist mode of production. It does not exist outside the class struggle any more than it exists outside capitalist relations of production, for the former is an inevitable consequence of the latter. Rather we are arguing that the state is *dominated* by capital, not only because the economically dominant class in society will seek to fashion and control the state in its own interests, but more importantly because the laws of motion of capitalist economies over time generate certain requirements for state action, as well as imposing considerable constraints on the state's ability to pursue policies that are inimicable to the interests of capital.

The state in a capitalist society, then, reflects the class nature of such a society. Those who own and operate the means of production also control the state. The state thus regulates capitalism on behalf of the capitalist class and in so doing reproduces capitalist relations of production in trying to maintain and create the conditions for profitable capital accumulation. As capitalism develops and changes its contradictions develop, thus requiring changes in the role of the state, both to remove the barriers to accumulation that arise and to reduce the social antagonisms and conflict that also arise as the contradictions deepen. Ultimate power thus rests with capital. Consequently we can make two further points of importance about the state and its actions. First, the superficial appearance of political democracy is a façade, for formal freedoms and equality rest on the class basis of society.[19] The scope for fundamental change, for challenging the power of capital, is severely limited as the state is subordinate to the interests of capital and dominated by it. Related to this point is, of course, that the state is much more than a 'democratically' elected government and parliament. Most state institutions never come up for election. Such permanent features of the state include the army, the police, the judiciary, the Civil Service and so on. The government is a body which is, as it were, called upon to run the state for a specific period of time.

Secondly, whilst the state is not the simple agent of capital and the changing balance of class forces can influence the actions of the state, it has to be realised that such actions win concessions only. Not only are they made only under pressure, but they do not tackle the roots of the problems, for they are inherent in the capitalist economy. An attack on the root causes is an attack on capital. This is ruled out by the state. There can be no threats to basic capitalist institutions and values like private property or individual freedom. Instead conflict is controlled and discontent diffused by the granting of concessions and reforms. Such concessions are not necessarily even against the interests of capital, for they help to conceal the objective conflict between capital and labour, and thus help to perpetuate the continuance of a society domi-nated by capital. Moreover, such concessions may be enough to remove barriers to the accumulation process caused by, for example, an inter-ruption in the production process due to the withdrawal of labour. In any case, the granting of concessions is not an automatic response to working class pressure. This is true particularly in periods of crisis when concessions to labour mean a further weakening of capital, as both cannot have an increased share of the same size, or smaller, 'cake'. In such periods the state may have recourse to its weapons of coercion and repression.[20] Thus the state regulates the struggle between capital and labour, through concession and repression, so that accumulation can continue, or be restored, without 'open' conflict.

Before turning to the analysis of the growth of the state in relation to our basic framework outlined above, a few words are apposite on the orthodox theory of the state so that the differences from a marxist view become clearer.[21] We have seen in the previous section that such orthodox 'economic' theories of the state, see it as intervening in the economy to correct market failures and deficiencies in the allocation of resources, as well as in their utilisation through stabilisation policies. The state is seen as being outside the economic system.[22,23] It is treated in isolation from the rest of the economy stepping into, and out of, it as required and there is no analysis of the state itself. Nor, not surprisingly, is there any mention of the class relations of society.

However, the 'political' counterpart to orthodox economics' 'theory' of state intervention is 'pluralism', which sees the state as trying to reconcile the different power and interest groups in society, and trying to find a 'consensus' between them. Within this view, however, there are differences between liberal and social democratic views of the state. The former, associated with, especially the right of, the conservative party, have a presumption against state intervention particularly in economic matters. The state should only undertake what private markets and private capital cannot, and where intervention is required, for example in macro-economic management, attempts are made to work through market institutions, for example as in monetary policy. Consequently the state is seen as providing the framework within which the market and private capital can 'freely' operate. The growth of state intervention is seen as a consequence of the election of 'socialist' governments. Social democrats on the other hand, associated primarily with, especially the right of, the labour party have a presumption in favour of state intervention in order to secure greater equality (at least equality of opportunity, if not of outcome!) in society. It is argued that private ownership of capital is not the key here, but rather state expenditure can be increased to redistribute income and expand public services. The state is thus seen as being benevolent and a vehicle for increasing working people's welfare. The growth of state intervention is seen to be a consequence of pursuing egalitarian and reforming policies.

4. The Growth of the State: Capital Accumulation and the Class Struggle

As can be seen from Table 7.1 the state in the UK has grown considerably over the last 50 years. State expenditure as a proportion of GNP has nearly doubled, from around 29% in 1921 to nearly 58% in 1975. Both expenditure on real resources (producing an output of actual goods and services) and on transfers (redistributing spending power between groups) have increased by similar amounts. State expenditure in 1978/9 (in 1978 prices) amounted to more than £51,000,000,000, of which around 50% was spent on the Welfare State services of pensions, social security, health and personal social services, housing and education. All this expenditure has to be financed either from taxation, the surpluses of nationalised industries charges from borrowing. It can be seen that revenue, primarily from taxation, has increased considerably over the period though spending has continually outrun it. Hence the borrowing requirement has risen. The problems posed by this large increase in the borrowing requirement are taken up in section 5.

Table 7.1: State Expenditure as a Percentage of GNP 1921-1975

	1921	1961	1975
Total expenditure	29.4	42.1	57.9
Total revenue	24.4	38.5	46.6
Borrowing requirement	5.0	3.6	11.3

Source: Gough (1979), Table 5.1, p. 77.

How can we explain this dramatic growth of the state in a capitalist economy like the UK? The state's primary function is to ensure and enhance the continuation of capital; to maintain and create the conditions for profitable capital accumulation. Thus the state provides the pre-conditions for accumulation which are impossible or difficult for individual capitals to undertake. It serves the common interest of capital in this way by providing the use values necessary for accumulation to take place, but which if undertaken by private capital would be unprofitable. It can do this because the actions are not immediately subject to market forces, competition and the dictates of accumulation. Moreover because of the existence of individual, separate, competing capitals and their never-ending search for surplus value and profit, capital as a whole may destroy the very source of its existence, the labour power of workers. Consequently the state provides services which aid the reproduction of labour power and keep it in a fit and healthy condition for future use (e.g. through provision for unemployment and illness) as well as educating, training and retraining it. Because labour power can be put to work by different capitals, and is continually attracted and repelled by capitals as market and technical conditions of production change, its skills are available to capital in general irrespective of which capital provided it. Such competition between capitals also requires regulation in order to provide for free and fair competition between them, and to guarantee the continuation of private property.

However as accumulation proceeds and the laws of motion of capitalist development unfold, *increased* state intervention and activity is required in order to overcome the barriers to profitable accumulation that arise.[24] First, as the productive forces develop and the concentration and centralisation of capital proceed, the minimum size and capital necessary to start up production and compete, domestically and internationally, increases. This, along with the existence of large 'lumpy' capital investments with long lead times and high risks, as well as the ever increasing pace of economic change, requires increasing state subsidies or even the state to carry out, or finance, such projects. Secondly, as capitalist development proceeds the social costs associated with it increase, for example urban development and the generation of pollution, which require controls and provision in relation to land use, infrastructure and public services inter alia. Thirdly, along with techno-logical changes in production techniques associated with the develop-ment of productive forces, the division of labour within factories increases and changes, generating further requirements to socialise some production costs in the fields of education and training, as a result of changing 'skill' requirements. Fourthly, the growth of wage labour and the corresponding reduction in the numbers of self employed and employers as a result of the competitive process and the continuous expansion of the capitalist mode of production, requires the state to increasingly provide social security. For if people have only their wage with which to purchase the means of subsistence then ill health, old age or unemployment deprives them of their sole source of income. Finally, and perhaps most importantly, as capital accumulation proceeds the tendency for the rate of profit to fall sets in generating economic crises.[25] The state's response to this is both to attempt to manage over-all demand levels in the economy through its expenditure and taxation policies in a Keynesian manner, and to mobilise the counteracting forces to the tendency for the rate of profit to fall.[26] Of particular importance are state actions to restructure capital in order to increase profitability and international competitiveness. This may involve reduc-ing the proportion of, and value of, constant capital that capital has to pay for, through subsidies and grants, or increasing the rate of surplus value through financing changes in production techniques and adding to the means of production. It may even involve the nationalisation of unprofitable industries. In addition to restructuring capital directly, the state may take action to reduce the cost of labour power, through in-comes policies (to reduce real wages) or anti-union legislation designed to reduce the bargaining strength of working people. The onset of crises, as well as the restructuring process itself, also requires increased state expenditure in other areas in order to retain social control in such times of increased social conflict. This can take the form of expanding welfare state services or even developing the state's apparatus of coercion and force.

It is worth mentioning in conclusion to our brief analysis of the increasing requirements of capital for state intervention as the contradictions in the accumulation process develop, that the progressive internationalisation of capital requires further state intervention in order to reorganise relations of production in favour of capital accumulation on a world scale, and may even require new forms of the state.[27]

However, whilst the state is *dominated* by capital, the actions of the state are not *determined* by it. For a fundamental feature of capitalist society is the antagonistic relationship between capital and labour. Capital has to struggle with labour to secure conditions for the extraction, appropriation and realisation of surplus value and thus the laws of motion of capitalism are modified by such a struggle. The state too comes into conflict with labour, representing as it does the interests of capital in general. Thus the class struggle and modifications in the balance of power between labour and capital can affect state intervention. How else can state policies which act against the interests of capital be explained? (E.g. the Employment Protection Act.) The long boom not only had the effect of reducing the size of the reserve army of labour and strengthening workers' organisations, but when the long boom broke the balance of class power had been modified, so strengthening the defensive power of the labour movement. Concessions and reforms can be won through concerted action by workers' organisations and through struggles to influence state policy by electing parties who represent workers' interests to parliament, who if they form governments, may introduce reforms. This is not to suggest that the power of capital will be or can be broken through such action, nor is it to suggest that the state can be used to transform society to socialism. It does however suggest that political struggle on this level is part of the class struggle if state policies are influenced by the ideologies of the party in 'power'.

We may conclude then that the growth of state intervention exhibits *contradictory* elements, for whilst it primarily reflects the interests of capital and the tendencies inherent in the capital accumulation process, the continuing class struggle ensures that the requirements of capital are not the only determinant of state policies. The state is no longer the simple agent of capital. The very developments of capitalist society, the increasing contradictions between the forces and relations of production, ensure that this is so by increasingly demonstrating to working people the enormous gap between what is possible in a classless society and what is possible under the capitalist mode of production. Hence the growth of state intervention is neither wholly beneficial to capital nor to labour, and attempts to reduce the level of state intervention is similarly neither necessarily wholly deleterious to capital nor to labour. This issue, inter alia, will be developed further in the next two sections.

But first, let us summarise the functions of the modern capitalist state, the functions that are essential to the process of capitalist production and reproduction. What contribution does the state make to sustaining the capitalist economy?[28] One major function is to manage the macro-economy through the regulation of demand. There is no inherent mechanism in the market economy to ensure that the total amount of goods produced will equal the total that people are willing and able to buy, at a level of utilisation of resources, both of labour power and means of production, that is not grossly wasteful.[29] Thus the state intervenes in the economy to regulate demand, through altering the balance between its taxation and expenditure, thus increasing or reducing as appropriate the demand for goods and services. It may also try to regulate demand through monetary policies, which again act so as to control the amount of spending, the level of demand, in the economy. As a result of these measures state expenditure and intervention has increased, as there is a chronic tendency to overproduction in capitalism, a tendency which implies economic crises. To avoid these the state almost continually runs a 'deficit' i.e. expenditure outruns revenue, in order to add demand to the economy. Nevertheless, whilst this approach may aid the realisation of surplus value it has little effect at the level of production i.e. on productivity and profitability.

Thus a second key function of the state is to aid the restructuring of capital. Whilst the state cannot abolish crises, either at the level of demand or production, as they arise in the sphere of production, it can remove some of the barriers to the escape from a crisis.[30] This can be done through promoting combinations of capitals, taking control of some capitals, regulating relations between different capitals, as well as regulating the relations between capital and labour changing the balance of power in favour of the former. This is all designed to increase efficiency and competitiveness, through increasing productivity and thus the rate of surplus value and profit. Another way in which the state can encourage the restructuring of capital is through breaking down the barriers to the operation of the law of value. By *reducing* state subsidies, loans, grants and so on, as well as other barriers to the free play of market forces, restructuring will be speeded up as the weakest capitals go to the wall under conditions of free competition, free trade and freedom of movement of capital. Though to the extent that previously 'socialised' costs now would have to be borne by private capital, profitability may suffer.

Many activities of the state are designed to socialise some of the costs of production that otherwise capital would have to pay. Again to the extent that the state undertakes such activities, it will improve the profitability of capital. The state socialises the costs of both means of production and labour power. With regard to the former, we have already referred to the subsidies, loans, grants, tax reliefs, research and development and infrastructure provision, provided by the state. All this 'social investment' increases the profitability of capital by reducing the cost of constant capital.[31] With regard to the latter, labour power, the state aids the reproduction of labour power through health care provision, training, social security provision and labour cost subsidies. All this 'social consumption' reduces the cost of variable capital.[32,33]

In the above ways the state clearly benefits capitals and the operation of the capitalist economy, but we must add to these 'economic' functions of the state a further 'political' function designed, too, to benefit capital and the capitalist economy. This role involves both the attempt to legitimise class society and to promote social stability, so that accumulation can proceed unhindered by social conflict between opposing classes and between labour and the state. Legitimation involves encouraging acceptance of the social order among those who own only their labour power. They must support a class society, or at least acquiesce to it, otherwise production and reproduction of the system will be continually interrupted by demands for radical social change and threats to the continuation of the system. This legitimation is sought not only through state propaganda, particularly in relation to the confined limits of economic and political options and debate, but also through the media, education and the family who encourage the view that only certain ideas are acceptable and that capitalism is part of the natural order of things. Alternative economic and social systems are not part of the political agenda in a democratic state like the UK! To the extent that this legitimation is achieved, this is a powerful force for consensus and stability in capitalist society. If, in addition, the demands of the subordinate groups in society can be confined and are capable of being accommodated within the system (increased wages, better working conditions, improved public services, better social security and so on), then though these 'social expenses' ultimately have to be financed[34] the conditions for state capitalist development are almost complete. Conditions similar to these seemed to pertain in the UK during the long boom, when a wide range of ideologues proclaimed the 'end of ideology' and the end of a 'class ridden' society. Then came the end of the long boom and with it the recognition by more and more people that capitalism and the interests and potential of working people were incompatible. Ideology, class and even marxism, have raised their ugly heads again! If a class society cannot ultimately succeed in legitimating itself and obtaining the acquiescence of those who own only their labour power, the state has one powerful instrument of class rule available. For securing acquiescence, there remains coercion; the apparatus of the law. This constitutes another part of 'social expenses'. In the last resort the role of the police, prisons, courts and army is to keep the oppressed, oppressed. Attempts to fundamentally change class society will be, and are, met by force and repression in the form of the state, acting as it ultimately has to, to protect capital.

5. The State and Capital: Contradictions and Responses

We saw in the previous section that the state has grown, both because of the requirements imposed by the difficulties that capital experiences in the process of capital accumulation, and as a result of the struggles between capital and labour, where concessions have been fought for and won. We will see in this section that there are limits on the ability of the state to perform the functions required of it by capital in general, and in particular that a series of problems in the capitalist economy emerge *because* of the growth of the state. There are thus contradictions in the growth of the state which, under certain conditions, lead to attempts to cut back on its growth and restructure its operations. This as we shall see briefly in this section, and in the next section on the Welfare State, leads to other problems.

Whilst the state performs vital functions for capital, for example in reorganising capital and the relations between capital and labour, it cannot ultimately transcend market forces or eliminate the tendency for the rate of profit to fall. It can only modify them and attempt to mobilise the counteracting forces. It remains ultimately subordinate to the laws of motion of capitalist economies. The power of the state is then limited, for it can neither directly determine the decision-making of private capitals nor be entirely separated from the exigencies imposed by the accumulation process. The quest for accumulation goes on, indeed may be speeded up, and the laws of motion that go with it. It cannot override the logic of capital, and it also has to contend with limits on its action contingent upon the class struggle and the balance of forces between labour and capital at any given point in time. Though, as we have seen the state can itself alter the balance of these forces.

There are limits on the growth of the state associated with the dynamics of capitalist development, limits which have been reached in the UK given the condition of the UK capital. The first problem, to which we will return in detail in the next section, is that of financing the growth of state expenditure. As we saw in Table 7.1 there has been a tendency for expenditure to outrun revenue and for the state to finance the deficit through borrowing. Both this method of finance, and the alternative of increased taxation, will exacerbate inflation, reduce profitability and accumulation or both. This so-called 'fiscal crisis' of the state, and the problems involved in financing expenditure are taken up in the next section.

Beneath the surface of this fiscal crisis lies a deeper problem, that of the relation between state expenditure and capital accumulation. Has the growth of state expenditure benefited capital accumulation or has it acted as a barrier to it? The motor of the capitalist economy is the extraction, accumulation and realisation of surplus value. Barriers to this process threaten the reproduction of the system. How has the growth of state expenditure, then, affected the extraction, accumulation and realisation of surplus value? At the level of realisation, clearly, increases in state expenditure will aid the realisation process by increasing the demand for goods and services produced by capitals, both from the state sector itself (by purchasing the output of capitals like pharmaceuticals, armaments, cement, paper and so on) and from workers spending their income from the state (whether as employees of the state or recipients of 'transfer payments'). However if taxation is increased to totally finance this expenditure the overall impact on demand will be neutral.[35] So we can state that a budget deficit will expand demand and aid realisation, whilst a budget surplus will diminish demand and generate realisation problems.[36] The same holds for increases in state expenditure (expanding demand) and reductions in state expenditure (reducing demand). What of the accumulation process, the production and expansion of surplus value?[37] Naturally, the greater the amount of surplus value generated the more rapidly accumulation can proceed. However to finance state expenditure, taxes are raised which ultimately come out of the surplus value.[38] Thus increases in state expenditure reduces the amount of surplus value available for accumulation. Here we see the contradiction of state expenditure – it is necessary to sustain capital accumulation, but it *inhibits* capital accumulation.

This however is an oversimplified view, which assumes that all state expenditure, because it is financed from a deduction from surplus value, acts as a drain on the accumulation process. But once we move away from the *financing* of state expenditure, and analyse the impact of state expenditure itself, a rather more complex picture emerges, for we have to know whether all state *expenditure* contributes to accumulation or is a barrier to it. Essentially some activities of the state, and thus some of its expenditure, do contribute to accumulation whilst others act as a barrier to it. We noted above distinctions between social investment, social consumption, and social expenses in state expenditure. Both social investment, in reducing the cost to capitals of purchasing and hiring means of production, and social consumption, in reducing the cost of reproducing labour power, clearly contribute to long run capital accumulation by raising the rate of profit over and above what it would otherwise be in the absence of such expenditure. Social expenses, on the other hand, whilst being necessary to promote social harmony and stability do not contribute to capital accumulation.[39]

In a period of crisis when accumulation and profitability are threatened, it is difficult to maintain the extent and pattern (in terms of the three categories above) of state expenditure and also to finance it, at the level it reached in boom conditions. Yet the requirements of capital, and the need for further social expenses in crisis conditions, remain. Such are the contradictions of the capitalist state. What implications does this have for state intervention in the current situation in the UK?

The crisis of capitalism in the UK is also a crisis for social democracy and social democratic parties. The constraints imposed on the expansion of state expenditure prevent the development and expansion of expenditure of the social expenses type, and raise problems associated with the financing of overall state expenditure. Social objectives are sacrificed in the face of the need to restore accumulation and profitability, and thus for capital to retain as much surplus value as possible. The state expenditure cuts initiated by the last labour government in 1976, the imposition of cash limits and the reordering of expenditure priorities (restructuring) bear witness to the limits of reformist policies in a crisis ridden capitalist economy. The election of a conservative government in 1979 has intensified the cutting and restructuring of state expenditure. A government with a positive commitment in principle to 'rolling back the frontiers' of the state and a (partial) understanding of the burden of state expenditure on capital accumulation, as well as the objective failure of social democratic state policies to restore the health of private capital, is fertile ground for further altering the extent and nature of state expenditure. In the light of our analysis, we would not only expect an overall reduction in state expenditure but a restructuring of it to more closely coincide with the needs of capital accumulation.

Together with a tighter overall centralised control over state expenditure through the application of cash limits, unadjusted to the level of inflation, within this one would expect a differential approach to state activities as between those that aid capital accumulation and those that constrain it.[40] One would also expect barriers to the free play of market forces to be removed, to encourage the restructuring of capital under market conditions and thus the reduction and removal of social investment and social consumption expenditure that *discriminates* between capitals; the denationalisation of profitable state-owned enterprises; and a reduction of social expenses expenditure to the extent which can be achieved without markedly increasing social conflict; and parallel with the latter an expansion of expenditure on the means of coercion in order to contain the conflict which does arise.

The state thus is increasingly drawn into the struggles between capital and labour in the crisis, as cuts in, and the restructuring of, state expenditure is one element in the struggle. The restructuring of capital, which is the aim of such state policies, to speed up accumulation and restore profitability, requires if it is to be 'successful' a change in the balance of power between capital and labour. Hence the development of state policies, requiring little expenditure, to reduce the power of working people and their unions in order to reduce their defensive strength in struggling against restructuring, both of capital and the state. However, strategies to cut and restructure state expenditure are not without their problems. First, such actions destroy the notion of the state's neutrality and the actions of governments being in the 'national interest'. They are clearly seen to be on the side of capital and thus struggles to maintain living standards will be directed at the state as well as capital. Secondly, and related to this, working people will not respond passively to such changes, as the objective conflict between the needs of working people and the needs of capital becomes clearer. Thirdly, cutting state expenditure gives rise to realisation problems for capitals as well as problems in the production of surplus value, for a tight monetary policy, which is a concomitant of cutting state expenditure, not only slows inflation through giving workers a 'choice' between wage increases and unemployment, but also increases the cost of purchasing means of production and financing expansion. Fourthly, the resulting restructuring of capital not only involves an 'attack' on working people but also on sections of capital, particularly small capital. Finally, of course, state expenditure cuts and restructuring may still fail to encourage faster accumulation and restore profitability for two reasons. First, generating conditions favourable to the production of surplus value may cause difficulties in realising it as state spending on private capitals output declines and overall demand falls. Hence the importance of policies of free trade and freedom of international capital movements. Secondly, in the midst of a world recession and increasing international competition, there are limited opportunities for profitable production, for surplus value has to be accumulated *and* realised.

6. Capital and the Welfare State[41]

This final section of the chapter draws on the analysis conducted above in a specific study of one crucial area of state expenditure, the Welfare State.[42] In so doing we concentrate particularly on the relationship between the Welfare State and the capitalist economy, and the current restructuring of the Welfare State.

As can be seen from Table 7.2, the Welfare State has grown dramatically in the UK over the last 60 years. Indeed it can be seen that welfare spending has increased more quickly even than overall state expenditure, and now accounts for about half of all state spending.[43]

Table 7.2: The Growth of Welfare State Expenditure in the UK (as a % of GNP)

	1921	1961	1975
Welfare State expenditure	10.1	17.6	28.8
Social security	4.7	6.7	9.5
Health and welfare	3.3	4.4	7.1
Education		4.2	7.6
Housing	2.1	2.3	4.6
Other state expenditure	19.2	24.4	29.1
Total state expenditure	29.4	42.1	57.9

Source: Adapted from Gough (1979), Table 5.1, p. 77.

Welfare State activities are structured by the same forces that structure state expenditure in general.[44] The Welfare State is ultimately subordinate to the capitalist mode of production, and its activities, both in extent and function, are dominated by the imperatives of the capital accumulation process.[45] However the class struggle provides pressure from below, and modifications in the balance of class advantage, gained through struggle, can increase the power of labour by enough to win concessions from the state in particular periods of time. Moreover, the Welfare State plays a key role in attempting to secure social stability and acceptance of the domination of capital.

Whilst the organised power of labour can, at best, partially modify Welfare State policies, the dynamics of the capital accumulation cannot be overruled whatever form Welfare State policies take. What then are the functions of the Welfare State? First, the state intervenes to modify the reproduction of labour power. As labour power is the source of surplus value this capacity must be maintained and reproduced for capital to reproduce itself. How is this capacity to perform labour maintained and reproduced? In exchange for their labour power workers receive a wage which allows them to purchase food, clothing, housing and other commodities whilst the services of non-working members of the family, in the form of cleaning, shopping, cooking and so on, also ensure that workers are fit and healthy enough to resume work in the next time period.[46] Into this process of reproducing labour power the state intervenes in a host of ways, most notably in providing health services; maintaining the unemployed through unemployment benefit and social security; providing the services of state employees to control and smooth relationships and behaviour within the family and between family members and the outside world; and perhaps especially important, providing education, training and retraining of members, or potential members, of the labour force to suit them to the changing requirements of the division of labour within society and the factory/office. Such state intervention to assist in the reproduction of labour is designed to benefit capital. For example, welfare benefits for the unemployed have to be kept below wages in order to guarantee the reproduction of capitalist social relations.

Secondly, the Welfare State maintains the non-working population: the aged, the sick, the disabled and those unable to work for other reasons. Some of the social product must be transferred to them in order for them to live. Indeed the overall effect of Welfare State policies is to redistribute income in this 'horizontal' way, rather than between social classes.[47] However, again, families, communities, voluntary bodies and even capital do provide a role here.

The expenditure involved in these functions can be seen in terms of the categorisation introduced earlier — social investment, social consumption and social expenses — which has important implications for the impact of Welfare State policies on capital accumulation. Whilst some aspects of Welfare State policies involve social investment, and thus increasing labour productivity (training and retraining, and some aspects of education), most fall into the category of social consumption, social expenses or both. For example, the maintenance of the non-working population clearly falls into the social expenses category; the provision of health services to the working population into the social consumption category; whilst something like the 'job creation programme' falls into both. The importance of seeing the functions of the Welfare State in this way, is not only that it integrates the Welfare State into the analysis of state intervention generally, but that it has important implications for understanding the restructuring of the Welfare State. Before we turn to this issue, however, we must consider the growth of the Welfare State and how it reflects the growing requirements of capital as well as the partial victories won by labour in the class struggle.

There are two 'superficial' contributory reasons to the growth of the Welfare State. First, the changes that have occurred in the structure of the UK population over time, as well as its absolute growth, have meant that the Welfare State has grown in relation to both its functions identified above. For example, over the period 1941 to 1969 whilst the working population increased by 4%, the numbers of those over the age of 60 increased by 54%. This has engendered a rapid growth in certain welfare provisions whilst the numbers of workers whose surplus labour provides the finance for them, has increased very slowly. Secondly, the relative costs of providing welfare services has increased over time, as most services are labour intensive and the rate of productivity growth has been slow. These two factors have been shown to account for, for example, over 70% of the growth in education spending, over 60% of the growth of spending on the health service and nearly 50% of the increased spending on the personal social services.[48] Such increases do not involve, therefore, a real 'improvement' in the standards of services for individuals.

How, though, can the rest of the growth of the Welfare State be explained? As capital accumulation proceeds new requirements emerge. We have already, in section 4, identified the tendencies that emerge in this process that require increased state intervention, but what developments require specifically the growth of Welfare State provisions? What new 'needs' develop in the course of accumulation? Indeed, how could welfare services increase without individuals being overall any 'better off' as a result? At least four main tendencies can be identified which generate new 'requirements'. First, as accumulation proceeds an increasing proportion of the population, and ultimately the great bulk of it, have only their labour power to sell and gain an income. In other words the working class grows. Thus if they become ill or disabled or when they grow too old to work, they are deprived of their only income.

Hence the requirement for the provision of some form of social security. Secondly, the existence of the capitalist mode of production brings with it the possibility of unemployment.[49] As the UK economy experiences 'crises' and as the level of unemployment at each successive boom grows, so the need for expansion of unemployment and social security payments increases. Thirdly, the development of technology, the increasing use of machinery and the ever finer division of labour require new and changing skills in the labour force and hence changes in the education and training fields. Fourthly, there are many 'social costs' of capitalist development associated with the speed of economic and social change, technical changes and dislocations in the pattern of life which generate 'social problems'. Mental illness, delinquent behaviour and broken relationships are but some examples of the costs involved.

It would seem then, that despite 'appearances' to the contrary: 'Rising cost, changing population structure and the emergence of new needs probably account for almost all of the growth of social expenditure since the Second World War. Very little, or conceivably none at all, represents a real improvement in the satisfaction of needs.'[50] Thus the influence of working class struggles on the development (though not origins) of Welfare State policies appears to have been minimal in creating real advances for working people. The Welfare State cannot be isolated from the economic system; it primarily operates to secure the necessary conditions for reproducing capitalist social relations i.e. reproducing labour power, maintaining the non-working population and ensuring social stability. However the *level* of spending on some services does reflect a struggle around the level of services by workers, parties and pressure groups, and certain provisions do reflect progressive thinking by 'social reformers'. And, there are progressive elements in many services. Again, the form of provision is important and has been affected by pressure from unions and working class parties. Most importantly, many of the social expenses type of expenditure directly arises from the magnitude of class conflict. A quiescent working class does not require considerable concessions from the state; a well organised, united and militant one does.

We now turn to the issue of whether the Welfare State ultimately benefits capital or whether it is a barrier to its development. Though, as we saw when analysing state expenditure as a whole, the Welfare State is primarily a response to the needs of capital, it is not certain that in all periods it acts so as to benefit capital. There are contradictions in the Welfare State.

As we saw in the previous section there are problems involved in financing state expenditure, for in raising finance through taxation the volume of surplus value available for accumulation is reduced. In periods of economic crisis, when accumulation is being held back because the rate of profit has fallen, expanding Welfare State expenditure will put further pressure on profitability and hence slow down accumulation even more, and intensify the crisis, in turn reducing the further potential for raising finance through taxation. However the requirements of capital accumulation make increased Welfare State expenditure necessary, and together with periodic crises which make increased expenditure necessary for social stability, and the defensive struggle of labour around the levels of provision, benefit and service, the state has had to revert to increases in borrowing which cannot be sustained indefinitely and in any case leads to expansion of the money supply and likely inflation.[51] Does the state have any alternatives to finance its welfare expenditure? Essentially there are four, but all of them (except the last) will increase inflation, reduce profitability, or both. There is no escape, welfare expenditure cannot be further increased given sluggish accumulation, low profitability, and the existence of an organised labour movement. The last of the four options effectively signals the end of the Welfare State. The options are:

(a) Increase direct taxes. For this to raise anything like the necessary revenue, increases are required which effectively reduce the real value of workers' wages. Given the defensive strength of the labour movement this will be rejected and money wage increases will be demanded to offset it. This, without corresponding increases in productivity, will increase prices, reduce profits or both. It will also increase state expenditure on wages.

(b) Increase taxes on the capitalist sector. This will reduce profitability further unless prices are raised, thus increasing inflation and encouraging further wage increases, inflation and/or lower profits.

(c) Increase indirect taxes. This directly increases prices, particularly on workers' means of consumption, and increases pressure for further wage increases (cf. the increases in VAT in the May 1979 budget).

(d) Increase charges. If this is to raise enough revenue, it puts welfare services increasingly on an 'ability to pay' market basis and further may put pressure on wages. Actually on a short term basis there is also the option of using tax revenue from North Sea oil, which will amount to at least £6,000 million in 1984. However this would mean it would *not* be available for capital investment or taxation reductions.

The only alternative is therefore to cut welfare expenditure. But this
has the effect of causing realisation problems and there are possible
dangers in this strategy with regard to maintaining social stability.
However the former can be mitigated by increasing the potential for
separation of accumulation and realisation by 'freeing' international
trade and capital movements, and the latter by simultaneously attempting to alter the balance of power between capital and labour (through
incomes policies, trade union legislation or whatever). Thus cuts are
possible,[52] but what of the requirements of capital? Welfare expenditure
will be *restructured* to more closely coincide with the needs of capital,
and cuts made in areas which restrain capital accumulation. Grafted on
to this restructuring and a switch in emphasis from the caring to the
controlling functions of the Welfare State, there is currently a different
political strategy from that of social democracy[53] which has been
dubbed 'right wing' restructuring[54] and which affects the forms that
restructuring takes. In part this restructuring is different because the
current crisis is deeper but also because the ideology behind it differs
from that of social democracy. The 'right' view sees the balance between
the demands of accumulation on the one hand, and the need for reproduction of labour power and expenditure of the social expenses type
on the other, in a rather different light. There is a belief in more self
reliance, more 'free choice', less paternalism and the restoration of
'incentives'. There is a general contempt for many welfare recipients,
seeing their problems as self inflicted. Associated with this is a belief in
the need to 'restore' law and order, strengthen national defence and
reduce the power of unions and the labour movement. If this can be
achieved, then the 'soft' alternative of state welfare expenditure to
contain social conflict can be diminished. Vital in this process is what
Leonard[55] terms 'ideological management' i.e. to get working people
to accept these views and to see them as being in the national interest,
common sense and there being no alternative.

Some aspects of the restructuring of the welfare state, associated
with these views, would include:

(a) Adapting educational and social security policies to be respectively,
    more 'relevant' to the needs of industry, and increase the will to
    work by widening the gap between unemployment and social
    security benefits, and wage levels.
(b) Moving some welfare services over to the private sector (e.g. in
    health, education, and especially housing) or into the voluntary
    sector, or back to the family (e.g. the elderly and the mentally ill).

(c) Increasing 'efficiency' by reducing employment, controlling wage increases and increasing 'productivity' and workloads and by increasing bureaucratic control and reducing the autonomy of 'professional' workers.

(d) Restoring women's 'role' in aiding the reproduction of labour power, thus simultaneously reducing welfare payments and un-employment and increasing family stability through reducing role conflict.

The state is now enjoined in the intensifying class struggle around the deepest crisis in the UK economy for 50 years. On the basis of the analysis presented here, it is not adequate to simply 'attack the cuts' and defend state expenditure on the Welfare State or elsewhere. For this implies that state action is beneficial to working people from expenditure on drugs, prisons, the special patrol group, germ warfare and nuclear power to social security benefits, council housing, nurseries, employment subsidies and preventive health care. State expenditure whilst containing both progressive and regressive elements, often within the same area of provision, is in the last analysis directed by the require-ments of capital accumulation. In this sense the state is an integral part of capitalist society. The task then is to link the struggles around the provision of Welfare State services, with a critique of Welfare State 'practice' and, especially, with the struggles of working people generally, both in the state and capitalist sectors and in the community, to en-courage the realisation that it is capitalism which stands between working people and our collective liberation.

Further Reading

For a critical analysis of the operation of markets in resource allocation and their implications for state intervention see Stilwell (1975). The functions of the capitalist state are outlined in Gamble and Walton (1976), Chapter 5 and Crompton and Gubbay (1977), Chapter 6, whilst an overview of the state in capitalist society is presented in Westergaard and Resler (1975), Part 3, which deals with growth of state expenditure and its relation to private capital, as well as the nature and role of the nationalised industries and the state's role in 'labour relations'. The section also includes a chapter which is a critique of pluralism.

The 'debate' between Miliband and Poulantzas is introduced in Urry and Wakeford (1973), Chapters 23 and 24, whilst a critique of both is outlined in Holloway and Picciotto (1978), pp. 3-10 and in Gough

(1979), Appendix A. A good critical survey of recent developments in the marxist theory of the state is provided by Jessop (1977), which could be followed up by an attempt to read Holloway and Picciotto (1978). This book of readings deals with the relationship of the state to the process of capital accumulation, and because of this and the implicit critique of viewpoints of the 'relative autonomy' of the state, is of considerable importance. See especially Chapter 1 (the introduction) as well as Chapter 5 by Hirsch, which sees the state in terms of the relation between labour and capital, and Chapter 6 by Blanke *et al.*, which sees the state in the context of the relations between capitals.

On the cuts and restructuring see CSE State Group (1979), the introduction, and for an analysis of the changes in individual areas (industry, education, fiscal control and so on) see the same book. There is also a short chapter on 'left strategy'.

With regard to the Welfare State, for a review of different perspectives see George and Wilding (1976) whilst Gough (1979) is by far the most important reference. Chapter 2 deals with the requirements of accumulation, whilst Chapter 3 outlines the functions of the Welfare State. Chapter 4 deals with the origins and development of the Welfare State, on which see also Ginsburg (1979). Chapter 5 deals with the growth of state expenditure, Chapter 6 with the 'contradictions' in the Welfare State, and Chapter 7 with the 'cuts' and restructuring. On which, particularly in relation to the present conservative government, see also Leonard (1979).

Notes

1. This is therefore a critique at the level of circulation, at the level of 'appearances'. See Chapter 1, section 3.
2. See also Chapter 1, section 8.
3. Except those where production is for personal use and there is no division of labour.
4. The decisions to be made are actually even more complex than this is, for in addition to decisions on what gets produced (the composition of output), there must be some way of deciding *how* commodities are produced (using what type of technology, what combination of resources), *where* they are produced, *who* gets what is produced, and *when* commodities are produced (for example, the balance between production of consumption goods and investment goods). See, for example, Stilwell (1975), Chapters 1 to 6.
5. Less of the surplus value embedded in the commodity will have been realised, or perhaps none at all.
6. For a more detailed description of how this market mechanism is supposed to work see Donaldson (1978), Chapters 2 and 11, and for an analysis based on value rather than price, see Harrison's (1978) discussion of the law of value,

pp. 36-43, 64-66.

7. In other words the theory of the market mechanism is based on certain assumptions. Only if these assumptions are a reasonable approximation to the real world will resources be allocated in the instantaneous, efficient, costless and automatic manner described.

8. See Chapter 3.

9. They do not however succeed in achieving maximum resource utilisation over time. See Chapter 6 on crises and unemployment.

10. See also Chapter 1, section 2.

11. In fact the situation is rather more complex than we make out here. For a further analysis see, for example, Peston (1972).

12. Social costs (benefits) are defined as private costs (benefits) plus external costs (benefits).

13. See, again, Peston (1972).

14. Sometimes, however, administrative controls are used instead of market adjustments e.g. as in the Clean Air Act of 1956.

15. See Chapter 1, section 2.

16. In addition the state intervenes not only to 'improve' resource allocation but also to alter the distribution of income (see Chapter 4) and manage the national economy.

17. See also Chapter 1, section 8.

18. See Chapter 2, sections 2 to 4 and the introduction to Chapter 3.

19. In the same way that at the level of appearance on the labour market, the relations between capital and labour seem free and equal. See, for example, Chapter 2, sections 3 and 4.

20. See section 4.3 of this chapter on the functions of the state.

21. One of the few books that explicitly adopts an analysis of UK society, including the state, based on contrasting 'consensus' and 'conflict' perspectives is Burden, Chapman and Stead (1981).

22. Ironically it has been suggested that two major contributors to the marxist theory of the state also fail to analyse the relationship between the political and the economic, and thus treat the state as being relatively autonomous. See the brief discussion on Miliband and Poulantzas in Holloway and Picciotto (1978), pp. 3-10 and in Gough (1979), Appendix A.

23. Orthodox economics could hardly treat the state as endogenous to the economic system, resting as it does on the normative theory of an essentially self-correcting and automatic market economy which renders unnecessary state 'interference' in market processes.

24. See Chapter 2, sections 5 and 6 and Chapter 5.

25. See Chapter 5, section 3.1.

26. See Chapter 5, sections 3.1 and 3.2 on these counteracting forces.

27. See Chapter 6 on the internationalisation of capital and its relation to developing supranational state forms.

28. Over and above its basic function of guaranteeing private property rights and establishing and maintaining the conditions necessary for free, competitive exchange.

29. See Chapter 5, section 3.1.

30. See earlier in this section, and Chapter 5, section 3.2.

31. The rate of profit is given by $\frac{S}{C+V}$, thus reducing C will increase the rate of profit.

32. See note 31 – this reduces V and will hence increase the rate of profit.

33. The terms 'social investment' and 'consumption' are taken from O'Connor (1973), Chapter 4.

34. The term 'social expenses' is taken from O'Connor (1973), Chapter 4. This

is a problem to which we will return in the next two sections of this chapter.

35. This is not strictly true. A so called 'balanced budget', where expenditure equals revenue, does in fact have a positive effect on overall demand in the economy because the state spends all its income, taxpayers do not.

36. Assuming unemployed resources.

37. Though not our concern here, the type of state expenditure will influence the proportion of surplus value that is accumulated rather than consumed by capitalists. To the extent that state policies encourage accumulation and re-investment, and discourage surplus consumption, they will aid accumulation.

38. See Fine and Harris (1976c).

39. It is however, as far as I know, not possible to go beyond this point and classify all state expenditure into these different types. As Gough (1979) and O'Connor (1973) note, many state expenditures contain elements of each.

40. This requires a detailed analysis of changes in individual state expenditure programmes.

41. This section is largely based on Gough (1979).

42. For an analysis of differing perspectives on the Welfare State see George and Wilding (1976) or for an introduction, Burden, Chapman and Stead (1981).

43. We define the Welfare State to encompass what has been termed 'social services' or the provision side, services and cash benefits, of social policy i.e. social security, education and training, health, social welfare provision and housing. In terms of marxist perspective we define it according to its functions in the capitalist economy, rather than specific policy areas. This we do later in the section.

44. See section 3 of this chapter.

45. Particularly in an era of relatively free trade and capital movement, where competitive pressures are felt all the more keenly.

46. Naturally this statement does not imply the agreement of the writer to such a domestic division of labour!

47. See Chapter 4, section 5 and Gough (1979), pp. 108-14.

48. All in real terms i.e. having discounted the effects of general price inflation. See Gough (1979), pp. 84-9.

49. See Chapter 5.

50. Gough (1979), p. 94.

51. See Chapter 6, section 4.

52. And indeed necessary. If taxes are to be reduced as well then expenditure reductions will have to be even greater.

53. It has to be remembered that the cuts in state expenditure undertaken in 1976 by the then labour government were greater than those currently being undertaken by the conservative government (1979-1980).

54. See Leonard (1979).

55. See Leonard (1979).

BIBLIOGRAPHY

Aaronovitch, S. and Sawyer, M. (1974) 'The Concentration of British
  Manufacturing', *Lloyds Bank Review*
—— (1975) *Big Business*, Macmillan
Allen, J.M. and Campbell, M. (1976) 'Employment Performance and
  the Structure of Industry in Leeds', *School of Accounting and
  Applied Economics, Leeds Polytechnic, Discussion Paper No. 3*
Amey, L.R. (1964) 'Diversified Manufacturing Business', *Journal of the
  Royal Statistical Society*
Atkinson, A.B. (1972) *Unequal Shares*, Penguin
—— (ed.) (1973) *Wealth, Income and Inequality*, Penguin
—— (1975) *Economics of Inequality*, Oxford University Press
Atkinson, A.B. and Harrison, A.J. (1978) *Distribution of Personal
  Wealth in Britain*, Cambridge University Press
Baran, P. and Sweezy, P.M. (1968) *Monopoly Capital*, Penguin
Barrat Brown, M. (1968) 'Who Controls the Economy' in Coates, K.
  (ed.) *Can the Workers Run Industry?*, Spokesman
—— (1974) *The Economics of Imperialism*, Penguin
Beharrell, P. and Philo, P. (1977) *Trade Unions and the Media*, Macmillan
Blackburn, R. (1967) 'The Unequal Society' in Urry, J. and Wakeford
  J. (eds.) *Power in Britain*, Heinemann
—— (ed.) (1972) *Ideology and Social Science*, Fontana
Braverman, H. (1974) *Labour and Monopoly Capital*, Monthly Review
  Press
Broadbent, T.A. (1977) *Planning and Profit in the Urban Economy*,
  Methuen
Brown, B. (1973) *Marx, Freud and the Critique of Everyday Life*,
  Monthly Review Press
Buckley, P.J. and Casson, M. (1976) *The Future of the Multinational
  Enterprise*, Macmillan
Burden, T., Chapman, R. and Stead, R. (1981) *Business in Society:
  Conflict and Consensus*, Butterworth
Burghes, L. and Field, F. (1977) 'The Cost of Unemployment' in
  Field, F. (ed.) *The Conscript Army*, Routledge & Kegan Paul
Campbell, M. (1978a) 'Recent Studies in the Economics of Urban and
  Regional Development', *British Review of Economic Issues*
—— (1978b) 'Review of OECD Structural Determinants of Employment

and Unemployment', *Environment and Planning*
—— (1979) 'Capital Accumulation, the Restructuring of Capital and the Future of Employment in the UK', *Paper presented to the European Congress of the Regional Science Association, London*
Carney, J., Hudson, R. and Lewis, J. (eds.) (1980) *Regions in Crisis*, Croom Helm
Casson, M. (1979) *Alternatives to the Multinational Enterprise*, Macmillan
Coffey, P. (ed.) (1979) *Economic Policies of the Common Market*, Macmillan
Counter Information Services (1979) *The New Technology*, CIS
Crompton, R. and Gubbay, J. (1977) *Economy and Class Structure*, Macmillan
CSE State Group (1979) *Struggle Over the State*, CSE Books
CSO (1972) *Annual Abstract of Statistics*, HMSO
—— (1976) *Annual Abstract of Statistics*, HMSO
—— (various dates) *Economic Trends*, HMSO
—— (various dates) *Monthly Digest of Statistics*, HMSO
Currie, D. (1979) 'The EEC: What It's Done for Britain and Can We Get Out?', *Marxism Today*
Dennis, R. (1978) 'The Decline of Manufacturing Employment in Greater London', *Urban Studies*
Department of Employment (1971) *British Labour Statistics Historical Abstracts, 1886-1968*, HMSO
—— (1977) *British Labour Statistics Year Book*, HMSO
—— (monthly) *Department of Employment Gazette*, HMSO
Desai, M. (1979) *Marxian Economics*, Blackwell
Donaldson, P. (1978) *Economics of the Real World*, Penguin
Dunning, J.H. (1973) 'American Investment in Britain', *Economic Consultants*
Edwards, R.C., Reich, M. and Weiskopf, T.E. (eds.) (1978) *The Capitalist System*, Prentice Hall
Engels, F. (1969) Letter to W. Sombart, 11 March 1965
Field, F. (ed.) (1977) *The Conscript Army*, Routledge & Kegan Paul
Field, M. Meacher, M. and Pond, C. (1977) *To Him Who Hath*, Penguin
Fine, B. (1975) *Marx's Capital*, Macmillan
—— (1980) *Economic Theory and Ideology*, Arnold
Fine, B. and Harris, L. (1975) 'British Economy since March 1974', *Bulletin of the Conference of Socialist Economists*
—— (1976a) 'The British Economy May 1975 – January 1976', *Bulletin of the Conference of Socialist Economists*

—— (1976b) 'Controversial Issues in Marxist Economic Theory' in
Miliband R. and Saville, J. (eds.) *The Socialist Register*

—— (1976c) 'State Expenditure in Advanced Capitalism: A Critique',
New Left Review

—— (1979) *Rereading Capital*, Macmillan

Fischer, E. (1973) *Marx in His Own Words*, Penguin

Freedman, R. (ed.) (1962) *Marx on Economics*, Penguin

Friedman, A. (1977) *Industry and Labour: Class Struggle in Monopoly
Capitalism*, Macmillan

Fromm, E. (1963) *The Sane Society*, Chatto and Windus

Gamble, A. and Walton, P. (1976) *Capitalism in Crisis*, Macmillan

George, K.D. (1975) 'A Note on Changes in Industrial Concentration in
the UK', *Economic Journal*

George, V.N. and Wilding, P. (1976) *Ideology and Social Welfare*,
Routledge & Kegan Paul

Ginsburg, N. (1979) *Class, Capital and Social Policy*, Macmillan

Gintis, H. (1972) 'A Radical Analysis of Welfare Economics and Individual Welfare', *Quarterly Journal of Economics*

Glyn, A. (1979) *Capitalist Crisis: Tribune's Alternative Strategy or
Socialist Plan*, Militant

Glyn, A. and Sutcliffe, R. (1972) *British Capitalism, Workers and the
Profits Squeeze*, Penguin

Gordon, D.M. (1972) *Theories of Poverty and Underemployment*,
Lexington

Gough, I. (1979) *The Political Economy of the Welfare State*,
Macmillan

Graaf, J. de V. (1957) *Theoretical Welfare Economics*, Cambridge
University Press

Green, F. and Nore, P. (eds.) (1979) *Issues in Political Economy: A
Critical Approach*, Macmillan

Gribbin J.D. (1974) 'The Operation of the Mergers Panel Since 1965',
Trade and Industry

Hannah, L. (1974) 'Takeover Bids in Britain Before 1950', *Business
History*

—— (1976) *Rise of the Corporate Economy*, Methuen

Hannah, L. and Kay, J.A. (1977) *Concentration in Modern Industry*,
Macmillan

Harbury, C.D. and McMahon, P. (1975) 'Inheritance and the Characteristics of Top Wealth Leavers in Britain', *Economic Journal*

Harbury, C.D. and Hitchens, D. (1980) 'The Myth of the Self Made
Man', *New Statesman*

Hardach, G., Karras, D. and Fine, B. (1978) *A Short History of Social-ist Economic Thought*, Arnold

Harrison, A.J. (1974) 'Income Inequality in the UK' in Grant, R.M. and Shaw, G.K. (eds.) *Current Issues in Economic Policy*, Philip Allan

Harrison, J. (1978) *Marxist Economics for Socialists: A Critique of Reformism*, Pluto Press

Harvey, J. (1977) 'Theories of Inflation', *Marxism Today*

Heilbronner, R.L. and Ford, A.M. (eds.) (1971) *Is Economics Relevant?*, Goodyear

Hobsbawm, E.J. (1969) *Industry and Empire*, Pelican

Holland, S. (1976) *Capital Versus the Regions*, Macmillan

—— (1980) *The Uncommon Market*, Macmillan

Hollis, M. and Nell, E. (1975) *Rational Economic Man: A Philosophi-cal Critique of Neo Classical Economics*, Cambridge University Press

Holloway, J. (1976) 'Some Issues Raised by Marxist Analyses of European Integration', *Bulletin of the Conference of Socialist Economists*

Holloway, J. and Picciotto, S. (eds.) (1978) *State and Capital: A Marxist Debate*, Arnold

Hood, N. and Young, S. (1979) *The Economics of Multinational Enterprise*, Longman

Horsman, E.G. (1975) 'The Avoidance of Estate Duty by Gifts Inter Vivos', *Economic Journal*

Howard, M.C. and King, J.E. (1975) *The Political Economy of Marx*, Longman

—— (eds.) (1976) *The Economics of Marx*, Penguin

Hughes, A. (1977) 'Births, Deaths and Survivals in the UK. Quoted Manufacturing Sector', *Mimeo, Cambridge*

Hunt, E.K. and Scwartz, J.G. (1972) *A Critique of Economic Theory*, Penguin

Hunt, E.K. and Sherman, H.J. (1978) *Economics: An Introduction to Traditional and Radical Views*, Harper and Row

Hutt, C. (1973) *The Death of the English Pub*, Arrow Books

Jacquemin, A.P. and de Jong, H.W. (1977) *European Industrial Organisation*, Macmillan

Jalée, P. (1977) *How Capitalism Works*, Monthly Review Press

Jessop, R. (1977) 'Recent Theories of the Capitalist State', *Cambridge Journal of Economics*

Kay, G. (1979) *The Economic Theory of the Working Class*, Macmillan

Kelsall, R.K. and Kelsall, H.M. (1974) *Stratification*, Heinemann

Kincaid, J.C. (1973) *Poverty and Equality in Britain*, Penguin

Kopits, G.F. (1976) 'Intra Firm Royalties Crossing Frontiers and Transfer Pricing Behaviour', *Economic Journal*

Labour Party (1977) *International Big Business*, The Labour Party

Labour Research (1973) *American Investment in Britain*

Labour Research (1974) *Foreign Investment in Britain*

Labour Research (1978a) *The Top 20 Companies*

Labour Research (1978b) *British Manufacturing Multinationals*

Labour Research Department (1977) *Inequality in Britain Today*, LRD Publications

Lall, S. (1974) 'Transfer Pricing and MNCs', *Monthly Review*

Lall, S. and Streeten, P. (1977) *Foreign Investment, Transnationals and Developing Countries*, Macmillan

Lampman, R.J. (1959) 'Changes in the Share of Wealth Held by Top Wealth Holders 1922-56', *Review of Economics and Statistics*

Lane, D. (1971) *The End of Inequality?*, Penguin

Larner, R. (1966) 'Ownership and Control in the 200 Largest Non Financial Corporations, 1929 and 1963', *American Economic Review*

Lebowitz, M.A. (1976) 'Marx's Falling Rate of Profit: A Dialectical View', *Canadian Journal of Economics*

Leonard, P. (1979) 'Restructuring the Welfare State', *Marxism Today*

Levinson, C. (1971) *Capital, Inflation and the MNCs*, George Allen and Unwin

Lindbeck, A. (1977) *The Political Economy of the New Left*, Harper and Row

Lindley, R.M. *et al*. (1978) *Britain's Medium Term Employment Prospects*, Warwick

Lipsey, R.G. (1971) *Introduction to Positive Economics*, Weidenfeld & Nicolson

Low Pay Unit (1975) *Bulletin No. 5*

Lukes, S. (1973) *Individualism*, Blackwell

—— (1975) *Power: A Radical View*, Macmillan

Lydall, H.F. and Tipping, D.G. (1961) 'The Distribution of Personal Wealth in Britain', *Bulletin of the Oxford Institute of Economics and Statistics*

McLellan, D. (1975) *Marx*, Fontana

Mandel, E. (1968) *Marxist Economic Theory*, Merlin

—— (1971) *Marxist Theory of the State*, Pathfinder

—— (1973) *An Introduction to Marxist Economic Theory*, Pathfinder

—— (1975) *Late Ca*

—— (1978) *Second Slump*, New Left Books

Manpower Services Commission (1977) *Annual Report and Plan*, HMSO

Marx, K. (1970) *The German Ideology*, Lawrence and Wishart

—— (1972) *Capital, Volume 3*, Lawrence and Wishart

—— (1976) *Capital, Volume 1*, Penguin

Massey, D. (1979) 'In What Sense a Regional Problem?', *Regional Studies*

Mauss, M. (1970) *The Gift Relationship*, Cohen and West

Meacher, M. (1971) 'Mr Barber's Wink to the Rich', *New Statesman*

Mermelstein, D. (1970) *Economics: Mainstream Readings and Radical Critiques*, Random House

Miliband, R. (1969) *The State in Capitalist Society*, Quartet

Mitchell, J. (1971) *Woman's Estate*, Penguin

Murdock, G. and Golding, P. (1973) 'For a Political Economy of Mass Communications' in Miliband, R. and Saville, J. (eds.) *The Socialist Register*

—— (1977) 'Beyond Monopoly: Mass Communications in an Age of Conglomerates' in Beharrell, P. and Philo, G. (eds.) *Trade Unions and the Media*, Macmillan

Muellbauer, J. (1974) 'Prices and Inequality: the UK experience', *Economic Journal*

Murray, R. (1975) 'Multinational Companies and Nation States', *Spokesman*

Nath, S.K. (1973) *A Perspective of Welfare Economics*, Macmillan

Nore, P. and Green, F. (eds.) (1977) *Economics: An Anti Text*, Macmillan

Nyman S. and Gilbertson, A. (1978) 'The Ownership and Control of Industry', *Oxford Economic Papers*

O'Connor, J. (1973) *The Fiscal Crisis of the State*, St Martins Press

OECD (1977) *Structural Determinants of Employment and Unemployment Vol. 1*, OECD

Ollman, B. (1978) *Marx and Reich: Essays in Social and Sexual Revolution*, Pluto Press

Open University (1975) *Patterns of Inequality D 302 Unit 15*, Open University Press

Papandreou, A. (1973) *Paternalistic Capitalism*, Oxford University Press

Parkin, F. (1971) *Class, Inequality and Political Order*, Paladin

Peston, M. (1972) *Public Goods and the Public Sector*, Macmillan

Pickering, J.F. (1974) *Industrial Structure and Market Conduct*, Martin

Robertson

Prais, S.J. (1976) 'The Evolution of Giant Firms in Britain', *NIESR Economic and Social Studies, 30*

Protz, R. (1978) *Pulling a Fast One: What the Brewers Have Done to Your Beer*, Pluto Press

Radice, H. (ed.) *International Firms and Modern Imperialism*, Penguin

Reich, M., Gordon, D.M. and Edwards, R.C. (1973) 'A Theory of Labour Market Segmentation', *American Economic Review*

Reid, I. (1977) *Social Class Differences in Britain*, Heinemann

Ricardo, D. (1951) *On the Principles of Political Economy and Taxation*, Cambridge University Press

'Rius' (1974) *Marx for Beginners*, Writers and Readers' Publishing Cooperative

Roth, A. and Kerbey, J. (1972) *Business Background of MPs*, Parliamentary Profiles

Rowthorn, R. (1975) 'Neo Classicism, Neo Ricardianism and Marxism', *New Left Review*

—— (1977) 'Inflation and Crisis', *Marxism Today*

Rowthorn, R. and Hymer, S. (1971) 'International Big Business 1957-1967', *University of Cambridge, Department of Applied Economics, Occasional Paper 24*

Royal Commission on the Distribution of Income and Wealth (1975-1979) *Reports 1-7*, HMSO

—— (1980) *The A-Z of Income and Wealth*, HMSO

Sawyer, M. (1971) 'Concentration in British Manufacturing', *Oxford Economic Papers*

—— (1976) *Income Distribution in OECD Countries*, OECD

Scott, J. and Hughes, M. (1976) 'Ownership and Control in a Satellite Economy', *Sociology*

Scott, P. (1979) *Corporations, Classes and Capitalism*, Hutchinson

Scwartz, J. (ed.) (1977) *The Subtle Anatomy of Capitalism*, Goodyear

Secretary of State for Prices and Consumer Protection (1978) *A Review of Monopoly and Mergers Policy*, Cmnd. 7198, HMSO

Sherman, B. and Jenkins, C. (1979) *The Collapse of Work*, Eyre Methuen

Singh, A. (1971) *Takeovers*, Cambridge University Press

—— (1975) 'Takeovers, Economic Natural Selection and the Theory of the Firm: Evidence from Post War UK Experience', *Economic Journal*

Sloan, P. (1973) *Marx and the Orthodox Economists*, Blackwell

Stilwell, F.J.B. (1975) *Normative Economics*, Pergamon

Social Trends (1980), HMSO

Swann, D. (1978) *The Economics of the Common Market*, Penguin

Sweezy, P. (1968) *The Theory of Capitalist Development*, Monthly Review Press

—— (1972) *Modern Capitalism and Other Essays*, Monthly Review Press

TUC (1976) *The Distribution of Income and Wealth*, TUC

Thrift, N. (1979) 'Unemployment in the Inner City: Urban Problem or Structural Imperative?' in Herbert, D.T. and Johnson, R.S. (eds.) *Geography and the Urban Environment, Vol. 2*, Wiley

Tipping, D.G. (1970) 'Price Changes and Income Distribution', *Applied Statistics*

Townsend, P. (1979) *Poverty in the United Kingdom*, Penguin

Union for Radical Political Economics (1978) *US Capitalism in Crisis*, URPE

United Nations Department of Social and Economic Affairs (1973) *Multinationals in World Development*, United Nations

Urry, J. and Wakeford, J. (eds.) (1973) *Power in Britain*, Heinemann

Utton, M. (1970) *Industrial Concentration*, Penguin

Van Parijs, P. (1979) 'From Contradiction to Catastrophe', *New Left Review*

Wedderburn, D. (ed.) (1974) *Poverty, Inequality and Class Structure*, Cambridge University Press

Westergaard, J. (1978) 'Social Policy and Class Inequality' in Miliband, R. and Saville, J. (eds.) *The Socialist Register*

Westergaard, J. and Resler, H. (1975) *Class in a Capitalist Society*, Heinemann

Winch, D.M. (1971) *Analytical Welfare Economics*, Penguin

Wragg, R. and Robertson, J. (1978) 'Post War Trends in Employment', *Department of Employment Research, Paper No. 3*

INDEX

accumulation of capital *see* capital accumulation

aggregate concentration *see under* big business

alienation 39, 68

balance of payments 143, 145-6, 152, 154

barriers to capitalist development *see* crises

big business 144, 167
- and aggregate concentration 60, 66-8
- and market concentration 60-6; in brewing 63-4; in the media 64-6
- causes of growth of 69-75
- consequences of growth of 68-75
- *see also* concentration *and* capital, concentration and centralisation of

capital 10, 17, 28, 38-40, 94
- centralisation of 47-8, 72-5, 174-5
- circuit of 41
- concentration of 47-8, 72-5, 174-5
- constant 42-4
- export of *see* internationalisation of capital
- organic composition of 48, 53, 117-20, 138
- technical composition of 117-18
- value composition of 117-18
- variable 42-4
- *see also* capital accumulation

capital accumulation 42, 45-9, 60, 78, 108, 113-14, 141
- and centralisation 47-8, 72-5, 122, 174-5
- and concentration 47-8, 72-5, 174-5
- and demand for labour 47-9, 113-21
- and rate of profit 47-8, 49-55
- and realisation 119, 123-5, 139, 141, 151
- and the state 173-81, 189

see also crises

capitalist state *see* state

class 23-5, 33-4, 35, 37, 83, 101-2, 103-4, 170
- conflict and struggle 28, 32, 35-6, 43-5, 52, 56, 82, 95, 109, 116, 118, 120, 124, 135-6, 153, 171, 176, 179, 183
- relationships 15, 16, 33, 37-8, 45, 68, 117
- struggle and the state 26-8, 171-2, 176-7, 182, 186, 188-9

competition between capitals 38-9, 46-8, 59, 68-9, 74, 78, 117, 133, 142-5, 149-51, 156

concentration 118
- causes of growth of 69-75
- consequences of 68-9
- diversification and 64, 71, 74
- growth of 60-8
- mergers and 63, 69-72
- *see also* big business *and* capital, centralisation and concentration of

counteracting forces *see under* profit

crises 49-55, 127
- disproportionality and 51-2, 115
- exhaustion of IRA and 52, 115-17
- overproduction and 50, 115, 119, 144, 177
- possibility of 50, 114
- profitability and 49, 109, 113-21
- realisation problems and 52-3, 119, 123-5, 144-5
- state expenditure and 175, 180-3, 188, *see also* restructuring and the state
- tendency for the rate of profit to fall and 53-5, 117-21
- wages and 52
- *see also* capital accumulation, profit *and* unemployment

dialectics 36, 56, 118, 171

economic base 35, 36, 59

economic development *see* capital

201

accumulation *and* crises
employment
   manufacturing 111, 129
   prospects for 128-32
   services 130-1
European Economic Community
      (EEC) 155-61
   impact on the UK economy
      158-61
   international competition and
      157-8
   internationalisation of capital
      and 155-7
   process of economic integration
      and 158-61
   supranational state and 156-7
exploitation 42, 53, *see also* surplus
      value
externalities *see under* free markets

free markets 37
   assumptions underlying 14-15,
      166-9
   efficiency and 13, 168
   freedom and 16, 22
   imperfections 14-15, 166-9
   normative model 14-15, 23
   optimal resource allocation and
      12, 13-15, 165-6
   self interest and 15-23
   state intervention and 28, 164-70,
      172-3; and externalities
      169-70; and public goods
      168-9
   see also neoclassical economics

historical materialism 32-6, 156

ideology 9, 12, 13-15, 22, 25, 29,
      36, 178-9, 188
income distribution *see* inequality
incomes policy 24, 48, 122, 125,
      175
individualism 20-3, 101
industrial reserve army 49, 54, 135,
      see also unemployment
inequality 29, 168
   class and 81-4
   education and 104
   health and 103-4
   income 90-6; from wages 94-5;
      from wealth 89-94
   inflation and 93
   orthodox views of 82-3, 93

power and 100-2
   state and 29, 97-100, 184;
      benefits 98-9; taxes 97-8
   wealth and 84-90; accumulation
      88-9; inheritance 88-9
inflation 23, 132-6
   class conflict and 135-6
   competitiveness and 136
   inequality and 93
   money supply and 133-4
   state and 134-5
international investment *see*
      internationalisation of capital
international trade 14, 142-8, 158-9
internationalisation of capital
      123, 127, 149-51
   EEC and 149, 151, 155-7
   nation states and 156-7
   see also multinational
      corporations (MNCs)

keynesian economics 10, 11, 25
   and crises 11, 109, 119, 137-8
   see also orthodox economics

labour
   as a commodity 37-8, 41-2
   necessary 42-4
   surplus 42-4
labour power 37-9, 41-2, 46, 59,
      82, 111-12, 116, 151-2, 178
   price of 38, 42, 43, 48, 94, 166,
      see also wages
   reproduction of 58, 174, 178
large firms *see* big business

market concentration *see under* big
      business
market system *see* free markets
means of production *see under*
      production
media 64-6, 101, 178
methodology *see* historical
      materialism *and under* orthodox
      economics
mergers *see under* concentration
money 41, 51, 53, 114, 119, 121,
      133-5
monopolies *see* concentration
multinational corporations (MNCs)
      147-55
   charateristics of 147-9
   consequences of: for home
      nations 152-3; for host

nations 153-5
explanation of growth of 149-51
locational flexibility and 153,
 159
state and 153-4, 156-7
strength of working class and
 155
transfer pricing and 154-5
see also internationalisation of
 capital

neoclassical economics 25
appearances and 10, 15-17
concentration and 72-3
ideology and 9, 12, 13-15, 22
state and 172-3
unemployment and 22, 109,
 137-8
see also orthodox economics and
 free markets
neoricardian economics 11

organic composition of capital *see
 under* capital
orthodox economics
appearances and 15-17
assumptions underlying:
 behaviour and motivation of
 economic agents 19-25;
 marginal analysis 24-5;
 preferences 20; social harmony
 23-5; state 25
ideology and 9, 12, 13-15, 22, 25,
 29
methodology of 17-18
value free 12
see also neoclassical economics
 and keynesian economics
ownership and control of capital
 75-8

perfect competition 166-7
poverty 92-3
power *see under* inequality
prices 40-41, 68-9, 165-70, *see
 also* free markets and inflation
production
 for profit 37, 51, 59, 113, 169
 forces of 33-5, 37, 108, 144,
 170, 174-5
 means of 33, 41, 59; ownership
 of 22, 34, 37, 38, 59, 82,
 84, 86-8, 100
 mode of 32-3, 35; characteristics

of capitalist 38-9, 59
relations of 33-40, 45, 82, 105,
 108, 170-1
productivity 33, 47, 54, 95, 116-17,
 119, 121-2, 124-5, 129, 177
profit(s) 15-17, 19, 55, 59, 68-9,
 82, 115, 165-8
divorce of ownership from
 control and 75-8
origins of 40-4
rate of 44, 49, 54, 120-2, 133, 135
realisation of 41, *see also under*
 capital accumulation
tendency for the rate of to fall
 53-5, 117-21; and accumulation
 53-5; and international investment 55, 118-19, 150, 152-3,
 156; and international trade 55,
 118-19, 144-5; and other
 counteracting forces 54-5, 118-
 19, 123
see also crises *and* capital
 accumulation

reformism 26-7, 45, 100, 164, 181
restructuring 118, 136, 152, 182
employment and 121-6, 127
industry 121-6
state and 125-6, 175, 177,
 182
the state 181-3
the welfare state 185, 188-9
see also under unemployment
rivalry *see* competition

simple commodity production
 36-8, 41
social change 34-6, 55-6, 57
economic change and 34-6
state 29
balance of class forces and 28,
 171-2, 176-7
capital and 170-7
capital accumulation and 173-80
class conflict and 27-8, *see also
 under* class
contradictions in 176-7, 179-83
fiscal crisis of 180
functions of 26, 174, 177-9
growth of in capitalist development 173-6
impact on inequality *see under*
 inequality

in orthodox economics 22, 25,
27-8
internationalisation of capital
and 157-8
realisation and 177, 180
reproduction of labour power
and 174, 178, 181, 186
restructuring the *see under*
restructuring
see also welfare state *and under*
free markets
superstructure 26, 36, 101, 171
surplus 33-4, 45-6
surplus value 42, 46-7
appropriation of 82
methods of increasing rate of
44, 54, 122-4, 150-1
origins of 40-4
production versus realisation
of 119, 123-5, 139, 141, 151
rate of 42-4
see also restructuring

unemployment 29, 108
accumulation and 113-21, 127
extent and duration of 109-13
functions of for capital 111-12
prospects for 128-32
restructuring and 121-6, 128
see also crises *and* industrial/
reserve army
uneven development 126-8

value
exchange 38, 40-2, 51
expansion of 41, 44, 59
labour theory of 40-1, 43
law of 51, 114-15, 125-6, 177
surplus *see* surplus value
use 38, 42, 51

wages 15-17, 38, 42-3, 48-9, 52,
82, 128, 135, 141, 188
wealth distribution *see under*
inequality
welfare state
capital accumulation and 183-4
class struggle and 183, 186
contradictions in 186-8
financing 187-8
functions of 184
growth of in capitalist development 183, 185-6
restructuring of *see under*

restructuring
see also state
women 56, 67, 96, 106, 111-12, 128,
138-9, 158, 189

For Product Safety Concerns and Information please contact our
EU representative GPSR@taylorandfrancis.com Taylor & Francis
Verlag GmbH, Kaufingerstraße 24, 80331 München, Germany